A HISTORY OF THE HUGUENOTS, FROM 1598
SHERGOLD BROWNING

-♣- -♣- -♣- -♣- -♣- -♣- -♣- -♣-

A HISTORY OF THE HUGUENOTS, THE TERMINATION OF THE LEAGUE TO THE PRESENT TIME.

CHAPTER I. CONDITION OF THE HUGUENOTS UNDER HENRY IV;— Biron's Conspiracy;—RESTORATION OF THE JESUITS.

The second period of King Henry's reign opened under circumstances which appeared favourable, only by comparison with the previous distracted condition of France; for the general state of the country was still deplorable. Distress, the exhaustion consequent on a protracted civil war, and the unsatisfied ambition of many chieftains, were serious barriers to the internal pacification of the kingdom. The dukes of Mercceur, Bouillon, and Biron, with other powerful nobles, endeavoured to re-establish the feudal sovereignties of the middle ages; and their interested efforts greatly impeded the operations of the royal government. At the same time, many of the gentry had become habituated to the restlessness of a partisan l warfare, and expected a continuation of the impunity which anarchy had sanctioned during a long series of years: this also materially retarded the returning prosperity of the country.

More than one instance on record will show the extent of this evil, and the length of time requisite torestore public order. Three gentlemen, of Brittany, named Guillery, sustained a siege against the King's forces. After an obstinate defence, the younger brother, who commanded, attempted to escape; but he was taken prisoner, and terminated his bold career on the scaffold, along with a considerable number of his adherents,. whose attachment to their leader had been stimulated by hopes of future booty, andencouraged by the success of previous depredations. Nor was a prospect of plunder the sole cause of violence, for angry personal feuds oc-

casionally broke out. In August, 1607, there was a combat on the borders of Poictou and Anjou, in which thirty gentlemen were engaged: twenty-five of the combatants were killed, and the others very much wounded,-j

Another serious inconvenience had arisen out of the civil wars: the leading characters of each party had contracted a habit of entering into treaties for assistance from foreign powers; and the frequency of such negociations proves that the state of affairs, by rendering them necessary, had destroyed their reprehensible character.

The rival pretensions of the house of Lorrain were annihilated, when Henry's right was acknowledged by the Pope; but the King's marriage with Margaret of Valois left him without any hope of posterity. The junior branches of the Bourbon family looked forward, with but ill-concealed impatience, to the succession; and the termination of the war was but half of what the nation claimed of its rulers. Still the King's personal character was a guarantee for firm government; and a series of valuable measures might be confidently expected, when the royal council comprised such men as Sully, Sillery, Jeannin, and Villeroy. It is however worthy of remark, that Sully complains of the jealousy of his colleagues, who wished to exclude him from all interference in foreign negociations; and, on 6ne occasion, Villeroy was so highly offended at the appointment of Bethune, Sully's brother, to the embassy at Rome, that the King was obliged to interpose, expressing himself greatly offended at such scenes in his presence.

Mercure Francais, 1608, vol. l, p. 289. f
Journal de Henri IV, in loc.

The heads of the Huguenot party at this time were Rohan, Soubise, La Tremouille, and Bouillon. The prince of Conde and the count de Soissons had been educated as Catholics, f Lesdiguieres, though nominally a protestant, was not considered likely to make any sacrifice for the cause. Duplessis-Mornay was their chief adviser; d'Aubigne their most active agent. Henry Chatillon de Coligny, the admiral's grandson, had inspired great hopes among the Huguenots; but he was killed at the siege of Ostend, in 1601. His rising qualities promised much; being noted for cool courage, prudence, comprehensive understanding, and an affability which won the affections of his soldiers. The King's mind was unhappily poisoned against him by various misrepresentations: he was reported to be ambitious without bounds; inspired by a fanatical impulse to surpass his lather and grandfather; and ready to sacrifice life for his religion. His relationship to one whom the king had professed to revere as a father; and his zeal against Henry's worst foes, the Spaniards, presented great claims on his behalf. But the King of Navarre had become King of France; and feared the dawning importance of such a dangerous spirit. According to the statement of his confidential minister, Henry appeared consoled by the news of Coligny's death; and manifested such a dislike to his family, that Sully desisted from any application in behalf of his mother and brother. Sully, liv. xii.

f Conde was so zealous as to give his livery servants fifteen sols each, every time they confessed; and, in order to claim the money, they were provided with certificates. Amelot de la Houssaie. *Mem. Hiit.* vol. ii,p, 140.

The fact of the protestants having Sully as their representative and advocate in the King's counsel, was less important, from the admitted necessity of public tranquillity: besides which, the stern character of that minister made him ready to suspect a seditious motive for the expression of conscientious scruples; so that he can hardly be viewed as one of their party,-j-And he has, in consequence, been charged with studying to gain the Pope's favour, " seeking," says an accusing writer," the applause of the Romish hierarchy, rather than the approbation of his brethren." Sully, liv. xii.

t Benoit says he was very jealous of the protestant leaders. *Hist, tie Vidit tie Nantes,* vol. i, p. 173.

The edict of Nantes, precious as it was to the protestants, was not free from defect; and during the year which elapsed between its signature by the King and its registration by the parliament, various attempts were made, on both sides, to alter its enactments. The protestants complained of their exclusion from many public charges; while the popish party considered its provisions awfully liberal; although the protestants were not, at first, permitted to baptize their children in Paris. In 1603, a greater latitude was allowed, on account of the danger to which infants were exposed in the journey to Ablon, a village three leagues from Paris, f This was the nearest protestant place of worship until August, 1606, when public service was performed at Charenton. Berthier, bishop of Rieux, in the name of the clergy, remonstrated against the latitude of the edict: that body contended that it should give the protestants no other privilege than that of sufferance: they were not to be questioned as to their opinions,. but should be prohibited from holding any assembly or synod, without the King's express permission; and forbidden to attend any such meetings in other countries. $

The university of Paris was not backward in the career of illiberality, and the rector demanded the exclusion of Protestant children from the colleges: but all opposition was fruitless; the edict was declared just and necessary,and in consequence passed through all the formalities requisite to make it valid. Nor was it beneficial to the protestants alone: for in above two hundred and fifty towns, and two thousand rural parishes, where the mass had been prohibited nearly fifteen years, the old ceremonial was restored; in some cases in spite of local influence; and particularly so at Thouars, where the duke de la Tremouille in vain endeavoured to maintain the ascendancy of his brethren in religion, f The public were in general satisfied: the majority from indifference to Romish interests; and the more expe-

rienced from a conviction that the hope of advancement would cause many of the Huguenots to abjure. $ *Arcana Gallica,* p. viii. London, 1714. 'j-*Journal de Henri IV. %* Cayet, *Chron. Septennaire.—HeScrres, Hist, de France,* vol. ii, Registered in parliament of Paris, 25 Feb. 1590. f Bournisseaux, *Hist, dela ville de Thouars,* p. 183. $ D'Aubigne *Hist Univ.,* vol. 3. p. 634.

The marriage of the King's sister Catherine with the duke of Bar, was an event of some importance from the elevated rank of both parties; the princess being at that time the presumptive heiress of Navarre and Bearn, and her affianced husband, heir of Lorrain. It assumed however a still more important character from the difference of religion. Like her mother, Jane d'Albret, the princess was most fervent and uncompromising in her attachment to the protestant faith; and would on no account assist at the celebration of mass as part of the marriage ceremony; which in its principles and nature presented ample materials for discussion, from the sacramental character claimed for it by one party, and as decidedly refused by the other. The duke of Bar was equally unyielding; and Du Perron was commissioned by the King to exert his eloquence in persuading the duke to be married according to the custom of the Huguenots, since the princess was determined to follow the example of her mother, and remain steadfast in the religion in which she had been educated. Whether the point in dispute might not have entirely broken off the marriage, is a problem; the King was at last fatigued with the unceasing theological controversies, in which were frequently mingled some allusion to his sister's firmness contrasted with his own abjuration. He resolved on a plan for settling the point in question, and summoned his sister and her future husband to his cabinet. The archbishop of Rouen, Henry's natural brother, was waiting to receive them; he had been induced to grant his ministry by Roquelaure, and at the King's command, performed the ceremony: the presence of the Sovereign being admitted by the clergy to compensate for the absence of the other solemnities which usually accompanied a marriage,-j-On quitting the King's presence, the princess conducted her husband to the Louvre, where she regularly maintained the proteslant worship in her apartments; and the nuptial benediction was there given by a protestant minisr ter. $

Meanwhile the agents of Spain and Savoy were actively fanning the discontent of those nobles, whose services gave them strong claims upon Henry's gratitude; while the recompenses they had obtained, by falling far short of their expectations, only extended their means of opposing the government. According to their connexions, they took measures for increasing their partisans, by well-timed appeals to the feelings, framed according to their respective principles. The Huguenot nobles invariably professed much anxious doubt, respecting the sincerity of the King's intentions towards them; and to maintain a corresponding tone in the minds of their followers, they described the humiliating condition to be apprehended, whenever the complete restoration of order should place them at the mercy of their unrelenting foes. The opposite party was also suspicious of the King's designs: the reality of his conversion was doubted, and his relapse into heresy declared most probable, whenever the time arrived for him to throw off the mask, and again declare himself a protestant. This party, guided and encouraged by experience, appealed to the bigotry and fanaticism, which had wrought such wonders in the time of the League. The riches of Spain were lavished to that end, but happily without their intended effect; each successive attempt at insurrection tending rather to strengthen than injure the royal power. Roquelaure, subsequently marshal, was the archbishop's boon companion, and had persuaded the King to elevate him to the see of Rouen. f 30 Jan. 1599. —Sully, liv. x.—Cayet— De Serres. $ D'Aubigne, *Hist. Univ.* vol. iii, p, 601. Among the discontented nobles of this time, the foremost was Charles Gontaut, duke de Biron, who at the age of forty

had obtained the rank of marshal, and was admitted to the councils, and even the intimacy of his sovereign; possessing in addition a splendid fortune, and enjoying a reputation for military excellence, equal to, if not surpassing, his father's. Brantome is exceedingly warm in the praise of this marshal, whom he calls the first in Europe; and adds, that "next to King Henry, he was the greatest cap"tain in Christendom; the bravest, the most daring, "and most valiant ever seen."

The celebrity of this first example of Henry's severity renders it almost superfluous to detail the particulars of his conspiracy and condemnation. He was lamentably insnared by the duke of Savoy, and don Pedro Henriquez de Azevedo, count de Fuentes. The latter was the recognized agent of Spain in Italy; and was so violent in his hatred to Henry IV, that he never mentioned his name without an opprobrious epithet; he gave a cordial welcome to all whose disaffection led them into exile, and is accused of having instigated several attempts against the King's life, as he deemed it impossible to renew the civil war in France so long as he lived,-f-Emanuel, duke of Savoy, had a personal dislike to Fuentes; but he cordially co-operated with that busy intriguer, whose plans, if successful, might enable him to extend his limited territory at the expense of France, whenever the dismemberment of that country could in any way be effected. He promised Biron the hand of his third daughter; and it was agreed with the King of Spain, that an independent sovereignty, consisting of Burgundy and FrancheComte should be vested in him, on occasion of the marriage. $ All these transactions were reported to the King, who was remarkably active in procuring intelligence concerning public affairs; and to such a degree, that he astonished the Spanish ambassador by his knowledge of what passed in the councils of Madrid. *Vie du mareschal de Biron et de son Fih.* f Malthieu, vol. ii, p. 814.

$ Sully, liv. xii.— Matthieu, vol. ii, p. 491.

Biron's discontent was in consequence,

early known: yet when it became necessary to use coercive measures with the duke of Savoy, he obtained an important command. He was already in league with the duke; and warned the governor of Bourg, that on a certain day and hour he would be attacked. "All this," observes Sully, "has been subsequently proved." The treachery did not however prevent the town from falling into the power of the King's troops. Nor was Biron's turpitude confined to disloyalty towards his sovereign; he most treacherously endeavoured to de liver Sully into the hands of the duke of Savoy.-f

The successful termination of this campaign was followed by Henry's second marriage. So long as Gabrielle d'Estrees lived, none of the King's advisers exerted themselves to obtain a dissolution of his first marriage: their ideas of a suitable union for the 44 eldest son of the church" made them shudder at the bare possibility of his raising a concubine to the throne; and such might have been the case, as Gabrielle possessed great influence over him, and appears by all accounts to have merited his attachment.

There was something very tragical in her death. She had quitted Fontainebleau for Paris, where she intended to perform her Easter devotions. After hearing *Tenebrce* at the church of Saint Antoine; she was seized with violent convulsions, from which she did not recover. She expired on the morning of Good Friday, after giving birth to a still-born child; her features being so distorted as to defy recognition. La Varenne (Henry's confidential agent in matters of gallantry) communicated this event to Sully in a mysterious manner, which leaves room to suppose that he thought she was poisoned; but whether this death was the effect of such machinations, or the general tribute of nature under a more terrific form than usual, can never now be known, as most of the circumstances were concealed from the King himself,-j The Nuncio, having asked the Spanish ambassador his opinion of the King, was told in reply: " Il scait tout, et m'a dit des choses te"nues au conseil d'Espagne, qui m'ont fait rougir pour les avoir niees, "et qui estoient tres vrayes: il est plus que le diable." *Journal de Henri IF,* Oct. 1608. j-Sully, liv. xi.

From this time the divorce encountered no obstacle; but Henry felt considerable repugnance to a second marriage; and in a conversation with Sully, after enumerating the qualities, which in his opinion were necessary to produce a happy union, he added with a sigh, "that he feared no such person could be found." He subsequently yielded to reasons of state, and conferred his hand on Mary de Medicis: the ceremony was performed at Lyons, in November 1600.

Ambition must have greatly hardened Biron's heart, or he would have been touched with his Sovereign's magnanimity on this occasion. Although Henry was fully persuaded that Biron was engaged in a traiterous correspondence with the enemy, he hoped by kindness to reclaim the faulty nobleman. Taking the marshal apart in the cloisters of a church at Lyons, he asked him under a promise of pardon, what was the extent of his correspondence and conventions with the enemies of the State? Biron, unhappily for him, made an incomplete avowal; the King promised oblivion for the past, but warned him that a repetition would have fatal consequences. Jsassompierre, vol. i. p. 61. — D'Aubigne, *Hist. Univ.,* vol. iii, p. 635. ."

f Sully, liv. x.
Still Biron continued to conspire; and the King, unwilling to consider him irrecoverable, was still inclined to try every means to reach his heart, but without effect. The marshal's unfortunate destiny hurried him to destruction. He was unhappy in the choice of his confidents: the baron de Luz was his bosom friend and instigator; an advocate, named Picote, was employed to flatter the marshal, and work upon his weakness; and a crafty wretch named Lafin, after urging him on in the tortuous path of treasonable correspondence, betrayed him to his offended sovereign. The Spaniards had endeavoured to corrupt Biron before the termination of the

war: their agents had discovered his foible, and flattered his hopes of obtaining one of the great fiefs into which France was to be divided. They perceived moreover, that Biron who had hitherto been very indifferent as to religious observances, now went into the contrary extreme. The Spanish agents encouraged this feeling; and it was repeated in his hearing, that he was the last and sole resource of religion and liberty. The late brilliant position of the Guises incited him to take their place, and become the champion of popery: as he imparted his views to others, discontented like himself, he could behold their ambition take fire at the prospect he unfolded; and he succeeded in forming an association for dethroning the King, by men who, above all others, were bound to serve and defend him. The duke of Bouillon, who had acquired the sovereignty of Sedan entirely by the King's support and recommendation; Charles, count d'Auvergne, brother of the King's present mistress, Henriette d'Entraigues; La Tremouille, Soubise, and Montpensier, a prince of the blood, were engaged in this cause; but Bouillon was considered the soul, d'Auvergne the trumpet, and Biron the arm of the conspiracy. However, so far as Bouillon and La TremOuille were concerned, it was all suspicion, for proof was wanting.-f-De Fresne-Canaye sent timely notice of their proceedings in Italy, but his intimations were disregarded; and it was by the treachery of-Lafin, that Biron's plot was discovered. That artful man, perceiving his patron's obstinacy and bad judgment, took immediate measures for his own safety, and solicited an audience of the King, when he delivered up the marshal's papers and correspondence. Sully being immediately summoned to Fontainebleau, was informed by the King that *he* was implicated by the marshal's letters. With a smile, he replied to Henry's enquiries respecting his knowledge of the affair: "If the others know no more of it than myself, your "majesty has no occasion to take any trouble about "the matter." "Nor have I paid anyattention to it," answered the King,

who then ordered him to assist Nephew of Espinac, archbishop of Lyons, a most violent Leaguer, and therefore easily accessible to Spanish influence.

Matthieu, vol. ii, p. 489. *f* Sully, liv. xiii.

Bellievre and Villeroy, in examining the correspondence. The result of their investigations was a summons for Biron to appear at court. Deceived by Lafin, he imagined that silence on his part would be sufficient protection; and set out for Fontainebleau, although informed by various friends that his lile was in danger,-f-When the King endeavoured to draw from him a confession of his guilt, he replied disdainfully, that he was hot come to justify himself, but to learn the names of his calumniators, and be avenged on them. Henry gave him clearly to understand that he knew all; conjured him to be candid; and promised a free pardon, $ His proud spirit would not submit: he left the royal presence, and was soon after arrested by Vitry, captain of the guards. When disarmed, he appealed to his past services; and being led across the hall of the guards, exclaimed: " See how good catholics are treated!" § These expressions almost suffice to account for his tragical end. The first proves his excessive presumption; the other indicates the source from which he expected to derive support. The rest of his history is a matter of notoriety.

How far Bouillon and d'Auvergne were implicated with Biron is unknown. Sully persuaded the King to be merciful, and privately advised all the parties involved to sue for pardon. Montpensier confessed his fault, and begged the King's forgiveness on his knees. The constable Montmorency, who was charged with being concerned, confessed a knowledge of the affair, though he denied having taken any part in it; he also asked and obtained pardon. The duke of Epernon made no attempt to conceal his friendship and intercourse with the marshal, but denied all knowledge of his designs; and Sully expressed much satisfaction at being able to declare his innocence. La Tremouille was summoned to appear, but made repeated excuses of confinement by the gout,-f Sully, liv. xii.-J-Cayet, p. 288.

:£ Henry, deeply affected, was heard to say, as he paced his apartment: " Il fautqu'il ploye ou qu'fl rompe." Matthieu, vol. ii, p. 500. § Sully—Bassompierre—Matthieu. He suffered 31 July, 1602. .'"' '.

The duke de Bouillon appears to have entertained great apprehension, as he passed the frontier, to avoid the consequences. In reply to a letter from the King, he states his willingness to set out in obedience to the summons; implores his Majesty to believe that his accusers are perfidious, disloyal, and false; and entreats him to be perfectly satisfied of his innocence. But instead of proceeding to Paris, he went to Geneva, from which place he wrote a second letter, again protesting his innocence. $ That this was a case of more than usual importance, is to be inferred from the fact of the French ambassador in London submitting to Queen Elizabeth the King's letter of summons, with a request for her candid opinion. Elizabeth immediately instructed her ambassador in Paris to see the King; to thank him for his frankness and confidence; and to assure him, that although she would rather decline giving an opinion, still the King's request demanded sincerity on her part. The following part of the instruction at any rate proves the interest Bouillon excited at the English court: "When we consider that a part of "the accusation is founded on his conspiracy with "marshal Biron (with whom we well know he never "had a good understanding, but rather enmity and "emulation), we hope that the King will find the ac"cusation altogether feeble; at which no one will "rejoice more than ourselves." The instruction continues with an argument upon the great improbability that the Huguenot leaders could be in league with the King of Spain, their mortal enemy. Girard, *Vie du due d'Espernon,* p. 208. f Sully, liv. xiii.—Bassompierre, *Nouveaux Memoires,* p. 181. 4: Both letters are in Villeroy, *Mem. d'Etat,* vol. v. The first is dated St. Cire, 30 Nov. 1603; the other, Geneva, 2 Jan. 1603.

Scarcely ever has there existed a plot with more ramifications, and combining a greater variety of opposing interests, than that which brought Biron to the scaffold. In the first place, the duke of Savoy promoted the undertaking in the hopes of extending his territory, and converting his duchy into a kingdom. Biron was himself seduced by a similar prospect; and to gain the Huguenot leaders to his party, some of the southern provinces of France were to be assigned to them, free from all control of the catholics. Bouillon being induced to co-operate, secretly summoned nine of the most considerable of his party, to whom he communicated the dangers which threatened the Protestants, and the means of deliverance which had been suggested to him. He declared to the meeting, that six months had elapsed since a proposal had been made, to which he long refused to listen; but which he would not altogether dismiss on his private judgment. The association which he had been invited to join, consisted of princes of the. blood, great officers of the crown, governors of provinces, and many persons of weight and respectability: that all of them, including the old members of the League, were indignant at the King's ingratitude to the protestants, who ought not to remain ignorant of an engagement lately formed, and signed by the King and the ambassadors of Spain and the empire, for a crusade to exterminate the Huguenots: that the time for the execution of the project, and the contingents of men and money which each should supply were specified, and the war was to be continued until the Huguenots were extirpated. After stating that the duke of Savoy, who was in possession of an authentic copy of the convention, bearing original signatures, was willing to place it in the hands of the protestant body, the duke de Bouillon unfolded the plan of territorial remuneration, proposed by the originators of this measure; and called upon d'Aubigne for his sentiments respecting the offer. That gentleman explained his views with eloquence, and severely criticised the character of the principal confederate,

Biron; who notwithstanding his education under a protestant mother, and a father who was an enemy to bigotry, had since his intimacy with the duke of Savoy, exchanged the licentiousness of an atheist for the superstition of a monk. He ridiculed the idea of such a combination against the protestants; and expressed his conviction, that if this pernicious offer were accepted, they would be quickly betrayed to the King. The company unanimously approved d'Aubigne's opinion, which the duke of Bouillon at once adopted as his own; and one of the party was sent to Lyons, where the King then was, with instructions to act according to circumstances: making such communication to Sully, as should preserve their fidelity from impeachment; yet concealing names, to avoid compromising the parties. Villeroy, vol. v, p. 129.

In 1603, the protestants were again made the tools of Bouillon's ambition. Persisting in his voluntary exile, he continued indefatigable in his negociations with James I and the Elector palatine; evidently with the design of inducing those princes to espouse his cause, by representing himself as the champion of the reformed religion. He even published pamphlets, apparently directed against the protestant body, with replies unfolding the great dangers which were impending. Duplessis-Mornay was so much deceived as to defend the duke's character, and enlarge on the value of his services; and at an assembly held at Gap,-f the discussions and resolutions were so animated as to threaten some insurrectionary movements. An effort was made to insert in the body of their articles of confession, that the Pope was antichrist. The King on hearing this, desired Sully to interfere, and put an end to such a scandal: at the same time, Lesdiguieres, Bouillon, and La Tremouille violently decried the loyal statesman, and represented him as corrupted by the court: yet he had sufficient influence with the Huguenot deputies, residing at Paris in pursuance of the edict of Nantes, to have the obnoxious article suppressed. Duplessis thus explains the cause of this proceeding. % After de-

scribing the condition of the *i* . ».
D'Aubigne, *Hist. Univ.,* vol. iii, p. 674. Oct. 1603. *$* In a letter to M. de la Fontaine, then in London: dated 26March, 1604.

French churches, in terms diametrically opposed to discontented feelings, he relates that a professor of divinity at Nismes had proposed as a subject for argument, *De antichristo;* for which he was summoned before the parliament at Toulouse, as a perlurbator. The protestant ministers seeing that they might be accused of sedition for their sermons, brought the matter before the synod for discussion,-j-The Pope was really alarmed, lest a declaration so hostile should become a matter of deliberation in all the European universities; but he availed himself of the circumstance to pretend great offence, and would not be pacified with anyt hing short of the recall of the Jesuits, whose re-establishment is the next event in which the liberties of the Huguenots were interested, $ Henry had been induced in the preceding year to promise their recall, and the Nuncio assisted the fathers Cotton and Mayus, in their efforts to realize that promise. Cotton had for some time been in the habit of preaching before the King, who thought favourably of his learning and talents. The Jesuits, in 1605, obtained permission to reside in certain towns: this did not however satisfy them; they required a formal recall, and the repeal of the decree against them. Henry had promised it when at Metz; and the parliament of Paris deputed their chief-president Harlay to remonstrate against the proposed measure. His address is a repetition of the general charges against the society. The authenticity of the King's answer, as reported by several writers, is hardly maintainable: it contains a rather laboured apology for the Jesuits, excusing their faults and concluding for their support, on account of their usefulness. But whatever may be the terms used by the King, it is evident they expressed displeasure at the sentiments uttered by the parliament; and whether he wished to conciliate, from a fear of their intrigues, or to act on genuine principles

of liberality, the result was equally favourable to the Jesuits. Sully opposed the measure in the council. He admits that Sillery excited his ill humour at the meeting, by a pretended compliment, which but ill disguised his jealousy. He called on Sully to open the consultation, both on account of his experience, and from being best acquainted with the King's views. To this Sully objected. "So it appears," observed Sillery, with a malicious smile, " we must wait for your opi"nion, until you have made a journey to the banks of "the Seine, lour leagues ofl," alluding to Ablon, where thc protestant ministers held their meetings. Sully replied with firmness, that in religious matters he was not led by man; the word of God being his sole guide: but in affairs of state he was entirely guided by the King's will, of which he must be more informed before he could pronounce.-f Ferrier, who afterwards abjured, was the professor implicated, lienoit, vol. i, p, 394. f Duplessis, *Mem.* , vol. iii, p. 49. $ Sully, liv. xvi.

The following day he conversed at length with the King upon the subject. After hearing his minister's objections, Henry summed up his sentiments in a manner that proved his intentions were already decided. He had been persuaded that by driving the Jesuits to despair, their audacity would have no bounds. This was clear from his reasonings; and instead of attempting further to refute his arguments, Sully declared that if the King's personal happiness and safety depended on the re-establlshment of the Jesuits, he would promote it as readily as the most decided of their partisans. This declaration illuminated the King's countenance with satisfaction; and he voluntarily pledged his royal word, that no influence of the Jesuits should induce him to make war against the protestants. The result of this interview was speedily communicated to the King's confessor elect, father Cotton, who the next day visited Sully, loading him with flatteries and commendations, f Harlay's speech, delivered 4 Dec. 1603, is preserved in the *Mercure Francais,* vol. ii, pp. 164 *et seq.* But the Jesuits published, in French, Latin, and

Italian, a *falsified abridgement,* with the answer attributed to the King. The latter pieces are to be found in Villeroy, vol. vii, and are referred to as unquestionable aulhorityby father Daniel, and others of the ultramontane school.
f Sully, liv. xvii. CHAPTER n. DEATH OF LA TREMOtlLLE. — D'aubigne's CONVERSATION WITH THE KING. — MEETING AT CHATELLERAULT. REDUCTION OF SEDAN. — DEATH OF HENRY IV.
Sully being named governor of Poictou, visited that province in the summer of 1604. He was well received " Ventre Saint-Gris! me repondez-vous de ma personne?" was Henry's reply lo one who endeavoured to dissuade him.
atRochelle; and endeavoured to convince the leading Huguenots of their error, in acting perversely towards the government. La Tremouille and Rohan hoth expressed unshaken loyalty to Henry; but the experienced statesman declares that in his opinion the followers of those noblemen were quite as refractory and discontented as they had been represented. Sully's voyage produced a very beneficial result to the regal authority, though it hastened the ruin of the protestant cause: by distributing pensions to the more pacific and moderate, he reduced the cabal in that province to insignificance, and La Tremouille's death, which occurred soon after, deprived them of their principal leader. This nobleman had married a daughter of the prince of Orange; and being thus allied to the duke de Bouillon, attained great importance in the protestant party, whose interests he so warmly espoused, that had he lived longer, it was the King's intention to bring him to justice.f Orders were sent at one time, to besiege him in his chateau at Thouars; and when La Tremouille was informed of the advance of some detachments towards his residence, he wrote to his tried friend d'Aubigne, reminding him of a mutual vow they had made, to share each other's dangers. D'Aubigne hastened to Thouars; and in conjunction with La Tremouille, commenced measures of defence, by collecting the gentlemen of their party. In one of their rides they

perceived the heads and bodies of some malefactors, left for exposure. La Tremouille changed colour at the sight; on which d'Aubigne took him by the hand, and observed: "You must learn to look at such melancholy" "spectacles with a good grace: for engaged as we are, "it is requisite to familiarize ourselves with death." Sully, liv. Jlyih. ƒ Bassompierre, *Nouveaux Mem.,* p. 181.

D'Aubigne declares that the death of this nobleman was the cause of his resolution to quit the kingdom; having no longer any one in whom he could conOde, for his defence against the secret manoeuvres of the court; all the other Huguenot leaders being corrupted by pensions. With this intention he had made preparations for his departure, and the greater part of his property was embarked in a small vessel, hired for the purpose. While his two last cases were being conveyed from his home, he received a letter from the King, and another from La Varenne; both assuring him that he was wanted at court; and would be well received. Those letters made him change his resolution, and decided his return to Paris where the King employed him nearly two months in superintending the preparations for some joustes and tournaments; yet without giving the least intimation of a desire to converse with him, respecting his conduct in the protestant assemblies, which was after all the real motive x of the invitation.

At length Henry took an opportunity of speaking to him alone; and endeavoured to persuade him to join the court party, by representing the selfishness and venality of his partisans. He admitted that d'Aubigne himself attended the meetings in good faith; but that the majority were corrupted, and that nothing would be henceforth carried against his wishes. "This is so true," added Henry, " that one of your "number, connected with the first families of France, "has cost me no more than five hundred crowns, to "serve as my spy, and inform me of all that passes "in your assemblies." D'Aubigne, *Mm.,* p. 154.

D'Aubigne in reply stated, that being elected a deputy, he felt bound to serve his constituents conscientiously; and the more so, since they had lost their royal protector; at the same time be well knew that with the exception of the late duke de La Tremouille, all the chiefs had sold themselves to the court. Henry then embraced his old companion in-arms, and recommended him to cultivate the friendship of Jeannin, observing: "He has managed all the affairs of the 4 League; and I shall have more confidence in you and "him, than in those who have played a double game." Henry was turning away, but d'Aubigne detained him; and firmly, though without disrespect, enquired what was the cause of his displeasure.—The King turned pale, as was customary with him when his feelings were moved, and replied: "You were too much at"tached to La Tremouille. You knew I hated him; and 44 still you gave him your affection. " "Sire!" replied d'Aubigne, " I have been brought up at the feet of "your majesty» where I learned never to abandon 44 those in affliction." Henry again embraced him, and they separated.

Henry sent a confidential agent to question Duplessis on d'Aubigne's friendship with La Tremouille, and other subjects affecting his character for loyalty. The agent's report to the chancellor was decidedly favourable. D'Aubigne, *Mem.,* pp. lis-152.

The conspiracy of the Entragues family does not enter into our subject, being an affair of private ambition, in which no Huguenot of distinction was implicated. The counts d'Entragues and d'Auvergne were condemned to death; and the marchioness of Verneuil was sentenced to perpetual imprisonment.-j- The King's promise, given at the dying request of Henry III, in behalf of d'Auvergne, effected a commutation of his sentence into confinement in the Bastille; $ and his passion for Madame de Verneuil caused the punishment of her father to be limited to banishment from the court, and an order to reside on his estate: the marchioness, as may be easily imagined, obtained a free pardon.

The chronicles of this period abound with incidents, which would be deemed insignificant if they did not serve as an index for judging of the state of public opinion. The conversions of monks and other ecclesiastics are carefully noted; as well as laymen, whose position ga ve them interest. But although we find only an occasional noticeof proselytes to the Romish churcb, it is too well known that court favour, the hopes of advancement, and the prospect of fortune, led many to desert their faith. In addition to those motives must be mentioned the effect of prejudice, which to many is irresistible; for the stake and the scaffold will excite firmness, when the silent contempt of connexions and neighbours will shake a well-founded resolution. The controversy between the rival creeds was zealously maintained; but principally by a few individuals, on behalf of the protelants. The English ambassador was for many reasons bound to stand forward; and on occasion of the *fite-Dieu,* he not only refused to place hangings before his hotel, in the rue de Tournon; but declared that he would set fire to any that might be placed, contrary to his will. The procession of Saint Sulplice, to avoid extremities, was in consequence ordered to pass by another street. Dated 8 March, 1605.—Duplessis, vol. iii, p. 91. f 1 Feb. 1605. $ Bassompicrrc, vol. i, p. *iHi.—Nouv. Mem.,* p. 190.

But unhappily the dispute was not always limited *o* opinions or protestations: in a moment of excitement, a placard was posted in different parts of Paris, inviting the university students to meet with clubs and other weapons, for the purpose of resisting the insolence of the *maudite secte hucjuenote et ablonisle.* An individual named Robert, returning from worship at Ablon, was attacked and murdered: his son who accompanied him, in desperation avenged his father, by killing the assassin on the spot, ƒ

The protestants having demanded a general assembly, by virtue of the edict of Nantes, the town of Chatellerault was named for the meeting; and Sully was appointed to receive the deputies, and address them in the King's name.$ This was a disappointment to those of the protestant nobility, who were influenced by political motives: they knew Sully's firm loyalty, and were well aware that his energy would enforce respect to the King's instructions, known to be directed against any renewal of the offensive proceedings at the - *Journal de Henri IV,* 23 June, 1604. f *Journal de Henri IV,* 18 Sep. 1605. $ His commission is dated 3 July, 1605. Sully, liv. xxi. f Sully, liv. xxi.

synod of Gap. None could be admitted as the deputy of an individual, not even from Lesdiguieres; and there was a positive prohibition against receiving letters from any foreign princes, and particularly from the duke de Bouillon: his conduct towards the King requiring some public mark of displeasure. In the event of the assembly manifesting a feeling of insubordination, Sully was instructed to avail himself of his authority, as governor of the province, and to inform the seditious members, that the King was well aware of their designs. A letter from Bouillon had in fact been intercepted, which proved the existence of irritated feelings; and manifested a prevalent desire on the part of many members, to improve the position of the body by a vigorous effort,-f

Sully's opening speech was not well received by the assembly. He endeavoured to convince the meeting, that the number of towns assigned to them under the edict of Nantes, so far from being to their advantage, was an injury to their cause;-as the dispersion of their forces would render them an easy conquest, if any serious design against them were meditated: even Lesdiguieres, their Achilles, could not hold out in such a case, although he should await compulsion to induce his submission; a thing not likely considering his interested views. This insinuation was intended to show how well the court knew the secret dispositions of all the party.

The assembly refused Sully the honour of their presidence, only two votes being given in his favour; and they commissioned d'Aubigne to inform him, that he must desist from appearing there, unless he had any thing to propose from the King. Such an affront where he had calculated on obtaining

marked distinction, renders-it necessary to make some deductions from his account of the proceedings, which he represents as very tumultuous. He excluded Duplessis from participating in the discussions, on the ground of his not being deputed by any province; and although the deputies of Dauphine exclaimed, that nothingcould be done in his absence, Sully enforced his authority, and compelled the assembly to forego the opinions of Duplessis, as well as those of the duke de Bouillon; who, together with Lesdiguieres, are severely censured in his Memoirs for their conduct at this period. In conjunction with d'Aubigne and others, they are charged with having signed a memorial, in which was laid the basis of a calvinist republic in France: the result of the meeting rendered the project useless; andDuplessis fearing the consequences, sent his excuse to the King, with a disavowal of the memorial, f

The mere conception of such a scheme was calculated to alarm the friends of the monarchy; and Sully endeavoured to learn the general feeling of the protestants on that point. The answer he obtained from the deputies with whom he conversed, was to this effect. If Henry were immortal, the protestants having full confidence in his word, would at once renounce all precaution, give up their places of security, and reject foreign support; but the fear of finding very different sentiments in his successors, compelled them to continue measures adapted for their safety. Sully-was satisfied that the partisans of the project did not exceed the number of six or seven persons; but the King was not so easily convinced, and was deeply struck with the danger to which the state would be exposed after his death.

D'Aubigne, *Mem.,* p. 154. f Duplessis, vol. iii, pp. 122—126. — Sully, liv. xxii.

This consideration had some share in originating the expedition for reducing Bouillon to submission. The duke was summoned; passports were sent to him; and he was even threatened with vigorous measures, in case of non-compliance, but in vain. He persisted, and it

was not until Henry was on his march to Sedan, that this proud subject showed any signs of submission. At first Bouillon boasted that he would bury himself under the ruins of his little principality. He then proposed to treat with the King on the footing of an independent sovereign; and finally requested that Villeroy might be sent to discuss the terms of surrender. The conditions were very lenient: Henry did not wish to ruin an old companion in arms, who had privately confessed his readiness to submit, provided he could do so with honour: he was satisfied with humbling him, by the means of hereafter keeping him in check. It was evident that Bouillon in rebellion, was less dangerous to his government while at Sedan than in the heart of France; and the duke although clear of criminal participation in Biron's conspiracy, was conscious that there was sufficient evidence in his correspondence with the marshal, to cause him trouble: a treaty was speedily concluded, by which Bouillon was restored to Henry's good graces without losing his territory—the King reserving only the right of placing a French garrison in Sedan. And afterwards when the Jesuits requested permission to establish a college there, they were informed that the consent of the duke de Bouillon was indispensable.-f Sully, liv. xxii.

Henry entered Sedan on the second of April, 1606, when the duke offered his homage and submission, $ He presented himself at the King's chamber, before he had risen, and conversed with him for some time on his knee. Henry afterwards placed in his hand a letter of abolition, on receiving the duke's renewed protestation of fidelity. From that time, observes a contemporary, he conducted himself with as much independence and hauteur, as if nothing had happened. §

Thus ended an expedition which caused so many remonstrances and complaints from the protestants, that an attempt to rise in the duke's favour was at one time apprehended. But.the condition of the place completely refutes the idea: a garrison scarcely amounting to three hundred men; the cannon in bad condition; and scarcely any supply of the most common requisites for maintaining a siege, are proofs that the protestant body had no intention of espousing the duke's personal cause, as at all connected with the interests of religion.

The affairs of the protestants during the remainder of this reign present no event of importance. Sully expresses his regret that the King too readily listened to the complaints of their enemies; at the same time it is impossible to deny that occasionally, their zeal led them beyond the bounds of propriety, no less than of good policy. It is needless to detail the routine of their periodical synods for electing deputies: they were uniformly accompanied by attacks upon the Romish doctrines, and frequently gave occasion for treating their Sovereign with disrespect. It is not hazarding too much to assert that this empty right, grounded upon the edict of Nantes, was highly injurious to their cause; for instead of contentedly sitting down " under their vine and their fig tree," they acquired a habit of meddling with state affairs, censuring the King's appointments, and remonstrating against his measures. In short, no government could complacently regard such an *imperium in imperio;* political necessity in consequence furnished a pretext for, and sanctioned the subsequent faithless conduct of the French crown towards the protestants. However, under Henry IV there was no fear of violence: persecution had given place to controversy; and with the exception of a certain degree of acrimony in some cases, wherein the Jesuits took part, their theological disputes passed off quietly. In 1607, father Cotton sent a brother Jesuit, named Gaspard Seguiran to Rochelle; but being certain of a refusal from the King, he privately obtained letters from the secretaries of state, f On reaching that city, Sully, liv. 23. —*Merc. Franc.,* v. i, p. 104.

f *Journal de Henri IF,* Sept. 1606. $ On the same day, Henry sent an account of Bouillon's submission to Duplessis. This communication was official and countersigned; but many of the King's letters were private, and written entirely

by him. Duplessis, vol. iii, p. 157.
§ Bassompierre, vol. i, p. 171.

Afterwards confessor to Louis XIII. f It must be borne in mind that this was a subordinate employ the father was rudely sent away, without being permitted to pass the gate. The partisans of the Jesuits took occasion to incense the King against such disrespect. Henry made a show of adopting the complainants' views, and appeared inclined to chastise the delinquents; but taking Sully aside, he admitted that the protestants were not entirely to blame; and that if he had known that such letters had been applied for, he should have forbidden them. "However," he added, 44 you must endeavour to settle this, without "disavowing the secretaries of state; for it may hurt "the importance of their other dispatches." Sully easily arranged the affair. He wrote to Rochelle, to explain that above all other considerations, the King must be respected; and that by yielding to his authority, they would more easily carry their point; especially as those letters were given without his sanction. Seguiran then presented himself a second time, bearing a letter signed by the King himself: he was admitted, and even allowed to preach; but in a few days after his arrival, he was recalled.

Sully's correspondence, it may be well supposed, was not made known to any other than the leading characters at Rochelle; and as the whole population felt deeply interested, a deputation arrived at Paris, when the speaker, named Yvon, *f* was so indiscreet, in his address, that the King charged him with sedition. This feeling of insubordination, which had grown out of their habits of warfare, blended with theological controversy, was their most offensive quality in Henry's eyes; and on a subsequent occasion, when Sully complained of the seditious sermons of the Jesuit Gontier, the King admitted that his complaint was well founded; but added, that the protestant ministers preached still more seditiously.-f not a cabinet minister. *Secretaire d'Etat* and *marechal de Camp,* translated literally, give a very erroneous idea of either of

those posts.

Arcere, *Hist, de la Rochelle,* vol. ii, p, 120.—Sully, liv. xxiv. f Paul Yvon, seigneur de l'Aleu, mayor of Rochelle in 1616. At the conclusion of the siege, he became catholic, and fixed his residence in Faris. He devoted his attention to mathematics, and has left two works on that science.

As the protestants had but few opportunities for advancing their tenets by means of preaching, we find their ministers much engaged in controversial publications; many persons in consequence became persuaded of the necessity and expediency of freeing the Roman catholic religion from various glaring errors and abuses. On the other hand, the staunch supporters of theRomish hierarchy were averse to all concession; and three preachers were engaged during the remainder of this reign, in vindicating its doctrines and rites. They were the Jesuits Cotton and Gontier, and a cordelier, styled *le Pere Portugais:* the latter was surnamed the *Doctor;* Cotton, the *Orator* ; and Gontier, the *Preach, er.* Gontier was patronized by the duke of Epernon, and made very violent attacks upon the protestants: he was at length so vehement, that the King deemed it requisite to intimate his displeasure. $ A reply to Gontier's sermons from the pen of the minister Dumoulin, was written with such caustic severity, that the sale was forbidden. *Journal de Henri IV,* 23 Feb. 1607. f *Journal de Henri IV,* Dec. 1600. $ *MercureFranc.,* vol. i, p. 377.

The press was tolerably free at this period; and although we not unfrequently meet with the suppression of a work, the condemnation of authors was rare. A publication, urging the convocation of a council, excited some attention, and drew forth several replies; which being supported by the authorities, obtained the honours of the dispute. A careful, observing contemporary remarks: "The King cared little about 44 those publications; his attention being devoted to "the general good, and the embellishment of his city "of Paris." f

The records of this period present several instances of great excitement, which arose altogether from religious prejudice. The cardinal de Sourdis, archbishop of Bordeaux, had acted with so much ill-judged tyranny; striking protestants for alleged disrespect to the cross, disinterring bodies, and other similar excesses, that a complaint was made to the King, who promised justice, and sent orders to put an end to the prelate's folly, $

The King's interference alone preserved the peace in a similar case where the judges of Orleans, with the approbation of the bishop, gave a decree for disinterring a protestant lady; on the pretext that the cemetery was too near the catholic burial ground. Above two hundred noblemen and gentlemen met at the grave, and vowed to expose their lives rather than suffer such an indignity. The King being informed, sent orders for all functionaries to keep away, and summoned the judges to answer for their decree. *Journal de Henri* IV, 8 May, 1609. f *Mercure Franc.,* 1607, p. 227. £ *Journal de Henri IV,* July, 1609.

An attempt was made about this time to reconcile the differences between the two religions; as there were sincere catholics, desirous of terminating the dispute by mutual concessions. The ministers Dumoulin, Chamier and Durand, were ardently engaged in the task; and d'Aubigne, whose character for argument stood high, was welcomed to their party. Having decided on the outline of preliminaries on which the discussion should be based, they agreed to reduce all their controversy to the discipline of the church during the four first centuries. With an authority to that effect, d'Aubigne proceeded to the King, who at once referred him to cardinal Du Perron. At first the cardinal objected that the Huguenot body would disavow the proposition; but d'Aubigne engaged his honour and life, that they would stand by the result. Du Perron then took him by the hand and replied: "Give us forty years beyond the four hundred." "I "seewhat you are aiming at," replied d'Aubigne; "you "want to have the council of Chalcedon in your "favour; but I will agree to it, so that we may "enter upon the discussion." To this the car-

dinal observed, that the elevation of the cross must then be admitted, as the usage was sanctioned by that council. *Journal de Henri IF,* July, 1609. D'Aubigne agreed to make that concession for the sake of peace, "but," added he, "you will never dare "to propose to reduce the Pope's authority to its li"mits during the first four centuries: on that head, *44* we can afford to give you two hundred years more." The cardinal terminated the conversation by a remark, that the question must be decided at Paris, if it could not be settled at Rome.

The King being informed by d'Aubigne of what had passed at the interview, asked him why he so readily consented to give the additional forty years, on commencing the discussion. "Because, Sire! in asking "for the additional period, the doctors of the Romish 44 church tacitly confess that the four first ages would 44 not be for them." Several bishops and Jesuits who were present, began to murmur at the reply; the count de Soissons condemned such remarks as improper; and the King abruptly turning away, withdrew to the Queen's chamber.

The affair, trifling as it may appear at this distance of time, was however, deemed so important by the King's friends, that he was advised, and even solicited to put to death, or at least imprison the indefatigable and zealous Huguenot. Henry desired Sully to confine him in the Bastille: but the threatened danger was warded off by a friendly hint from Madame de Chatillon; and d'Aubigne having boldly sought an interview with the King, gave a detail of his long services, and concluded by requesting a pension. That was a sufficient submission to induce the monarch to countermand the order, which d'Aubigne was afterwards assured by Sully himself, had been really given for his imprisonment. D'Aubigne, *Mem.,* pp. 156—161.

The close of Henry's reign was signalized by extensive preparations for some military expedition, the object of which is shrouded in mystery. To suppose h is passion for the princess of Conde would have been a motive is

most preposterous; and the settlement of the duchy of Cleves was not of sufficient importance. "The enterprise," observes Sully, "being limited to "that single object, would be insignificant." The protestants all rejoiced in the possibility of a war, which they believed was destined to curtail the Austrian power; and the ultramontane or popish party spread reports, that the King's object was to assist the heretics. Some accounts of the time would almost induce the idea that Iienry aimed at the empire of the West.

Even Sully can only conjecture this monarch's design: the various hypotheses built on the project are therefore valueless. During several months Henry could think of nothing else; many of the sparkling phrases and anecdotes which have been handed down to us, may owe their origin to deep laid political precaution; and in some measure to the prudent suggestions of Sully, who relates, that on one occasion he took the liberty of pulling the King's cloak, in the midst of a public conversation, when he was rather too communicative, f D'Aubigne, *Mem.,* p. 162. + Sully, liv. xxvii.

At length the arrangements for his departure were completed: the Queen's coronation and its attendant festivities were at hand; and Henry, addressing one of his intimate friends, observed " I will sleep at St. De"nis on Wednesday; I shall return on Thursday; "Saturday I will hunt, Sunday my wife will make her "public entry; on Monday my daughter's wedding; "Tuesday the feast; and on Wednesday to horse!"

Yet this tone of confidence did not prevent his being assailed by painful apprehensions, which have been repeated by every writer who has treated of this period. Astrology and prophetic declarations had then great hold upon the imagination; and there is a prevalent idea of his having been told, that the first display of pageantry, in which he was concerned, would prove fatal. He frequently cursed the approaching ceremonial; and Sully endeavoured during three days to persuade the Queen to renounce the honour, but in vain, *f*

After receiving intimation from many quarters of an intended attempt against his life, the predicted blow was finally given, and on the fourteenth of May, 1610, the Great Henry felt under the knife of a fanatic.

That Ravaillac was the mere instrument of some party appears beyond doubt: his feelings had evidently been worked upon, in the same way as those of his precursor Jacques Clement; and this supposition will admit of his remaining completely ignorant of his instigators, in which respect his answers were uniform. Both in the common interrogatories, and under the torture, he always denied having any accomplice, and declared his sole motive was that he heard the King was about to make war against the Pope; and when at the last extremity, the wretched man implored absolution, which his confessor refused to give until he had revealed his accomplices, he begged it might be given, even with a reserve that his damnation should be certain, if he spoke falsely. His ejaculation at the Place de Greve, "that he had been deceived, and "thought the people would be pleased," is by no means in contradiction with his denial of accomplices, if we assume that his imagination had been inflamed by artful devices of spectacles, which he considered supernatural visions, and by violent sermons on the causes which would justify regicide.-f Matthieu, vol. ii, p. 804.

f Stilly, liv. xxvii. According to Matthieu, the Queen did not care for the honour of the ceremony, yet felt slighted that she alone, of all the Queens of France, should be excepted.

This fatal and infamous instigation has for two centuries weighed heavily against the Jesuits: not from historic proof, for it cannot be had; but in a great degree from the prevalence of certain opinions at this period cherished by the society; and which opinions not only led Ravaillac to commit the crime, but caused others to envy the wretched distinction he thus acquired, and to avow a readiness to imitate him. At the time, public feeling was unequivocally against the Jesuits. The clergy both regular and parochial, impugned them in their sermons; and the accusation found an echo in lay publications. In the courts of law and at meetings in the market place, that societywas alike believed to have prompted the assassin.

Journal de Henri IF. Mercure Franc., vol. i, pp. 440—441.
There would be a cruel injustice in contributing to perpetuate this sentiment, in the absence of regular evidence, if the Jesuits had not subsequently been in a situation which enabled them to justify the reputation of their body. The two succeeding Kings had Jesuits for confessors; and although every thing tended to facilitate the elucidation of this event, not the least effort was made to render public the investigations and statements, which the parliament of 1610 had consigned to secrecy. It would be useless to repeat the numerous incidents, or rather anecdotes on record, concerning the death of Ring Henry; which, however true, would be rather grounds for inference than bases for an accusation. It will be clearly seen that justice was impeded, in tracing the proceedings of the parliament of Paris; and our entire ignorance of the influence then wielded gives immense latitude to conjecture.

Sully, after alluding to the information communicated by the female, so conspicuous in the judicial annals of this epoch, as La Coman or d'Escouman, and who charged the duke of Epernon, the marchioness of Verneuil and others with preparing a plot, adds: "The incident will not be overlooked by those who "are inclined to attach importance to the suppression

"Among other curious hypotheses, one of the most remarkable is the accusation raised against the Queen and the prince of Conde; they are charged in a recent work with having instigated Ravaillac, who is said to have met the prince at Brussels a short time previous. Roederer,Me'm. *pour servir a VUistoire de la Socielepolie enFrance,* p. 15. Paris, 1835.

"of the particulars of the trial," and his editor (the abbe de l'Ecluse) remarks, in a note, "that this con"cealment of the proceedings by the parliament, was 44 universally known. "

A widow named St. Matthieu denounced a soldier named Martin. He had accosted her on the Sunday before the King's death, as he was proceeding to public worship at Charenton. He told her, that within a week there would be strange doings in Paris; and, those would be fortunate who were away. He admitted that he was not going to hear the sermon; but to form an opinion of the Huguenots' means of defence; that all the beggars and cripples about, were thieves and spies of the King of Spain; and that there was one in particular, whom he was surprised not to see there. The appearance of Ravaillac completely agreed with the description he had given. When the King's death was known, this man to her great surprise, called at her house, and engaged her to leave Paris: she consulted her friends, and had him arrested. But the lukewarm manner in which this affair was treated became so notorious, that L'Estoile observes thereon: "The cowardly proceedings adopted in the "investigation of this important fact (in which it 44 would seem they are afraid of finding what they seek) "will be probably without result. "--And at a subsequent date, the same writer states: "The trifling "enquiry made at this time, into the late King's "death, and the little desire shown to bring the guilty "to justice, offended many persons, and caused ani"madversions."

'Sully, liv. xxvii.
f *Journal de Henri IF,* 17 May, 1610.
While in prison, Ravaillac dictated a testamentary confession; but the clerk employed to take down his words, wrote it in a manner that defies the most skilful decipherers:-j-a circumstance which must at once strike every reader as most singular, since no man thus employed would have dared to act so, unless assured of impunity.

The decision of the parliament of Paris respecting LaComan, is of the same character. During that trial, the duke of Epernon acted so indecorously as to excite the indignation of the chief president Seguier; and when the public officers of the crown proposed their conclusions, viz: to defer judgment till after more ample enquiry; to liberate the accused, and imprison the accuser, there was a general assent to that decision. Seguier's reply to the Queen's inquiry, respecting his views of the question, proves the importance of the real criminals. £ Sad as is the misfortune for a nation to produce such wretches as Clement and Ravaillac, it is still more serious calamity to have a servile magistracy. What induced the parliament to incur this reproach, is now an unfathomable mystery. As a body, it could not be suspected of any bias in favour of the Jesuits; the opposition of its members to the recall of the society being a sufficient guarantee. The secret influence must therefore have been individual in its nature: the Jesuits, supposing them innocent, were deeply interested in making known that motive; but this they have declined doing. What their conduct was, with a consciousness of existing suspicions, will next claim our consideration.

Journal tie Henri IF, June, leio. f Fontanier, *Portefeuille,* No. 456, quoted by Capefigue, *Hist, de la Reforme, de la Ligue el de Henri IF,* v. viii, p. 372.. $ *Journal de Henri IF,* Feb. 1611.

When the news of the King's assassination reached the Louvre, father Cotton, as if conscious of a coming accusation, instinctively aimed at diverting suspicion from his party; and exclaimed: " Ah! who has killed "this good Prince; this pious, this great King? Is "it not a Huguenot?" Afterwards when he visited Ravaillac in prison, he cautioned him against incriminating *les gens de bien.*

Father d'Aubigny, another Jesuit who had been consulted by Ravaillac, was particularly questioned by the chief president, respecting the secret of confession. But the wary ecclesiastic answered only by sophisms; he stated "that God, who had given to "some the gift of tongues, to others prophecy, etc., "had conferred on him the gift of *forgetting* confes"sions." f

The decided expression of public opinion caused father Cotton to make an effort, surpassing in impudence any thing of the kind on record. Accompanied by two other Jesuits, he went to the attorney general; and in the name of the society intreated him to sanction the publication of an apology; with a prohibition for all persons, of what quality soever, to contradict or reply to it. The application was too monstrous to be received.

Journal de Henri IF.— Sully, liv. 28 *ad init.* f *Journal de Henri IF,* 19 May, 1610.

The liberty of the press was sufficiently established to expose the Jesuits to some tery rude attacks; but at a later period the monarchy became absolute: nothing could then be published without an *imprimatur*; and writers on French history either slur over this important event; or else adopt the good natured conclusion of the archbishop of Paris. "If I am "asked, who were the demons that inspired this "damnable idea, history answers that she knows "nothing: even the judges who interrogated Ravail"lac did not dare to open their mouths upon the sub"ject; and never spoke of him otherwise than by "shrugging their shoulders, "-j-L'Ecluse, the commentator on Sully, is likewise imbued with this feeling. Because father d'Orleans, in his life of Cotton, says nothing about his caution to Ravaillac, he maintains that it is not true; and since Pasquier, a great enemy of the Jesuits, is silent, it must be assumed that they were considered innocent by that writer. The Jesuit d'Avrigny's argument is all of this negative kind.$

To conclude—supposing the Jesuits' guilt fully established, their successors are not to be held responsible for a crime, in appreciating which, the barbarity of the times must be taken into account. The principles of the Jesuits may be still the same; but the mighty revolutions which have since occurred, render them less dangerous: they were long called the *Pope's militia;* and in many cases withstood the progress of reformed religion; but the rights of conscience are now admitted; and a general apprehension of their intolerant and grasping policy has essentially promoted a feeling in favour of protestantism.

Journal de Henri IV, June, 1610. f Peréfixe, *Hist, de Henri le Grand.* % Me-

moires chronologiques el dogmatiques.

Henry IV occupies too conspicuous a place in the annals of religious contention, to allow us to enter upon his successor's reign, without an attempt to portray his character as a man, as a captain, and as a

In the first point of view, his biographer has the painful task of recording many blemishes, chiefly attributable to his passion for the fair sex. His unblushing attachment to the princess of Conde is at once disgraceful and disgusting. The aged Constable Montmorency had selected Bassompierre for his son-in-law; and in that marshal's Memoirs we have a glowing description of his joy at the unexpected honour thus accorded to his personal merit. So long as Henry believed the gay soldier was chiefly enamoured of the brilliant alliance, and that there was a chance of his being a complacent husband, he encouraged the match; but j)n discovering the existence of a sincere affection for the beautiful Charlotte de Montmorency, he interfered; and declared his wish, that she should be the wife of his cousin Conde. Bassompierre could not conceal his disappointment; and at the wedding, Henry maliciously held him close to the bridal pair. The prince of Conde, aware of the Ring's intentions, kept his wife from the court as much as possible; but neither this intimation of vigilance, nor the affairs of state, nor the variety with which Henry's disposition was pampered, could divert him from his base design. He degraded himself so far as to engage the prince's mother in his interest. He had great.claims on her compliance; having destroyed the proofs against her, when charged with her husband's death. This may palliate her conduct a little; but she was severely punished when Henry taunted the prince, who complained of his tyranny: "I never acted as a tyrant, but when I "caused you to be declared what you are not;"-j-an abandonment of generosity, at variance with the character popularly attributed to him. A few months afterwards, when the prince set out privately for Flanders, the King's rage was excessive. $ Yet they are still formidable. The recent refusal of ecclesiastical sepulture to the count de Montlosier, entirely on account of his *Memoire d consulter,* is a proof that an undoubted attachment to the Romish Church does not compensate for a dislike to the Society.

Yet Henry's character had some redeeming points; and several who long knew him intimately, have left thier testimony in his favour. Sully revered him; d'Aubigne invariably bears witness to his goodness of heart, attributing his severity and ingratitude, to the misrepresentations of envious courtiers; and Bassompierre even when relating the loss of his betrothed, calls him "the best of men." Bassompierre, vol. i, p. 222. f *Journal de Henri IF,* June, 1609. % Bassompierre, vol. i, p. 28J. Respecting Henry's military talents there is no difference of opinion. His enemies admit his consummate courage and unrivalled skill. Many of his battles surpass the most celebrated actions of antiquity, if we consider how cruelly his means were limited, in comparison with the importance of his object; and in the details of those engagements, his prowess was almost romantic; so much so, that his bravery nearly amounted to temerity.

But it is as a sovereign that his character must be submitted to investigation. The eclat of a victory will still censorious judgments on the merits of a cause; but state decisions, and the severe exercise of authority after long commotions, cannot escape the complaints and cavils of unsuccessful competitors for power. The administration of justice was excessively rigorous; capital condemnations following offences of almost every kind and degree. But those laws were not of his enacting; he unfortunately found society overrun with numbers of reckless individuals, and the enactments appear more severe from their frequent application.

An expression is attributed to the most celebrated of his successors, when accused of usurping the crown. "*Comment usurpce? Je l'ai ramassee dans la bone!*" Henry of Navarre, the lawful heir of the crown of France, was also treated as a usurper, and compelled to

win his right by his sword. Had the monarchy been altogether prostrate, his task would have been comparatively easy; but he had to contend against the most formidable European powers; with what success is notorious. We make no attempt however, to draw a parallel between Henry and Napoleon: each re-established a fallen throne; and the memory of both is cherished by the nation over which they successively reigned; but the similarity extends no farther.

To form a due estimate of Henry's domestic policy, it should be placed in comparison with that of Louis XVIII. Henry consulted the sympathies of the conquered party — the catholic majority. He shewed himself their paternal monarch, and braved the charge of ingratitude by neglecting his old supporters, the protestants. This restoration was permanent. Louis on the contrary was unwilling to convince the nation that he placed public affection in the foremost rank, by confining within the bounds of private generosity his regard for the emigrant nobles, indebted like himself to foreign support. His sovereignty took no root in public feeling, and the natural consequence was experienced by his successor.

In foresight and political judgment Henry IV was very great. Accustomed from his boyhood to parry the intrigues of a hostile court, he was nurtured in the difficulties of government, and made use of corruption as a weapon for counteracting opposition to his sway.

There are several points of view in which he may be placed in comparison with our Alfred: the Danish invasion bearing some analogy to the League. But Henry's abjuration places him in an isolated position; no other prince having sacrificed religious principle to secure the possession of the crown; and this suggests an inquiry into the sincerity of his conversion.

During his life there was a very general doubt of his being a decided Romanist; yet several instances attest his orthodoxy. He endeavoured to persuade Sully to change his religion; and as an inducement proposed on one occasion to make him Constable; on another, that

his natural daughter Mile, de Vendome should marry the marquis de Rosny. After the public debate between cardinal Du Perron and Duplessis-Mornay in 1600,--Henry wrote to the duke of Epernon, that the victory of the diocese of Evreux over that of Saumur, was one of the greatest advantages obtained by the church of God for a long time; and that by such means more protestants would be reclaimed, than by fifty years of violence. $ During the siege of Montmellian in 1600, Henry accompanied by the count de Soissons and several nobles, having ventured rather close to observe the works, a masked battery was suddenly opened on them, which caused the King to cross himself. 44 By that," observed Sully who was present, " I recognize the good catholic."§

To these evidences of his catholicity, we can only oppose one slight incident, to mark any remembrance *Journal de Henri IF,* Nov. 1608. Sully,liv. xxv. f Usually termed the *conference de Fontainebleau:* there is a long account of it in the *Chronologie seplennaire.* Duplessis was too much shackled by the King's restrictions to hope for success. D'Aubigne" composed a Treatise on the occasion, entitled *De dissidiisPatrum;* but though Henry undertook that Du Perron should refute it, the Cardinal made no attempt. D'Aubigne", *Mem.,* p. 148. $ Sully, liv. xi. § Ibid. of his protestantism: he refused to hunt on St. Bartholomew's day, on account of the peril to which he had been exposed in his youth.

Voltaire observes that Henry could not but yield to adverse circumstances and abjure' having the Pope, the King of Spain and three-fourths of his subjects against him. Gustavus Adolphus or Charles XII would have been inflexible; but they were essentially soldiers, while Henry IV was a politician, f CHAPTER III. REGENCY OF MARY DE MEDICIS.—ASSEMBLY AT SAUMUR. STATES GENERAL. —INSURRECTION OF 1616.

Henry's position had been embarrassing, he was obliged to conciliate opposing interests, and was in consequence exposed to the distrust of each. The protestants complained of his disregard of their long services: the catholics were incensed at his tolerance of heresy. The moderate party composed of the principal judges and advocates, had not acquired sufficient influence to turn the wavering balance. At a subse Bassompierre, vol. i, p. 1'62. f *Essai sur les Mceurs,* rem. 15. *Journal de Henri IV,* in loc.

quent period their opinions gave importance to the Gallican and Jansenist parties; but at Henry's death the intolerant faction prevailed, andEpernon triumphed over Sully. The former, assured of the Queen's support, had already taken his measures; while the latter was waiting the King's visit by appointment. The news of the assassination overwhelmed him; and when he left the Arsenal, he was so deeply affected, that L'Estoile represents him as more dead than alive.

Having collected his attendants, and being subsequently joined by his personal friends, he set out for the Louvre on horseback; but as he advanced, several intimations of danger had been given; and after consulting with Vitry whom he met at the *Croix du Trahoir, f* he decided on returning to the Arsenal. He then sent a message to the Queen, with the assurance of his ready obedience; and informed her, that he watched with additional vigilance over the Bastille, the Arsenal, and other places in his charge. However, before he had regained his quarters, he was pressed by several in the Queen's name, to go as quickly as possible to the Louvre, and be attended with but few persons. Sully's distrust however increased as the message was quickly reiterated. He maturely weighed the warnings he had received, with the information since brought, of archers being seen about the gates of the Bastille, and sent an excuse deferring his visit till the following day. His wife was so commissioned, with a view to observe the state of the court. -f-Bassompierre, after describing his meeting with Sully in the rue St. Antoine, states: "He shut himself up in "the Bastille, sending at the same time to seize all "the bread he could find in the market, and in the "bakers' stores. He

also dispatched a messenger to "his son-in-law, the duke de Rohan, to march upon "Paris with six thousand Swiss, under his com"mand."$ But this excessive caution which has exposed Sully to a charge of disloyalty is scarcely reprehensible, when every feature of the case is brought into view. Notes arrived at the Bastille from many quarters, containing most alarming intelligence; a great consternation had seized the protestants, many of whom could remember the St. Bartholomew; and rumour revived and magnified reports, threatening a repetition of that dreadful scene. The King's death was no sooner known, than many protestants quitted the capital $ and more would have gone, if they had not been deterred, some by persuasion, others by force, until their alarm was proved to be groundless. §

'J-At the corner of the rue de l'Arbre-Sec, a place where executions often took place.

The Count de Soissons hastened to Paris on learning the news of Henry's death: he came well attended, and confident of unlimited influence over the duke of Epernon; but on reaching St. Cloud, he had the mortification to learn that the regency was already disposed of. He would not probably have opposed it; but wished to have made certain conditions. Although a community of feeling existed between Soissons and Epernon on various points, and particularly in hatred to Sully, the young prince failed in his attempt to gain the aged courtier to his views; and to his astonishment the duke made him desist from his project of murdering Sully in the court of the Louvre,-f Sully, liv. xxviii. —Matthieu, *Hitl. de Louis XIII,* p. 3. 'J-*Memoires du marechal d'Estrees,* p. 3. :£ ltassompierre, vol. i, p. 284. $ *Mercure Franfais,* vol. i, p. 463.

Such violence being contemplated, there was reason to apprehend serious consequences from the rumours in circulation among the protestants. Every day beheld an increase of the evil; and a trifle would have sufficed to inflame the kingdom. This was observed by Epernon, who deemed it adviseable to calm the public mind, by a declaration con-

firming the edict of Nantes. $

Mary de Medicis was certainly indebted to Epernon for the post of sole regent. That nobleman took ample measures for suppressing all opposition to his plans, by placing guards on the Pont-Neuf, and in the streets surrounding the convent of the Augustins, where the parliament was to hold its sittings. The president Seguier, with whom he had consulted on the intended measure, had no sooner assembled the members, than Epernon entered, holding in his hand a sword, still sheathed. He appeared agitated and confused; and informed the assembly that his sword was as yet in its scabbard, though he apprehended, that unless the Queen was instantly declared regent, it must be drawn, and might cause great trouble and confusion. The boldness of his proceeding astonished the assembly, and the proposal was adopted forthwith. D'Estrees, p. 5.

f Girard, *Vie du due d'Epernon,* p. 246. Le Vassor, *Hist, de Louis XIII,* vol. i, p. 19; 4to. Amsterdam, 1757. $ Girard, p. 252. The declaration, dated 22 May, 1610, is in the *Mercure Francais,* vol. 1, p. 463.

The prince of Conde, then at Milan, was excited by Fuentes, the Spanish ambassador, to make an effort to obtain the crown. The assistance of the Spanish government was promised as an inducement, f He arrived on the fifteenth of July, accompanied by fifteen hundred gentlemen; which gave some alarm to the Queen, who was fearful that Sully might deliver into his hands the Bastille, the cannon, and treasures of the late King. The prince, on his side had considerable apprehensions: three or four letters were delivered to him, stating that the Queen, instigated by the count de Soissons, intended to arrest him and the duke de Bouillon; and notwithstanding his favourable reception, he continued for some days in a state of readiness for quitting Paris, at the first disturbance which might arise; but when this apprehension was at an end, he advanced his claims to power. $ Girard, pp. 241—243.

t D'Estrera, p. 5. % *Hist, de la Mire*

et du Fils, vol. i, p. 102. This work, published under the name of Mezeray, is very generally attributed to the pen of Richelieu, who is thought to have composed it during the administration of Luynes. Father Daniel is of opinion that Richelieu retouched and corrected it.

The prince, his cousin the count de Soissons, and Epernon, were each at the head of a distinct faction. The duke de Bouillon advised the prince to return to the reformed church, and declare himself its protector. The want of an ostensible head had greatly injured the protestant body, as a party; and if the prince had listened to Bouillon's suggestion, the cause of the Huguenots might have been placed on a very flourishing basis; but that result could only have been effected by establishing an independent government. Sully could not forget what he owed his country; and Conde was not destined by nature for so distinguished a career.

We have the testimony of a respectable contemporary, by no means their partisan, to the quiet deportment of the Huguenots during this crisis. 44 Instructed "by experience, they then displayed great modera"tion, and made no pretensions to innovation *;Jeign "ing* to have no wish to undertake any thing, pro44 vided they were allowed to live according to the "edicts. This produced the King's declaration, that "to maintain harmony among his subjects, it was his "desire that the edict of Nantes should be inviolably "respected." They were, according to this author, so well treated that they had no pretext for agitation.-f

The vast preparations. for Henry's expedition terminated in the taking of Juliers, which surrendered to marshal de la Chastre on the second of September. Sully's opinion respecting this campaign was disregarded: it was useless for him to struggle any further in competition with Epernon; and to use his own expression, the conduct of the Regent completely destroyed all hope of his ever being able to bring back the council to a wholesome line of policy. He retired to the country; but was in a short time invited to return. An agent

communicated her Majesty's desire to have him for her confidential adviser, on the same footing as under the late King. Le Vassor, vol. i, p. 27. Rohan, *Memoires,* liv. i, p. *4.* t Bernard, *Hist. de Louis XIII,* p. 12, Paris, 1646.

Had Mary de Medicis been sincere, and candidly followed up this proposal, her fortune would in all probability have taken a different turn. But a spirit of bigotry was prevalent among the new ministers; and at an early meeting of the council, Villeroy, in expressing his opinion, took occasion to tell the Queen, that the Huguenots were the worst enemies she had to fear; as they had the means and probably more serious intentions than ever, of making an attempt against the government: he concluded by an insinuation against Lesdiguieres. Unhappily a conspiracy had been formed before the King's death, to take arms in Poictou; for which Du Jarrige, a protestant, and two accomplices were hanged in Paris;-f-and the circumstance gave importance to Villeroy's remark. Sully was engaged in conversation at that moment; but his colleague's observations were reported to him: they confirmed what he had heard of a secret council held at the house of the Nuncio; and he was indignant at an attempt, evidently intended to revive the wars of religion. He advanced towards the Queen, who was still talking with Villeroy, and complained of his unfair insinuations against thep rotestants. This breach was never healed; and at the beginning of the following year, Sully was deprived of his post of superintendant of finances, and governor of the Bastille; but he continued governor ofPoictou, and Grand Master of the Artillery,-j Sully, liv. xxix.

f *Journal de Henri IV,* 4 Sept. 1610.

The edict of Nantes had, unfortunately for the interests of the protestants, conferred a political existence upon that body; and the Queen was no sooner named Regent by the parliament of Paris, than her government was formally acknowledged by all the protestant provincial assemblies. The whole kingdom was divided into fifteen provinces; and at the assembly of Saumur there

were present seventy deputies: viz thirty nobles, twenty ministers, sixteen elders, and four delegates from the corporation of Rochelle. In addition to the deputies, Sully, Rohan, La Tremouille, and others of equal importance were invited to be present. £ The Huguenots were so much pleased with occasions of meeting for discussion and mutual encouragement, that it is asserted they held them on every pretext. § D 'Aubigne attempted to raise an opposition in the assembly of Poictou, on the grounds that such an election should have been submitted to the Statesgeneral, and not to the parliament of Paris. This ill judged aet of independence did not prevent his being deputed to assure the Queen of the submission of that province. He was already known for his persuasive qualities; and with his unflinching principles, it was useless to attempt corruption: an effort was therefore made to ruin him in the opinion of his party. The Queen summoned him to Paris, to consult him in private; he remained alone with her for two hours at a time; and soon after, when he set out for the assembly at Saumur, he received such attentions from the government agents, that the Queen's object was in a great measure effected. Sully, liv. xxix.

f *Journal de Henri I.*—Bassompierre.— *Merc. Francais,* and *Uill. de la Mere et du Fils. $ Mercure Francais,* vol. ii, p. 73. § Bernard, p. 18.

This assembly had been convoked for Chatellerault; and its removal to Saumur was an unequivocal proof of the rising jealousy and ill will, which soon after gave a mortal blow to the Huguenots' cause. Indeed their enemies assert, that great designs were to be prepared by them at this meeting, which caused much alarm,-j-Chatellerault was jn Sully's government; and the duke of Bouillon had sufficient influence to effect a change, calculated to hurt the feelings of one whom he considered a rival, if not an enemy. £ At the same time, the Queen being impressed with apprehensions of an insurrection, ordered Duplessis to be watchful in his government, as the deputies were attended by an unusual number of armed followers. Bouillon was corrupted at the very commencement of the regency. Immediately after King Henry's death, he made an attempt to awaken Conde's ambition; but the Queen aided by the marquis de Cceuvres, and skilful negotiators, won him to her cause: his policy then assumed a diametrically opposite character; and being constantly in opposition to Sully, he sided with the court against the protestant party; his own interests at the same time urging him to hasten the ex-minister's ruin, as he was promised the reversion of his employs, f D'Aubigne, *Mem.,* p. 167.

f Daniel, *Hist.de France,* vol. xiii, p. 54. 4: *Veritable Discours de ce qui s'est passe en VAssemblet politique des Egliset reformers de France, tenue a Saumur.*

The memorials prepared for the consideration of the assembly, being confided to the duke of Bouillon, were by him communicated to Yilleroy; and in consideration for a promise of the government of Poictou, with three hundred thousand livres, and some minor stipulations, he undertook to have all the resolutions changed in the discussion; and engaged that every thing should pass off to the Queen's satisfaction, $

A contemporary nobleman relates that Bouillon Tvith his secret instructions, received money to recompense those deputies whom he could gain over; and proceeded to Saumur, where the results justified his assertions. The prudence, skill and firmness he displayed on this occasions, were considered signally serviceable to the state. § 25 May, 1611. Duplessis, *Mim.,* vol. iii, p. 294.

t D'Estrdes, pp. 65—66. Rohan, *Mim.,* liv. i, p. 11.
§ D'Eslrees, p. 66.

This treacherous conduct could not be entirely concealed from the protestant deputies; and although the duke made great efforts to obtain the presidence, Duplessis was elected by a great majority. The vicepresident chosen, was Chamier, a most zealous and courageous Huguenot minister; the same who had assisted in drawing up the edict of Nantes. Bouillon's disappointment

made him give utterance to violent expressions of resentment, declaring that no trouble he had ever experienced, affected him like that. The interference of friends became necessary to pacify him.; and during an interview with Sully, who in expostulating complained of the removal of the assembly from Chatellerault to Saumur, Bouillon replied by complaints against his rival, for having aided an expedition, the object of which was to ruin a church so renowned as that of Sedan. An apparent reconciliation was however effected; and Bouillon declared that he should ever be as ready to bring his cannon from Sedan, Jo defend the cause of religion, as Sully had been to bring those from the Bastille to ruin him.

Bouillon's animosity towards Sully, and his jealousy of Duplessis being too evident to admit a doubt, a common interest excited those individuals, who had long been kept apart by mutual diffidence. Sully was apprehensive that Duplessis might be led by his zeal into projects hostile to the French monarchy; while the latter had openly represented the situation of confidential adviser to an apostate King, as incompatible with a sincere attachment to the protestant religion. The friends of Duplessis also contributed to widen the breach, by insinuating the existence of envy at his acknowledged talents. However the events of the preceding year convinced them of Sully's integrity; and the whole protestant body took an interest in his personal welfare. They entreated, and even enjoined him not to give up his charge; especially that of grand master of the Artillery; and promised their united aid in his support. This demonstration greatly annoyed the duke de Bouillon, who made such a representation to the Queen, that she wrote a letter to the assembly in the King's name. The nature of this communication may be inferred from the fact, that DuplessisMornay deemed its suppression necessary, through fear of the irritation it would cause,-j *Writable Discours,* etc., pp. 24—27.

To return to the proceedings of the assembly, the King's commissioners

announced the favourable intentions of the government towards the protestant body; but when the *cahier* or statement of demands was presented, they declared it indispensable to consult the King's pleasure; their powers not authorizing an approval of the changes proposed. This statement astonished the assembly; and during the tedious negociation which followed, the court agents actively pressed the nomination of the deputies who were to remain at Paris, that being the ostensible cause of the convocation. The more experienced Huguenots were however resolved to wait for a reply, as they foresaw that the assembly would be dissolved as soon as the deputies were named. The duke de Bouillon meanwhile insidiously attempted to injure the protestant body, by representing the exertions he and his friends had been compelled to make, in order to preserve peace; and it was maliciously reported to the Queen, that Sully, Rohan, d'Aubigne, and others were anxious to renew the civil war.

Merc. Franc., vol. ii, p. 27.—Rohan, *Mem.* liv. i, p. 17. i Supplement to Sully, by the abbe de l'Eclusc.

The demands of the assembly comprised above sixty articles, which it is needless to recapitulate,-jThe eighth is one of the most remarkable: in that the protestants complain of their being compelled to qualify themselves in all acts and deeds, as members of *la religion pretendue reformee.* To this grievance they obtained no redress; as the government replied, that they must use the term adopted in the edict of Nantes. Their eleventh article requests that preachers may be punished for abusive and seditious attacks upon them in sermons; and for interdicting all social intercourse with them, under threats of perdition. The government reply is evidently directed against the petitioners; for it enjoins *all* preachers to abstain from exciting language, confining themselves modestly to what will instruct and edify their hearers. A spirit of equivocation pervades the answer to each article; and bears testimony to the bigotry of the age, which is at once its explanation and excuse. The answer to the *cahier* is dated twenty-third of July, 1611.$ On its arrival at Saumur, the duke de Bouillon obtained a power from the Queen, authorizing the minority consisting of twenty-three members, to elect the deputies without the concurrence of the others. Such a measure was excessively irritating; and a contemporary writer who makes no attempt to disguise his partiality, accuses Duplessis of filling an adjoining chamber with armed men, to massacre those who were willing to comply with Bouillon's recommendation; but that the determination of the minority, who filled the courts with their friends and attendants, foiled the plan, and secured a general acquiescence; in consequence of which the deputies were elected, and the meeting separated on the third of Septentjber. *Veritable Discours,* etc., p. 65.

T *Merc. Franc.,* vol. ii, pp. 88 *et seq.*
:£ Printed at the end of the *rentable Discours, etc.*

The readiness of this writer to use opprobrious epithets against the protestants is perfectly consistent, and converts his approbation of Bouillon into a complete corroboration of the venality laid to his charge. The government, he observes, was very well satisfied with him; and on his return he had the grant of an hotel in the Faubourg St.-Germain; but he was not equally satisfied, for he fully expected a greater reward, and calculated on being received into the cabinet; he threatened revenge, and from that time instigated the prince of Conde to hostilities,-f

During the animated discussions at Saumur, the intimate friendship which for many years had subsisted between Bouillon and d'Aubigne, received a violent shock. The latter relates that it was in a great degree through his exertions, that Bouillon failed in the election for president; and that he warmly opposed all his proposals, which were palpably intended to gain favour at court. D'Aubigne's remarks were often severely cutting, particularly on occasion of a pathetic appeal to the loyalty of the deputies; in which Bouillon advised them to renounce their cautionary towns, and rely altogether on the good

faith of the government; his address concluded by exhibiting great want of tact, in alluding to the glory of voluntary exposure to martyrdom. This remark, by admitting the existenceof danger, completely destroyed the effect of his argument; and d'Aubigne, after criticising his project, observed that it was certainly the duty and characteristic of a truB christian to be ever ready to suffer martyrdom; but to expose others, and facilitate their destruction, was to act like a traitor or an executioner.
Hist, de la Mere el du Fils, y. i, p. 13. f Ibid., p. 147.

The tenacity of the protestants at Saumur was calculated to make them more odious to the court. That meeting was looked upon as the first token of disaffection;--and the feeling against them was greatly heightened by the publication of an attack on the papacy, entitled *le Mystere d'iniquite,* by DuplessisMornay. Immediately on its appearance, it was condemned by the Sorbonne; $ and a bookseller was sent to prison for the publication. § It is however worthy of note, that the advocate-general, Louis Servin, being requested to reply to the obnoxious work, after consenting to undertake it, declined the task.
D'Aubigne, *Mem.,* p. 169.
'f Bernard, p. 19.
.$ *Mere. Francais,* vol. ii, p. 109.
§ *Journal de VEtloile,* 19 July, ten.

From this time abjurations became very frequent among the protestant nobles and ministers; and the duke de Rohan was so disliked by the government for his conscientious exertions, that he retired to St.-Jeand'Angely, where he assembled some friends and followers. D'Aubigne at the same time, withdrew to a fortified mansion at Doignon, suspected by the Queen and ministers, and feared by the bigoted party for the sarcasms of his writings, and the energy of his disposition. D'Aubigne's motions were watched with suspicion, and Rohan was obliged to act with vigour, to maintain his rights against an attempt of the Queen, at Rouillon's instigation, to infringe on his privileges. Rohan had proceeded to Paris to justify himself from the charge of seditionat Saumur;

but the court, prepossessed in Bouillon's favour, secretly took measures for placing a mayor at St.-Jean-d'Angely, opposed to Rohan's interests. The Duke being informed thereof, and feeling that this measure, if successful, would ruin his importance, quitted Paris under a pretext of news that his brother Soubise was ill; and though the government agent had arrived before him, he succeeded in regaining his authority, after the threat of an armed force to subdue the town. Two gentlemen whom he had sent to Paris were arrested; and his mother, wife and sisters were forbidden to leave that city. But the affair was peaceably arranged by Themines, governor of Quercy, to the disappointment of Rouillon; who con *Journal de l'Estoile,2t* Aug., 1611.
fessed he had so acted, to take revenge for the affront he received at Saumur.

We pass by the intrigues and negociations, which attended the project of a double marriage between the French and Spanish crowns. Bouillon was sent to assure King James, that England had no cause of apprehension from the alliance. He availed himself of the opportunity to accuse Rohan and the Huguenot leaders as rebels; and endeavoured to obtain from the English monarch a condemnation of the proceedings at Saumur; declaring that the Pope's views towards the lost protestants, were limited to their conversion by preaching and good example. James, naturally averse to hostilities, was ready to believe any thing calculated to promise the duration of peace; and in what concerned the alliance with Spain, Bouillon's mission was successful. Rohan however had a confidential friend who accompanied the ambassador, by whose means, the King was informed of the position and conduct of the protestants; he therefore advised Bouillon to be reconciled with Rohan. A synod was held soon afterat Privas, when an accommodation was signed by all the protestant nobles, f The Jesuit d'Avrigny observes: 44 Rohan was a sincere Huguenot, "and aimed at the good of his party. Sully was not "very devout, but felt sore at being excluded from "public affairs. Bouillon was politic, making reli"gion forward his interests; and doing more harm to "the catholics than to the protestants." *Merc. Franc.,* v. ii, pp. 382—385. Rohan, liv. i, p.. 37. f 16 Aug. 1G12.—Rohan, *Mem.,* liv. i, p. 38.

The dissehtions among the leaders of the party were terminated, but the designs of the court, against the reformed religion, were still suspected by the protestant body, and a meeting was summoned at Rochelle, which gave rise to a tumult, on the interference of the government to prevent it. However, nothing serious followed; for the King gave another edict, confirming that of Nantes, and coupling an entire amnesty of the latedisturbance with a prohibition against such assemblies,-f

The year 1614 witnessed an attempt of the prince of Condeto excite a revolt. Jealousy of marshal d'Ancre was the ground of his discontent; but he was urged on by Bouillon, and encouraged by.the adhesion of many leading nobles, who quitted the court soon after his departure from Paris. $ In the hopes of deriving advantage from the co-operation of the protestants, he sent the lieutenant of his guards to the duke de Rohan, conjuring him to take arms, and promising to conclude no treaty which had not his approbation. Rohan however was not only aware that Bouillon was of the party; he knew that even before hostilities had commenced, there had been preparations for a treaty; he sent a confidential friend to deliver a verbal reply, and learn the prince's exact position: at the same time he wrote to the Queen, stating his unchanged attachmeitf to the reformed interest, and assuring her that by satisfying the protestants' claims she need not fear the disaffected party.

D'Avrigny, *Mem. Chronologiques,* vol. i, p. 68. f *Merc. Franc.,* vol. ii, pp. 476 — 487. The tumult occurred in September, and the King's declaration was dated 15 December, 1612. 4: *Merc. Franc.*, vol. iii, p. 306.

The prince lost no time in publishing the reasons for his conduct, in a letter to the Queen-Mother, f in which he complained of the disordered state of the government, and the exclusion of the princes and peers from public affairs: they were sacrificed, he asserts, to the interests of three or four individuals, who in self-defence excited distrust and ill will among the nobility: he concluded by demanding that the statesgeneral should be convoked.

About the same time a messenger was sent by Conde to Duplessis, to win him over to the cause, but in vain. Duplessis replied by expressing his confidence that the prince would choose lawful means for redressing public grievances; and would avoid violent measures, which were worse than the ills to be removed. At the same time he informed the Queen of the political aspect of his province, giving a faithful account of the movements and meetings that came to his knowledge; he likewise addressed the pastors and principal protestants, recommending quietness and loyalty. The Queen was highly pleased, and informed him that she approved of his answer to the prince. £ Rohan, *Mem.,* liv. i, p. 4 9.

f Dated 19 Feb., 1614. *Merc. Franc.,* p. 317. $ Duplessis, *Mem.,* vol. iii, p. 557 *et seq.*

No one has ever impugned the authenticity of the Letters and Memoirs of Duplessis-Mornay; yet the enemies of the reformed religion (and such were all authors whose works could be published in France during a long period) agree in passing over this and similar incidents, unnoticed, and actually charge the protestants with having caused the evils which originated with their opponents. On the other hand it is beyond doubt, that if Rohan and Duplessis had listened to Conde's proposals, France would have speedily become the scene of a general insurrection.

The court was seriously alarmed at the extent of the conspiracy, and from the prevalent readiness to suspect those who are oppressed, it was generally feared that the Huguenots would join the malcontents, and plunge the country into a civil war of some duration; but Epernon who had passed through the troubles of the League, was satisfied that a want of the means of war would preserve the kingdom from that extremity: he urged the propriety of sending a strong force to suppress.the insurrection, and concluded by assuring that if the Ring were to accompany the troops, there would be an easy conquest. The ministers thought the experiment dangerous, and Epernon lamented the disgraceful, conciliating line of policy adopted in preference: the Queen being so ill advised, as to purchase a peace, which a little.vigour would have enabled her to dictate. The treaty of Ste.-Menehould, where Conde had been secretly negotiating from the time he left Paris, was signed on the fifteenth of May. Conde obtained Amboise; the other confederates were gratified in various ways; and the convocation of the statesgeneral was agreed to. The King's marriage with the Infanta was also to be postponed; but of that the prince received a previous assurance, in a letter from the Queen.

Girard, *Vie A'Epernon,* p. 260.

The states-general, which continued its deliberations from the twenty-fourth of October, 1614, until the end of March in the following year, was at length dissolved without a single measure being voted. The interested disputes of the nobility neutralizingevery individual effort of the more enlightened members. The clergy displayed the full measure of their undiminished bigotry, by demands which could not be acceded to, without a complete abandonment of humanity and justice. Their obstinacy in urging the publication of the council of Trent may be excused, as those decrees are a compendium of popery, and have become its infallible canon, in opposition to the right of free commentary, claimed by protestants. In this instance they were consistent and reasonable; yet in the worst period of popish illiberality there has been a determined opposition to the reception and sanction of those decrees, by the French parliaments. But it is difficult to mark with adequate abhorrence some of the proposals, gravely made and seriously maintained by the clergy: a few will suffice as a specimen. They demanded the condemnation of all books injurious to Che pope; authority for bishops to condemn to the galleys; prohibition against printing any books without the bishops' licence; that protestants should not speak or write against the sacraments of the Romish church, under severe penalities; that their ministers should not visit the sick, and that their colleges should be suppressed. As an argument for justifying these demands, which were fully satisfied at a later period, Richelieu, then bishop of Lujon, laid stress on a recent tumult at Milhaud, in the diocese of Rodez, where the consecrated ornaments, and even the host had been trampled under foot. The King's indignation was kindled on hearing of such a sacrilege; but notwithstanding his vow to avenge the outrage, the affair was entirely laid aside. It was found on investigation, not only that the accounts had been mischievously aggravated; but that the popish party had committed even greater excesses in the same diocese,-j *Mere. Franc., P-427 et sea.*

The president of each state having delivered his *cahier* to the King, all the suggestions were referred for the sake of form, to the council, but without any intention of their being examined. However, among the deputies of the *tiers-etat,* the demands of the clergy were so seriously scrutinised, that there was an outcry against the prevalence of heresy in that body.; there were protestants among the deputies, and the alarm which they manifested at the great zeal of the clergy, induced Louis to publish a declaration, renewing and confirming the edict; hypocritically expressing a hope, that the divine mercy would unite all his subjects in one faith, since violent measures were useless. The states-general were then dissolved, and the inutility of such assemblies being completely evident, the institution may be said to have been from this time abolished; for the states of 1789, though bearing the same appellation were altogether different in character and object; the monarchical power being then virtually overthrown, and instead of the body alluded to being the representation of general interests, it proved the medi-

um for announcing that noble, feudal, and ecclesiastical privileges had been all swallowed up by the increased importance of the popular body.

"Arcana Gallica, p. 46.
t *Merc. Franc.,* p. 398.—Benoit, v. ii, p. 149.— *Arcana Gallica,*

The duke de Bouillon had indulged a hope, that with the assistance of the states-general, he could drive marshal d'Ancre from his post. The aspect of the assembly favoured his views: many of the deputies were indignant at the manner in which Ravaillac's trial had been conducted; and contended that his accomplices could have been discovered, if sought for in earnest. Marshal d'Ancre was detested throughout France; and the majority of lawyers who had been elected by the tiers-etat, were offended at the indifference of the court, which was construed by them into disdain. The parliament was in consequence easily induced to adopt a measure, intended to assert its dignity, which was in some measure violated by the dissolution of the States without knowing the opinion of that body upon the proposals presented; and a decree was passed for assembling all its members, inviting the princes, peers, and officers of state to join in deliberating on certain proposals for the general good. This step was met by an intimation of the King's severe displeasure; and a prohibition so positive, that the parliament made no other opposition than a remonstrance, indicating a long series of inconveniences, (many being merely social or municipal) which it was desirable to remedy.

As the princes had founded their hopes on the energy of the tiers-etat and the firmness of the parliament, this conclusion brought back affairs to the condition in which they stood, prior to the treaty of Ste.Menehould. Conde again displayed the standard of revolt, withdrew to Creil, and sent his cannon to Sedan. The King wrote several letters urging his return to court, and afterwards sent the aged and experienced Villeroy to persuade him; but Conde in reply, denounced Ancre and his partisans as enemies of the state. This was

followed by a general proclamation from the prince, addressed to all orders of the state, f

But before that address was made public, the King had sent against him an army of ten thousand infantry, and fifteen hundred cavalry, under marshal BoisDauphin; while another force, commanded by the duke de Guise, escorted him to the Spanish frontier, where he was to meet his affianced bride. $ *Mere. Franc.,* vol. iv, pp. 6—HO.—*Hist, de la Mereet du Fits,* pp. 327 *et seq. f Merc. Franc.,* vol. iv, p. 197.—Rohan, *Mem.* , liv. i, p. 63. $ Bassompierre, vol. i, p. 392.—Rohan, *Mem.,* liv. i, p. 64.

Conde, being informed of the favourable disposition existing among many of the principal inhabitants of Rochelle, proceeded there in December; and was received with every demonstration of honour, by those who revered his father's memory. The minister Merlin was led to hope for his conversion, from the candid admissions elicited during his conversations with the prince. But a selfish ambition was his motive; and in treating with that jealous municipality, he consented to greater restraints, than he would have endured in the lawful service of his King.

The protestants at the same time held an assembly at Grenoble; and Conde deputed thither a gentleman named La Haye, to request their co-operation with him, in effecting a reformation of all abuses. His promises were calculated to ensnare a considerable number of the Huguenot deputies; who were stimulated by Bouillon, to perceive much advantage in the proposals. On the other hand, Lesdiguieres was in correspondence with the Queen, and exerted his influence to prevent the meeting from acceding to the offers, f Rohan and Sully varied in their determination, according to circumstances; but Duplessis-Mornay was decidedly averse to mingling the cause of religion with politics. His letters to the Queen, Villeroy and Jeannin; and his representations of the danger to which his government would be exposed, if the prince marched into Poictou, are unquestionable proofs of his loyalty: on the other hand, the official replies from the King and his ministers prove that such honourable conduct was justly estimated.

Arcere, vol. ii, p. 139. f Bernard, p 52. — *Merc. Franc.,* vol. iv, p. 193.

In one of his conferences with the chancellor Sillery he observed: "Since the Jesuits in their sermons, "openly declare that the object of the double mar"riage is to root out heresy, can you be surprised that 44 our churches take the alarm?" Yet he endeavoured to tranquillize his friends; and when a proposal was made to transfer the assembly to Nismes, in order to escape the interference of Lesdiguieres, he considered their proceedings legally null; as the royal sanction was requisite to give their votes validity. The King, being solicited, consented to their meeting at Montpellier; but Chatillon was a protestant of the same dubious character, and the deputies persisted in selecting Nismes for their sittings.-J

Among the French nobility none was more decidedly inveterate against the reformed religion, than the duke of Epernon; but to the surprise of all, his son, the count de Candale declared himself a protestant. $ His position created great interest, and gave him considerable influence. He recommended the union with Conde; and a treaty was voted, though only by a majority of two votes. Conde who really hated the protestants, was lavish in his concessions to the party; but Mayenne, whose interests were similar, refused to grant any thing likely to benefit Calvinism. § The government duly appreciated the conduct of the minority, in a royal declaration which appeared soon after; and the effects of this prudent conduct make it the more to be regretted, that it was not followed by measures of a similar character; for the majority of the Huguenots disavowed the assembly at Nismesj as a complete party affair.

Duplessis, *Mem.,* vol. iii, pp. 812—835. f *Arcana Gallica,* pp. 74—75.— Bernard, p. 54. $ *Merc. Franc.,* vol. iv, p. 279. % 27 Nov. 1615.—D'Avrigny, vol. i, p. 92.

D'Aubigne was induced to take a part in this revolt; and was chosen by Conde for his marechal-de-camp; but that gentleman declined the prince's commission, and would only receive his appointment from the assembly at Nismes. This war, as he observes, gave rise to no event worth recording; and was soon concluded by the treaty of Loudun.-j-Conde had in council, called him his father; but ultimately behaved to him most dishonourably: he never reimbursed a large sum which d'Aubigne advanced for supplies; and on returning to Paris, denounced him to the King, as one capable of troubling the government. When the treaty of Loudun was signed, Conde knowing that d'Aubigne's character would still keep him from court, exclaimed: "D'Aubigne! begone to your fort at Doignon!" To which the veteran replied: "And you to the Bastille!" The prediction was very soon realized.$ 7 Dec. 1615. *Merc. Franc.,* vol. iv, p. 331. The president Jeannin thus wrote to Duplessis: "Vous vous estes conduict, pendant ceste miserable guerre, en sorte que leurs Majestes en'ont contentement, et y reconnaissent votre prudence et fidelite." Duplessis, *Mem.,* vol. iii,p. 856. f 3May, 1616. The negociations are minutely detailed in the *Mercure Francais.* $ D'Aubigne, *Mem.,* p. 174. CHAPTER IV.

Condf, Arrested.—Death Of Marshal D'ancre.—RE-ESTA RLISHMENT OF THE ROMISH RELIGION IN BEARN.—NOTICE OF D'aubigne.

The negociations for the treaty of Loudun were conducted principally with a view to draw Conde from the path of revolt; and the deputies who attended to defend the protestant interests, were treated as mere cyphers. The Queen is represented, by one who knew her well, to have aimed at winning the prince to her party; but as she could not refrain from making him feel his dependence upon her favour, her plan failed. She changed her ministers: Barbin, a man of inferior condition, but great talents, became comptroller of finances; the seals were given to Du Vair; and to gratify the prince, marshal d'Ancre was ordered to exchange the government of Picardy for that of Normandy, f

But notwithstanding these concessions, the harmony of the court was far from being established. Epernon was in a manner disgraced; but an attempt to enlist the dukes of Bouillon and Mayenne against that nobleman, having completely failed, marshal d'Ancre found his position at once uncertain and dangerous.

Bassompierre, *NouveauxMem.,* p. 19C. f *Hist, de la Mere el diC Filtj* vol. ii, p. 20.

The extraordinary elevation of Concini was a source of jealousy to the French nobles. This Florentine whose principal merit was that of being a favourite, had been raised to the rank of marquis d'Ancre, and the dignity of marshal; and Conde's efforts were directed to his overthrow, on principles similar to those of his grandfather, in opposition to the house of Lorraine. The prince's cause was warmly espoused by Mayenne, Longueville, and Vendome; but his chief strength was in the influence of the duke de Bouillon, which assured him of the friendly feeling of the protestants, even supposing he could not command assistance from that body. The treaty of Loudun having changed his relative position, he was no longer d'Ancre's enemy.

Notwithstanding the change in Conde's deportment, d'Ancre was not ignorant of the dangers of his position: gifted with acute perception, he knew that the transfer of authority from the Queen Mother to her son, would be attended with his disgrace: still his haughty demeanour was calculated to increase the popular odium, already directed with violence against him. Under such circumstances a trivial incident sometimes becomes important; and an unfortunate encounter arose, in which d'Ancre's name was blended, though without the least blame accruing to him. The marshal proceeding to his house in the faubourg St.-Germain, was stopped for want of a passport, at the Porte de Bussy, by a shoemaker named Picard, on duty as serjeant of the quarter. The marshal was compelled to return, after submitting to some most insulting remarks; and a threat of firing was even made, if he did not go back. As this occurred before the conclusion of the peace, the shoemaker was justified by the instructions for garrison discipline during the war; and there the affair might have terminated, as the humble condition of the individual would sufficiently have protected him against the marshal's resentment. It was however publicly stated, that the insult was intentional; that the serjeant was one of Conde's partisans; and that he boasted in public of what he had done. An esquire of the marshal's, indignant at such conduct, employed two valets to waylay the serjeant, and beat him so unmercifully, that he was left for dead. The valets were taken, and hanged a few days afterwards. The excitement arising out of this circumstance had not subsided when Conde arrived in the capital, and was conducted in triumph to the Louvre by the people, who took that opportunity of shewing their hatred of the marshal. He was induced by the situation of affairs to come to Paris, notwithstanding the danger to which he was exposed. About this time lord Hay, afterwards earl of Carlisle, arrived with a splendid embassy to ask the hand of one of the princesses, for the prince of Wales. He was most magnificently received; each of the leading nobles endeavouring to outvie the others, in the sumptuous entertainments given in his honour. At the fete given by the prince of Conde, the marshal appeared, accompanied by about thirty gentlemen; this step has been commented on as very bold, for it is well known that his enemies were then assembled, and were anxious to take advantage of the opportunity to kill him. The prince, however, had pledged his word for the marshal's safety; but the following day, Conde sent the archbishop of Bourges, a mutual friend, to inform him of the extreme difficulty he Had experienced in keeping his adherents within bounds; that they all threatened to abandon him if he did not discontinue his protection; and in consequence, he advised the marshal to retire to his government in Normandy.

June, 1610. *Merc. Franc.,o.* v.—Has-

sompierre, vol. i, p. t6».

The Queen Mother became alarmed at the aspect of affairs: Conde's influence was very menacing; his confederates were known to be already making preparations for another campaign; and Longueville obtained possession of Peronne, a town belonging to d'Ancre. *ƒ* In addition to these overt acts, the archbishop of Bourges informed the Queen, that the conspirators intended to seize the King's person, and place her in a convent. $ She might have disregarded this intimation, from a feeling by no means rare among individuals of high spirit, which prompts them to neglect what is to their personal advantage; but she could not disregard the advice of Sully, who forgot his injuries, and demanded an audience for the purpose of making known the danger of her situation.

Bassompierre, p. 462.—Rohan, *Mem.,* liv. i, p. 85.—D'Estr&s, p. 216. f Aug. 1616. *Merc. Franc.,* p. 180. $ *Hist, de la Mire et du Fits,* vol. ii, p. 72.

That experienced and loyal statesman declared that he did not deem her safe in Paris, but should consider her much better off, with her children in the country, attended by a thousand horsemen, than in the Louvre in the present state of the public mind; and frankly exposed the fatal consequences of a want of energy on her part. Bassompierre, then colonel-general of the Swiss Troops, was. presently admitted; and his opinions coinciding with those of Sully, he was ordered to make arrangements for a vigorous measure.

It was intended to arrest at once, the prince of Conde and the dukes of Vendome, Mayenne, and Bouillon; but the first alone fell into the Queen's power. A marshal's baton recompensed Themines for arresting him in the Louvre, while receiving the homage of a crowd of courtiers. Mayenne and Vendome were warned in time to leave Paris; and Bouillon, who had gone to public worship at Charenton, learned the news of Conde's arrest on his return: he hastened to join his friends, and take measures for their common safety,-j

The princess dowager of Conde rode

through the streets, accompanied by several gentlemen; and excited the people to avenge her son, who she said was murdered by marshal d'Ancre. An infuriated mob rushed to his hotel in the rue de Tournon; it was exposed to pillage during two entire days; and property was destroyed to the value of two hundred thousand crowns. At the same time the nobles and gentlemen of Conde's party threatened to murder Sully, as the instigator of the measure. This has been assigned as the cause of a very inconsistent remark, which escaped him in the Queen's presence, when the state of affairs was passed in review. Villeroy and Jeannin were both of opinion, that the prince should be liberated; and Sully, forgetting his recent recommendation, declared that whoever had thus advised the Queen, had ruined the state. f The prince alone being arrested, he may have viewed the affair as a failure; and perhaps wished in consequence, to retrace his steps; for Duplessis-Mornay wrote to the duchess of Rohan, that the advice was given out of hatred to M. de Bouillon, $ Bassompierre, v. i, p. 466.

f » Sept. 1616. *Merc. Franc.,* p. 198. —D'Estrees, p. 218.—Bassompierre, p. 478....

From this time d'Ancre was exposed to the vengeance of Conde's partisans, whenever his ill fortune should enable them to resent the injury. In a conversation with Bassompierre, he confessed his desire to return to Florence; or at any rate to remove to Caen, whence an embarcation for Italy could be easily obtained. At one time he had every thing prepared for departure; but a sudden illness prevented his wife from undertaking the voyage. § He fortified his residence at Quillebœuf, and came to Paris no more than was absolutely necessary; but a new enemy had arisen to supplant him in the royal favour, Albert de Luynes, who became a most formidable instrument to effect his ruin. This young man rapidly gained the King's confidence, by his fascinating manners and adroit pliancy to the feeble monarch's wishes: his next step was to undermine the Queen's influence over her son; and to that end some inferior functionaries were employed to give him, as if unde-signedly, a most exaggerated account of public affairs. Louis at first entertained a dislike to his mother for her misgov-ernment; he then burned with ambition to take the reins into his own hands; and as among the courtiers there were many reckless individuals, impatient for the marshal's overthrow, a dastardly project was formed for murdering the Queen's favourite. Vitry, captain of the guards, was selected for this dishonourable deed; and the rank of marshal was again made the price of violence: his com-mission was executed on the twenty-fourth of April, 1617, when the unfor-tunate d'Ancre received the contents of three pistols, as he entered the Louvre. The atrocious act was followed by shouts of *Vive le Roy,* on which the King presented himself at the palace window, to acknowledge the loyal service.

Bassompierre, p. 481.—Rohan, liv. i, p. 87. f *Hist, de la Mire et du Fils,* vol. ii, p. 94. :£ 6 Sept. 1616. Duplessis, vol. iii, p. 989.

§ Bassompierre, p. 501.—*Hist, de la Mere et duFUs, vol. ii,* p. 67.

This put an end to the regency: the Queen was closely guarded; and the marshal's widow and partisans were ar-rested. The scenes, which followed at-test the brutality of the French populace. D'Ancre's remains were disinterred, ex-posed with the greatest indignity, and publicly torn to pieces. The unfortunate widow, Eleonora Galigai, was after-wards treated with a severity which can hardly be justified, even if all the charges preferred against her, were well founded. The parliament of Paris was unfortunately affected by the ferocious spirit of the age.

Hisl. de la Mere el du Fits, vol. ii, p. 185.

Blois was selected as the scene of the Queen's exile, or rather captivity; for she was debarred every vestige of lib-erty, and experienced repeated insults. After some time she wrote to request an interview with her son, but the policy of Luynes rendered it necessary to prevent the meeting, if possible; and the Jesuit Arnoux was sent to dissuade her from reiterating the proposal. Various argu-

ments were used to persuade her, fol-lowed by threats of harsher treatment; and she was finally induced to make a declaration on oath, that she would nev-er go to the King, unless sent for; and that being sent for, shewould not inter-fere with public affairs. A declaration to this effect was signed at the Jesuit's pro-posal.

Yet even this did not satisfy the Queen's persecutors, who thought of imprisoning her in the castle of Am-boise: which intention being communi-cated, added to the vexations of captivi-ty, caused her to meditate some plan for the recovery of her liberty. Her confine-ment, which lasted-nearly two years, was at length terminated in February, 1619, by a spirited exploit of the veteran duke of Epernon; who executed a most romantic expedition for effecting her re-lease.-f *Hist, de la Mire ei du Fils,* vol. ii, p. 212.

f Relation de la Sortie de la Reyne Mere de Blois, par le cardinal de La Valette. This piece is inserted in the *Memoire$ pour servir d I'Histoire du cardinal de Richelieu,* par Aubery.

A tedious series of negotiations and in-trigues followed; and in September the King met her near Tours, after which, Angers was selected for her abode. She resided in that town until the following year, when it became a rendez-vous of discontented nobles to such an extent, that the King was obliged to bring an armed force before it. As the troops ap-proached, the Queen's friends showed a disposition to negociate; but Conde who had recovered his liberty, was en-deavouring to make himself valuable to Louis; and being probably instigated by resentment against the Queen-Mother, pushed affairs to an extremity, by at-tacking the Pont-de-Ce, a small place in the neighbourhood of Angers. The re-sult of this engagement quickly induced a surrender. Still the King was disposed to act leniently towards his mother's ad-herents; and a convention was signed, by which the prisoners were liberated and an amnesty granted,-f

The King was advised to take advan-tage of the present moment, when he had a respectable force at his disposal,

to subjugate the province of Bearn; where the protestant religion had taken deep root, and attained almost general adoption, under the protection and en-couragement of Jane d'Albret. These protestants were obnoxious, not only on account of the heretical notions they held, in common with the general body of the Huguenots; they had besides been so favoured by their zealous Sovereign, that all the church property was in their hands: in consequence every ecclesias-tic having access to the Royal council, would urge the prosecution of a mea-sure for removing such a scandal. Conde approved of the plan, principally because he was anxious for a war, in which he might gain importance; and the King was easily persuaded to at-tempt what coincided so well with his feelings. This epoch is, on that account, important in the annals of the protestant religion; for upon the fate of this under-taking' depended the subsequent pros-perity of the reformed religion in France.

7 Aug. 1620. f *Hiit. de la Mire et du Fih.* —*Merc. Franc.*—Bassompierre.

To preserve a greater degree of per-spicuity in this narrative, the more im-mediate affairs of theprotestants have given place to events which, however important in themselves, were far less interwoven in the proceedings of that body. It will now be requisite to return to the year 1616, when the prince of Conde, after involving many Huguenots in a contest with the crown, took es-pecial care of his own interests in the treaty of Loudun; and unfeelingly left his dupes to their good or ill fortune.

The character of Duplessis-Mornay stands too high to allow any suspicion of his integrity; but his aversion to resis-tance, and his constant dissuasions from vigorous efforts, even when all hopes of averting the threatened ill had passed away, caused incalculable injury to his party. The line of conduct he pursued from conscientious loyalty, was fol-lowed by other Huguenot chiefs from sordid motives; and it is established be-yond doubt, that the constable's sword and a mar shal's baton were the bribes for detaching Lesdiguieres and La

Force from the protestant interest. Even Chatillon could not be deemed staunch in the cause for which his ancestor had been a martyr. It was probably a knowledge of the sentiments entertained by the leading Huguenots, which made Duplessis write to the assembly at Rochelle, that the churches would sooner or later be afflicted.

The disposition to molest them was evident; Epernon's conduct in the province of Aunis was a specimen of the treatment to be expected at a future time; and when lord Hay came to Paris on a mission in 1616, he begged the Queen to withdraw that haughty nobleman' from the province, as the protestants of Rochelle had sought the assistance of Great Britain, which could not be refused if they were molested in their religion. The Queen, who expected a communication relative to the demand of her daughter in marriage, was quite surprised at his observations; yet she replied in general terms of a satisfactory nature,-f

A few days afterwards, when the tidings of Conde's arrest reached Rochelle, the inhabitants were greatly apprehensive of some violent measure to their prejudice; and as a precaution for securing the navigation of the Charente in the event of a war, they seized upon Rochefort, a small town in the neighbourhood. Blanquet, Gaillard and some other *Huguenot pirrates,* observes the courtier Bernard, had assembled four ships of war and some small vessels, with a iew to command the mouth of the Charente. They were defeated by Barraut, vice-admiral of Guyenne, and the ill-fated Blanquet and Gaillard were broken on the wheel at Bordeaux. Cameron, the minister who attended theni previous to execution, published an account of their last moments; which was condemned by the parliament of Guyenne to be burnt by the executioner. It was not clearly shewn whether the expedition was a private scheme of the individuals concerned, or a measure sanctioned by the party. But as the vessels were chiefly fitted out at Rochelle, the proceedings afforded Epernon a pretext for attacking that town; and at the same

time justified his levying men, for protection against the known hatred of d'Ancre's party, f However his expedition altogether failed; and instead of surprising the city, of which he hoped to get possession, he withdrew to Guyenne. It was subsequently feared by the court, that Rochelle would take an interest in Conde's captivity, and declare in his favour. Villette, son-in-law of d'Aubigne, was in consequence sent to assure the protestants, that the edicts would be punctually observed, and the stipulations of the treaty ofLoudun fulfilled. $ 17 Dec. 161C— Duplessis, vol. iii,p. 1025. f 27 Aug. 1616.—Bassompierre, vol. i, p. 470. Bernard, p. 147. f Girard, p. 280.—Arcere, vol. ii p. H3.

From this time until the period of the expedition against Angers, nothing of moment occurred. The protestant synods andassemblies were frequently held—too frequently for their own prosperity; because when the King's sanction was not given, they met as if in defiance. Yet with the exception of the affairs of Bearn, their discussions were entirely on questions of divinity and discipline. But the condition of that province had occupied the attention of the government for some years. Henry IV seems to have wished to leave the principality as he received it from his mother; but from 1614, representations were repeatedly made on the subject. The states-general of 1614 demanded the restoration. of the Romish religion, and the annexation of the province to France. The bishop ofBeauvais made a similar demand in the name of the French clergy. In the state councils, at the assemblies of the clergy, and in short, on almost every occasion, the government was exhorted to re-establish the catholic worship, and restore the church lands. The bishop of Macon assured the King, that christians were better treated in mahometan countries than in the principality of Bearn; where the property of the church was applied to the support of its enemies. The King was greatly moved by the appeal; and his ideas of piety caused such a direct sanction of heresy to lay heavy on his conscience,-j *if.* Arcere, vol. ii, p. 147.

An *arret* was soon after given by the King, in council, for the complete restoration of the Roman catholic worship in Bearn, with a resumption of the church lands: which was followed by a declaration of the assembly at Orthez, that the execution of this decree should be resisted; and the president Lescun, who was deputed to remonstrate with the government, was so far led away by the warmth of his feelings and party zeal, that although the King permitted him to expose his arguments, he obtained no other result than an edict confirming the previous *arret.* From that time his violence against the government exceeded all bounds; he was the most active promoter of the opposition at the assembly at Loudun in 1619, where according to the statement of catholic writers, he proclaimed the ne-' cessity of taking arms to prevent the resumption of the church property. This show of resistance only served to increase the efforts of the clergy in persuading the King to adopt strong measures for vindicating his own prerogatives, no less than for serving the cause of religion,-f *Merc. Franc., in loc.* f Bernard, p. 149.

The King being in the field at the head of an army, travelled southward; and on reaching Bordeaux, resolved to proceed in earnest to terminate the affairs of Bearn. $ The parliament of Pau refused for some time to register the King's edict for restoring the church lands to the catholics; and on the tenth of October, 1620, Louis set out from Bordeaux to compel the submission of that body. The advocate-general of the parliament accompanied by La Force, met the King on the road, and presented the decree which had been voted on hearing of his determination. That did not however prevent the King's advance: he reached Pau on the fifteenth of October; and ordered the Romish worship to be celebrated in the cathedrals and churches, Lescun was subsequently executed for high treason. *.f Histoire des Troubles du Beam, au sujet de la Religion, dans le* 17" *siicU,* par le P. Mirasson, Barnabite, pp. 20—45. % Berule, afterwards famous as cardinal, resorted to a pretended inspiration, in order to confirm the King's resolution. At a private audience, he assumed a prophetic tone, and declared that the Almighty would conduct him; that his appearance alone would overcome all opposition; and that complete success would attend his purpose, for restoring the authority of Jesus Christ. Mirasson, p. 47. from which it had been excluded sixty years. Within five days from his arrival, a decree was registered for incorporating Bear n with France.

The campaign of 1620 was calculated to discourage altogether the disaffected of every class and party, from the facility with which the Queen's adherents were subdued. D'Aubigne, who had declined an invitation to join that party, was nevertheless exposed to suspicion, and marked as a subject for persecution. The approach of the Ring in person with a formidable force, was serious to one so circumstanced: he decided on retiring to Geneva, and quitted St.-Jeand'Angely with twelve horsemen well armed. Although orders for his arrest had been given in every direction, and the commanders were furnished with his portrait, in order to recognise him, he completed his journey in safety. After a series of unusual difficulties and dangers he arrived at Geneva on the first of September, where he was received with every demonstration of respect, which the authorities of that city could devise for one whose ardour for religious liberty was unrivalled. f

In addition to an inflexible disposition, which rendered d'Aubigne obnoxious to the court, he had recently become still more so by the freedom of his publications. His *Histoire Universelle* was burnt by the common hangman, almost immediately after its appearance. £ Having been an eye-witness of the most important military operations during the long civil wars; moving in a sphere, which enabled him to converse with the leaders of each party; and enjoying a reputation for great probity and discretion, which won their confidence, he was well qualified to relate the eventful scenes in which he had taken part. But ihe naked truth appeared in the light

of an accusation; and the work was condemned. The Jesuits had persuaded Henry IV to forbid the composition; but cardinal du Perron had that order countermanded: the hostility displayed by those ecclesiastics at its subsequent publication is quite natural. D'Aubigne wrote likewise several humorous pieces, in which an extraordinary vein of satire was remarkable. *Le baron de Foenesle* in particular, was severely cutting upon the duke of Epernon, whose party was powerful, and who was a warm friend to the Jesuits. D'Aubigne's voluntary exile was therefore easily accounted for. During his residence at Geneva, the general assembly of Rochelle sent messengers to testify their regret at the injustice he had received from that body in his private affairs; to express their sympathy in his exile, and the loss they suffered by his absence; and to authorize him to negotiate with the Swiss and Dutch protestants for levies and supplies. He also received proposals from the Venetian ambassador at Berne, to take employment in the service of that republic, as general of the French troops in their pay. The latter proposal was nearly agreed to, when Miron, the French envoy, sent word that the Venetian republic would not fail of incurring the extreme displeasure of Louis, by employing a man he held in abomination. Thus tacitly avowing the importance of this excellent man, of whom *Merc. Franc., v.* vi, pp. 350—354.

f D'Aubigne, *Mem.,* pp. 189—192. $ 4 Jan. 1617, D'Aubigne, *Mem.,* p. 193—200. it may be truly said, that his uncompromising principles alone prevented him from obtaining the highest honours. His prospects in youth being more than usually favourable, from the personal friendship of the King of Navarre; and his acknowledged merit surpassing that of many who obtained the rank of marshal.

Theodore Agrippa d'Aubigne was born at St.-Maury in Poictou, in February, 1550; he died at Geneva, in April, 1630. CHAPTER V. *r* ASSEMBLY AT ROCHELLE. —RIOTS AT TOURS.—ST.-JEAN D'anGELY SUBDUED.—SIEGE OF MON-

TAUBAN.—VIOLENCE OF A MOB IN PARIS.

The abolition of the provincial independence of Bear n was the pretext of a general assembly at Rochelle. It was to no purpose that the King published a declaration, forbidding the meeting: the huissier sent to signify the publication to the mayor received no other answer, than that he might leave when he pleased. This conduct was regretted by the principal Huguenots, who foresaw the natural effect would be to irritate the government. The duke de Rohan did all in his power to persuade his friends to submit, but in vain; he was accused of being sold to the court. La Force, Chatillon, and Favas, from interested motives urged the deputies to be firm; and a solemn fast preceded the opening of the session, on the twenty-fifth of December,-j *Merc. Franc.,* vol. yi, p. 459.

Even if the limits of the present work did not preclude the attempt, it would be useless to detail every proceeding of this assembly, represented by the duke de Rohan, as the source of all the ills which followed, $ Warnings and monitions were addressed from every side. ' Telinus, a minister of great celebrity, published an address; La Tremouille assisted Rohan in the endeavour to persuade; and Lesdiguieres wrote three times, exhorting the Huguenot body to desist from setting the royal authority at defiance. § Duplessis was not discouraged by several failures: he persevered in sending his memorials to the assembly; commissioned his son-in-law Villarnoul, to deliver a final address; and wrote a private letter to the mayor of Rochelle, in which he exhorted him to reflect seriously on the consequences of his dangerous policy.

The threatening aspect of affairs made it important to secure the co-operation of Lesdiguieres; and the King offered to revive the dignity of constable in his favour, on condition however that he became a catholic. Lesdiguieres received the intimation at Grenoble, and immediately hastened to Paris, to express his sense of the obligation, and give evidence of his loyal zeal, by endeavouring to convince the assembly at Rochelle of their error. He could not however decide upon abjuring his religion; and declined the proposed honor, with a recommendation of Luynes as a more fit person to fill that important post. Conde and Guise approved of the selection, and the nomination of Luynes was registered by the parliament of Paris.

Rohan, *Discours sur les derniers Troubles,* p. 101. f Arcere, vol. ii, p. 155. £ Rohan, *Discours,* etc., p. JO).

§ His letters are given at length in the *Merc. Franc.* Arcere, v. ii, p. 163.

There had been some movements at the close of 1620, in the Vivarais and Beam, which made it more requisite to enforce respect for the authority of the crown; and the King took the field with a force adequate for suppressing the insurrectionary bodies; as well as for humbling the obstinate assembly of Rochelle, At the same time, to encourage the loyal portion of the protestants, he published a declaration, assuring them of his intention to maintain the edicts in their favour.f

It was the King's intention, on leaving Fontainebleau, to remain some time at Blois, from which central position the moral effect of his presence with, an army, might render military operations needless. He was however induced to hasten onto Tours, where a conflict between the protestants and catholics had threatened to produce serious consequences. It originated with the funeral of a protestant, named Martin Le Noir, an inn-keeper whose character was not calculated to honour the religion he professed, if a correct opinion can be founded on a popular refrain. As his body was taken to the cemetery, a number of children followed, singing the couplets alluded to; and in the market place the people hooted at the procession. At the place of burial, the children continued singing; on which some of the party turned, and striking them, caused two of the disturbers to fall into the grave. The consequence of this was an interference on the part of the populace: the protestants were attacked with stones, and compelled to seek shelter.

The ignorant people, ever ready to gratify the brutal feelings engendered by prejudice, and on this occasion urged by revenge, rushed to the cemetery, and took up thebody of Martin Le Noir, with the intention of hanging and burning it. At the same time the houses and stores of the protestants were broken into and devastated. The magistrates were unable to quell the tumult; the body was however deposited in the grave; and such of the goods as were not destroyed were placed in safety; but it was beyond their power to restore order. The following day the mob set fire to the protestant temple, and prevented the authorities from interfering to stop the conflagration. The sedition continued with shortintermissions until the King's arrival, on the sixth of May. A species of fury animated the mob, who renewed their attacks on fresh pretexts, each succeeding day; till at length nearly thirty of the ringleaders being arrested, the future tranquillity of the town was secured by a severe example. Five were condemned to walk barefoot from the prison to the market place, where they were hanged, and their bodies burned: which sentence was executed without any disturbance. The remainder were pardoned, and soon afterwards set at liberty.

22 April, 1621. *Merc. Franc.,* v. vii, p. 277. f 24 April, 1C21. Ibid., vol. vii, p. 286 Le plus grand cornar
Qui soit en la France,
C'est Martin Le Noir:
Telle est ma croyance.
Merc. Franc., vol. vii, p. 291.

From Tours the King proceeded to Saumur, where he remained five days,-j- His authority was there exercised rather severely. Duplessis, whose loyalty and moderation had been uniformly praised at court, was ordered to resign the keys of Saumur: impartiality will however admit some excuse for this harsh decision; it was reported to the King, that the assembly of Rochelle purposed sending a body of six thousand men to hold Saumur, and cut off all communication with the capital. $ That such a violent measure was really contemplated is not proved; but there is evidence

of readiness to adopt it, in the organisation of the Huguenot forces, by dividing France into eight circles, with a commander appointed to each. § It was in fact establishing a feudal republic, only without entirely disclaiming a nominal allegiance; and such a defiance was necessarily followed by energetic measures on both sides.

The siege of St.-Jean-d'Angely was commenced on the sixteenth of May, by count d'Auriac with a division of four thousand men. The town was well defended; and the inhabitants showed themselves worthy of their ancestors, who had sustained three sieges of considerable celebrity. Even the women shared the labours and dangers, working night and day at the fortifications, and preparing cartridges. The duke de Soubise commanded the place; f and his brother Rohan, within three days after the beginning of the siege, threw in a reinforcement of a thousand soldiers, and above one hundred gentlemen; after which he proceeded to Guyenne, the circle entrusted to him by the assembly, $ 10 May, 1621. *Merc. Franc.,* pp. 291—304.—Bernard, pp. 209 —211. f From 12 to 16 May. $ *Merc. Franc.,* vol. vii, p. 304.

S Bernard, liv. vi, p. 221 *etseq.*

A royal ordinance was issued, § declaring the inhabitants of Rochelle, St.-Jean-d'Angely, and their adherents, guilty of treason. Subsequently a herald called upon Soubise to open the gates to the King, under penalty of being declared a traitor; with degradation from his nobility, and the confiscation of all his property. Soubise having explained that he was there on behalf of the assembly at Rochelle, gave the following answer: "I am the King's very humble ser"vant; but the execution of his command is out of my "power.—Renjamin De Rohan."

Meanwhile the King's army had been joined by reinforcements of men and artillery; and the place was severely cannonaded. The besieged made several bold sallies; but without succeeding in destroying the preparations for an assault: and although their danger became daily more evident, they maintained the defence with spirit, until Haute-Fontaine, the confidential friend of Soubise, was killed. That loss, and the fact of some extensive mines being prepared, made Soubise more willing to capitulate. He accordingly wrote to the King's minister Luynes, who had recently been named constable; and after several discussions on matters of form, the King sent word that he should make no treaty, but at the humble supplication of the inhabitants of St.-Jean, he would give a full pardon to every one on the sole condition of its being asked, and on their swearing fidelity and obedience for the future. The offer was accepted and the gates were thrown open. The fortifications were destroyed, and the place completely dismantled; not only as a measure of precaution, but also of punishment: the royal ordinance declaring, that in times of trouble, the inhabitants of St.-Jean-d'Angely were always the first to revolt.-f *Mere. Franc.,* p. 533 f Benjamin de Rohan, seigneur de Soubise, was elevated to the dignity of duke in 1626; but his patent was never registered by the parliament: he is however generally known by that title. :£ Rohan, *Mem.,* liv. ii, p. 122. § Dated Niort, 27 May, 1621. *Merc. Franc.,* v. vii, p. 526. During this siege, the King's authority was established in all the towns of Poictou, Saintonge, and the adjoining provinces. The duke of Vendome reStored order jn Brittany; Bouillon wrote with submission to the King; La Tremouille went in person; Chatillon and La Force were either paralized in their operations or seduced by promises. Rohan and his brother alone remained faithful to the protestantcause; and their fidelity was the more meritorious, as Luynes had married their niece, and great efforts had been made to win them to the court interest. 25 June. f The ordinance, given at Cognac, was registered at Bordeaux, e July, t62l.

The historian of Rochelle, a father of the congregation of the Oratoire, complains of the inconsistent conduct of the protestants, who were clamorous for the execution of the edict of Nantes, and yet violated its conditions, by refusing to allow the celebration of the Roman catholic worship,and oppressing the followers of that creed with constant odious vexations. The Oratorians were the only catholic clergy in Rochelle; they had formed an establishment in 1614, but the advance of the King's forces, and the alarming state of affairs, caused a strong feeling against them. In consequence, a vote of the assembly ordered them to quit the city. "The more violent," says father Arcere, "were for burning them in their church, or pitching "them over the remparts." The mayor however assisted them in retiring from the city; and lamented his inability to protect their continued stay. To avoid the clamours of the multitude, they quitted the town at dinner time, in a boat prepared by that magistrate.

Previously to the King's departure for Guyenne, he ordered Epernon to press Rochelle, by sea as well as by land. That nobleman decided on blockading that town; and therefore kept parties of horsemen constantly in the neighbourhood, to prevent the arrival of provisions.-f-Skirmishes often took place, and all supply from the land was cut off. Rut it was different on the sea coast: the ships stationed at the mouth of the harbour, not being able to prevent the entrance of small vessels. In general the confederates were superior at sea to the King's forces; and their success induced them at a later period, to attempt a measure of some importance, and bar the entrance to Brouage, by sinking some vessels laden with stones at the mouth of that port. St.-Luc, the royalist marine commander, having intimation of the design, hastily threw up a redoubt at the water's edge, Which effectually prevented the approach of the Rochellese. Arcere, vol. ii, pp. 167—168. f Girard, *Fie A'Epernon,* p. 3G4. Arcere, v. ii, p. 175. The King's progress in the south of France was almost every where hailed by submission. La Force and his son, who intended to make a stand at Bergerac, retired to Nerac, where the Huguenots hailed him as commander of the circle, f Being joined by Rohan, the catholic counsellors of the justice-chamber were dismissed; and after establishing La Force in that place, the duke set off for Montauban, where he arrived in the middle of July. In that journey he was obliged to take a circuitous route of thirty-five leagues, to avoid marshal Themines, at the head of a considerable force, $

The dukeofMayenne, governor of the province, was then laid up at Bordeaux with a fever: not a levy had been made, nor any order given for repressive measures, in consequence of this insurrection. La Force availed himself of Mayenne's inactivity to strengthen his army; but on the news of his operations reaching Bordeaux, the emergency of the case, and his serious responsibility as governor, caused the duke to disregard his illness: he set out in the night to join the duke of Eperaon, and ordered two regiments to follow him. Nerac held out with spirit for some days: as a diversion, La Force obtained possession of Caumont, and besieged Sept-Fons: but the King's forces were so much superior in numbers, that ultimately the insurgents were every where defeated, and Nerac surrendered on the ninth of July. .J-3 June, 1621. *Merc. Franc.,* vol. vii, p. 601. $ Rohan, *Mem.,* liv. ii, p. 124. Clerac, another Gascon town detained the King from the twentieth of July until the fifth of August, after which the siege of Montauban was resolved on. -f Rohan had apprehended this decision, from the tidings he received of such general submission to the King; and early in July he had visited Lower Languedoc, to rally his friends, and obtain supplies for the assistance of Montauban; which town was invested on the twenty-first of August, by the King in person, attended by the constable, the duke of Mayenne, and marshals Praslin,Chaulne, Themines, and Lesdiguieres.4: Sully, who had for some time withdrawn from public life to his states at Quercy, came to the King's head-quarters, and offered to use his influence with the inhabitants, whom he imagined he could persuade into submission; but his intentions were frustrated by the zeal and firmness of the town-council, of which body the minister Chamier was president. Sully's recommendations were disregarded, the council being determined on the question of refusing to submit; they were willing however to treat with the King, in the name and with the approval of their party at large; which of course could not be conceded by a monarch flushed with success. The obstinacy of this body unequivocally arose out of their warm attachment to the cause they had espoused; and the selfish and interested conduct of many noblemen of their party, made them distrustful of Sully's advice. Having so often experienced fetal effects from too much confidence; and being stimulated by a desire of rivalling the assembly at Rochelle, they would admit no compromise in the contest for religious liberty. But unfortunately, that sacred cause received an irreparable injury from their well meant zeal. The republican character of their institutions, and their self-government, altogether independent of the crown, became obvious; and from that time the interests of the monarchy demanded a hostile policy, so far as the protestant body was concerned.

Merc. Franc., vol. vii, p. 603. f Ibid., p. 658. $ Rohan, *Mem.,'*p. 129.— Bassompierre, vol. ii, p. *tot.*—Merc. Franf., p. 822.

Montauban was courageously defended; and Bassompierre, who was present, has related some spirited scenes that took place. Rohan was, on his side, actively engaged in bringing a reinforcement to the besieged; and in the middle of October sent fifteen hundred men, under the command of Beaufort, a courageous man, to enter the town, if possible. The King was informed of the project, and the guards were doubled; which did not however,' prevent eight hundred of Beaufort's division from breaking through the camp. This incident was closely followed by several sorties, which greatly discouraged the King's troops.

Both attack and defence were well sustained, till the end of October, when the constable decided on raising the siege. He. had invited Rohan to a private conference at Castres, but the public feeling being opposed to a negociation, they met at Reviers, within a league of Montauban, when Luynes used the most friendly arguments to win over the protestant commander. He even appealed to the alliance between their families, the duchess of Luynes being of the house of Rohan. But the conference produced no result, because the constable would not hear of a general treaty; his object being to detach the leader from his party. Rohan's firmness was ill requited by his confederates; and he had reason to complain of their interestedness before the end of the war.

Merc. Franc., vol. vii, p. 826. t Rohan, *Mem.,* liv. ii, p. 133.—*Mem. dePontis,.* i, p. 147.

When Luynes communicated to Bassompierre his design of raising the siege, he was told in reply, that he did right to relinquish a plan, in which he was unintentionally engaged; as it was entered upon with a full assurance from Bourg-Franc, the commander, that he would open the gates,-j-This incident affords an explanation of the prevailing readiness to surrender on the King's approach, so different from the unvarying practice of the Huguenots in former civil wars; and Rohan observes: "from Saumur to Montauban, there "was a general submission; with no resistance, except "at St.-Jean-d'Angely, which my brother defended as "long as he could. And the peace of Montpellier "comprised no chiefs of provinces, except my brother "and myself; all the others having made their treaty "separately and on advantageous terms."£ Rohan, *Mem.,* pp. 135 *et seq.* f Bassompierre, vol. ii, p. 232.:£ Rohan, *Discours sur les derniers Troubles,* p. tot.

After the conversation already alluded to, between Luynes and Bassompierre, a conference was privately held with some of the besieged, but without producing any result; and the King withdrew his troops early in November. He confessed to Bassompierre, with tears in his eyes, how bitterly he felt the unfavourable turn of affairs. Bas-

sompierre's division had been conspicuous, and Louis declared that no other part of the army had given him equal satisfaction. In short he had resolved on giving him the chief command. During the siege a considerable number of nobles and gentlemen were killed: among the besieged, the minister Chamier was struck by a cannon ball, while defending a breach.-f-The most eminent among the assailants was the duke of Mayenne, mortally wounded in the left eye by a musket ball, while examining the trenches with the duke of Guise and count Schomberg. He was conveyed to his tent, and died almost immediately after reaching it. $ The greatest honours were paid to his remains, in every town through which they passed; but the Parisians appear to have fancied nothing so congenial, as to attack the protestants. There were in circulation some menacing reports, during several days after the news of his death had reached the capital; and on the Sunday following, the road to Charenton was well guarded, to protect the protestants in going to and from their temple; the duke of Montbazon, governor of Paris, the chevalier du Guet, the provosts, lieutenant civil, etc., being stationed at the porte St.-Antoine. The morning service passed off quietly; but in the afternoon a band of vagabonds, concealed among the vines, commenced an attack on some carriages returning to the city. When the archers hastened forward to protect that party, another band fell upon some protestants on foot, at a little distance. As they were armed with swords and pistols, a skirmish ensued, in which several were mortally wounded. The affray, once commenced, was not confined to the outside of Paris; the confusion was still greater within the gates, and an aged female protestant was murdered near Mayenne's hotel.

Bassompierre, vol. ii, p. 235. f Merc. Franc., vol. viii, p. 605. t n Sept. 1621. Ibid, vol. vii, p. 849.

Nor were the protestants the only victims; for the mob became more and more outrageous in their proceedings; and as many catholics were taking their Sunday walk in the country, they were robbed of whatever they had about them: the populace pretending to search their persons for crosses and rosaries, as evidence of their being catholics.

The mob then proceeded to Charenton, being strengthened by a reinforcement of bad characters of every kind; with a swarm of apprentices and workmen, free for the day, and ready for any kind of mischief. The door of the temple was forced open; the benches, desks and books were piled up in a heap; the houses of the consistory and guardian were pillaged; and the temple itself set on fire: after which the mob, about four hundred in number, returned to Paris, shouting *Vive le Roi.* It required all the watchful care of the authorities to prevent still more serious conse quences, for many of the populace were bent upon killing the Huguenots. Companies were however formed, and stationed in each quarter; and the night passed off quietly. The following day the parliament issued a decree, authorizing the prosecution of the delinquents, and placing the protestants under the protection and safeguard of that court. Yet the mob persisted: houses belonging to protestants were plundered; and four men being arrested in the act of carrying away clothes, were summarily punished by a decree of parliament, given the following day:—Two were condemned to be hanged; and their companions to be whipped and banished for nine years. The sentence Was executed the same day at the Place-de-Greve, and the severity of the example restored order,-f CHAPTER VI.

MILITARY MOVEMENTS IN THE SOUTH. — EXPEDITION TO THE ISLE OF RUtS, UNDER SOUBISE.—LA FORCE SUBMITS TO THE KING. — SIEGE OF NEGRE-PEL1SSE AND MONTPELLIER.—RICHELIEU NAMED PRIME MINISTER.

During this civil war, the affairs of the Huguenots became so extensively diversified, that it is scarcely possible to give a connected view of the events, occurring among the many divisions comprised in their confederation; for the interest is no longer arrested by one body, around the history of which, the episodes of its satellites can be succes-

sively unfolded; but proceedings of nearly equal importance claim and fix attention in opposite directions. On one side Soubise, regardless of his recent oath, appeared in arms at Oleron, where he committed serious devastations, levied contributions, and destroyed the churches. At Nismes, the assembly of deputies passed a decree for depriving Chatillon of the command, entrusted to him by the assembly at Rochelle.-f-The complaint against him comprised ten heads of accusation, which in substance declared that his loyalty and sense of duty were impediments to his usefulness for the party. This decision drew forth a long apology from the accused nobleman, whose aim and desire were described as directed to the preservation of peace in Languedoc; at the same time he charges his accusers with selfish and seditious motives. $ 27 Sept. 1621.-t *Merc. Franc,* vol. vii,pp. 851—857.

At Montpellier, the catholic clergy were ordered to discontinue their worship, and close their churches: the following day a pillage commenced, and many sacrilegious outrages were committed. § The government of Languedoc devolving on Rohan, when the assembly deprived Chatillon of that command, he was received with great demonstration of respect at Montpellier. The vigour with which the King had besieged Montauban, was a presage of what might be expected there; and great activity was displayed in preparing for defence. Lesdiguieres, who had succeeded in suppressing an insurrection in the adjoining province, was ambitious of figuring as mediator with the insurgents of Montpellier; and accordingly sent Ducros, president of the parliament of Grenoble, to converse with Rohan on the best means for effecting a pacification. The president had been selected on account of the high consideration he enjoyed among the principal protestants; but unhappily some violent partisans circulated a report, that his object was to detach Rohan from their cause, and a plan was arranged for killing him. It was executed with the atrocity of an age of violence and fanaticism; and Rohan deemed it necessary to punish such

an outrage, by having four of the ringleaders hanged,-f 8 Nov. 1621. Arcere, vol. ii, p. 174.

f 21 Nov. *Mercure Franf.,* vol. vii, p. 686. :£ Ibid., vol. viii, p. 93.

§ 2 Dec. 1621. Soulier, *Hist. du Calvinisme,* p. 471.

Monheurt, a little insignificant town on the Garonne, was likewise a point of considerable interest at this period, as the King besieged it in person. The explosion of some mines produced a sufficient impression upon the besieged to make them desirous of capitulation: that however the King would not permit, and insisted upon an unqualified surrender. However in the evening the besieged received an assurance of the monarch's desire to shew clemency, and that all who submitted would be at liberty to retire. Th§ offer was generally accepted; after which the town was given up to plunder, and then burned.

Rohan, *Raisons de la Paix faicte devant Montpellier,* p. 92. t *Merc. Franc.,* vol. viii,p. in.—Soulier, p. 480.

During the siege of Montauban, the English ambassador had endeavoured to persuade Rohan to consent to a treaty, calculated to establish a general peace, compatible with the dignity of the French crown. At first the duke referred the proposal to the assembly at Roehelle; but as there appeared to the ambassador a probability of the loss of Montauban, he persuaded Rohan to meet the constable on the subject. Luynes being confident of taking the town, assumed a high tone, and expressed a determination to exclude it from the edict of pacification, unless a citadel were erected: in consequence the matter was dropped. Afterwards, when Rohan had thrown in supplies, and the chances of success were diminished, Luynes invited him to renew the conference. When the siege was raised, the constable consented that Rohan should obtain the approbation of the protestant assembly, which was a great point gained; but the negocia tions again failed of producing any result. The death of Luynes opened a new field of ambition and intrigue; and the friends of Gonde, who then acquired influence, persuaded the King that the fact of receiving authority to treat in the name of the assembly, could not be too severely reprobated, f The same influence may have originated the King's decree, declaring Rohan guilty of high treason.

The constable's death removed the Queen's bitterest enemy, and Conde's chief rival; and if we may rely on the testimony of Bassompierre, the event must have afforded some satisfaction even to Louis himself. In treating of the siege of Montauhan, the marshal observes: "The King's dislike to the constable aug"men ted; while he took less pains to keep In favour," "either from feeling assured of his Majesty's affection, "or because important affairs on hand prevented his '4 thinking of it; or because his greatness blinded him; "so that the King's discontent increased very much, "and every time that he spoke of him in private, he "displayed more and more violent resentment." 12 Dec. *Merc. Franc.*, vol. vii, pp. 827—9. *f* Rohan, *Raisons*, etc., p. 85.

Though the King had returned to Paris for the remainder of the winter, the confederates pursued their isolated operations; which became important from their extent, as the Huguenot force was not less than twenty-five thousand men. f The marquis de La Force quitted Montauban, to establish his authority in Quercy and Lower Guyenne; where he was received with ardour, and treated as a sovereign, notwithstanding the decree of the parliament of Paris, which condemned him and his sons to be beheaded in effigy, deprived them of their nobility, and confiscated the family estates. *$* La Force far from being alarmed by this proceeding, levied money by virtue of his commission from the general assembly of the Reformed Churches; and transported to Ste. Foy, the chamber founded at Nerac, pursuant to the edict of Nantes, declaring its authority equal to that of the other parliaments. The duke d'Elboeuf and marshal Themines had been already sent by the King to reduce the province to submission; and early in January, 1622, they took the field. The results of the subsequent military movements were long

doubtful. Elbceuf found it requisite o abandon the siege of several places, and the town of Clerac was taken by the marquis de Lusignan, co-operating with La Force,' who himself obtained possession of Tonneins. The latter town afterwards sustained a long and arduous siege, in which the garrison displayed uncommon resolution: their difficulties being aggravated by want of provisions. La Force made two attempts to relieve the place, in which his son Montpouillan, commanded; but was driven off by the duke d'Elboeuf. The siege lasted till May, when the garrison obtained a favourable capitulation, but the town was burned as an example.
Bassompierre, vol. ii, p. 257. f *Merc. Franc.,* vol. viij, p. 418.-*if* 15 Nov. 1021.

The assembly at Rochelle was encouraged by the energetic resistance of their leaders, and Soubise, whose operations were in their own neighbourhood, gave the royalists full occupation, both by sea and on shore. Woodford, the English Ambassador's secretary, was sent to complain of the misconduct of their naval captains, who plundered the English vessels trading to Bordeaux. The envoy took occasion to represent how utterly improbable it was, that their sovereign would ever treat with revolted subjects, even on the mediation of foreign powers; and advised submission. The assembly, in reply, expressed a readiness to adopt his recommendation, and begged him to obtain a safe-conduct for their deputies. The measure was however laid aside; and instead of submitting to the King, a body of three thousand men under Soubise marched into Lower Poictou; where he obtained possession of several places, and sent five standards to Rochelle as trophies. His progress was stayed by the count de La Rochefoucault, who kept him in check by a superior force, hastily levied, consisting of four thousand infantry and six hundred horsemen,-j *Merc.Franc.,* vol. viii, pp. 445 *et seq.* There is a minute detail of the operations and skirmishes in the *MSmoires de Pontis,* liv. iv.

The King again quitted Paris, to pur-

sue the advantages which had attended his military journeys, the preceding years. On reaching Saumur, he found that the protestants did not conceal their hopes of a change of circumstances, from the successes gained by Soubise. The fortifications were in consequence destroyed, and the town annexed to the government of Anjou.

Soubise meanwhile had taken a position in the isle of Rie; § where he appeared full of confidence, and ready to resist the attacks of the Royal army. The surrounding country was difficult of access, being intersected by canals; and a moderate degree of precaution, in establishing posts at the few practicable passes, would have given him an impregnable position. Under cover of the night, the King's troops crossed over to the island at low water, and Soubise endeavoured to retreat from a force so superior to his own, at a moment when it would have been much less hazardous to engage. Four thousand of his men, who perceived the irremediable fault of their commander,and despaired of gaining the ships at anchor, laid down their arms. About fifteen hundred were killed by the soldiers of La Rochefoucault, and by the peasantry, who were highly incensed against them, as the causes of the war; from six to seven hundred fugitives were made prisoners; among whom were one hundred and fifty gentlemen. Soubise arrived at Rochelle with about thirty horsemen, the wreck of a respectable body of cavalry; and out of seven thousand infantry, not four hundred effected their escape. 9 Jan. 1622. Arcere, vol. ii, p. 175.
f *Merc. Franc,* vol. viii, p. 530.— Arcere, vol. ii, p. 175. *3p* April, 1622. *Merc. Franc.,* vol. viii, p. 547.
§ Rife" or Ries must not be confounded with *Jthe or Re:* the former, in Poictou, is separated from the main land by a fordable stream; Rhe is divided from Aunis by an arm of the sea.

The results of this expedition announced a change in the views of the government, by an unusual display of severity. The sentence of death passed upon rebels was perfectly conformable to the practice of all civilized nations;

but in every other case during this war an act of grace had followed the success of the King's arms; and there was no reason why the unfortunate followers of Soubise should have suffered the consequences of an exceptional rigour. The prince of Conde persuaded the King to punish with firmness. His Majesty, says a contemporary, left the affair to his council. Persons of quality were treated as prisoners of war; but as for the soldiers,five hundred and eighty-eight were conducted to Nantes—thirteen were hanged; and the remainder sent to the galleys. 16 April, 1622. Bassompierrc, v. ii, p. 306. — *Merc. Franc.,,* vol. viii, p. 554.

With a view to improve the advantages of the late victory, by seizing vessels belonging to the Huguenots, or at any rate destroying some of the sailors, La Rochefoucault ordered several of his prisoners to run along the bank, and call for help. The commanders immediately stood in towards the shore, to receive their companions, while La Rochefoucault's soldiers advanced to wait the proper moment for action. A resolute and devoted protestant, named Job Ferran, perceived the danger to which his friends were exposed; climbing a high rock, he called out, "Treason! Treason!" and precipitated himself on the shore. Some Huguenot sailors who had already landed, carried him to one of their ships, where he died a few days afterwards, from the effects of his fall; his last moments were however soothed by the reflexion, that his death had saved the protestant flotilla, *f*

About the same time the Huguenots had to lament the loss of the county of Foix, where their interests had been well secured by Jane d'Albret, and the appointment of successive protestant governors. In December, 1621, the charge being resigned, La Forest, a catholic, was named; and the Jesuit Villatte was employed to convert the population. In an account published at Toulouse, it is stated that the Huguenot minister Molinier confessed his inability to resist the Jesuit's arguments; and the majority of his flock abjured their errors, as an evidence of their sincerity.

For the suitable celebration of Easier they consented to demolish their temple. To perpetuate the memory of that event a declaration was signed by a hundred and twenty-two converts; and at the head of the list was Pierre Fer, an individual who went to Geneva for the purpose of receiving from Calvin himself, a minister to preach the reformation at Foix; and having attained the age of a hundred-and-ten years, was induced to concur in its suppression. 27 April, 162?. *Merc. Franc.,* vol. viii. pp. 554 *et seq.* f Arccre, vol. ii, p. 178.

Royan, situated at the mouth of the Gironde, was besieged by the King, in the beginning of May. The assembly at Rochelle sent supplies and reinforcements by sea; but it was to no purpose, for the assailants surmounted every obstacle; and on the sixth day of the siege the garrison demanded and obtained a capitulation, by which they were allowed to withdraw by sea to Rochelle, with arms and baggage; leaving behind them only the cannons and ammunition,-j

La Force who had taken up his head quarters at Ste.-Foy, beheld different divisions of the royal army directing their march towards him; and concluding from the fate of other places, that his citadel must be subdued, he wrote to de Lomenie, the King's secretary, expressing a deep regret for his rebellion, and presented articles of capitulation for himself, his children, and the nobles and gentlemen who had followed him. These terms would in the present day, be deemed extravagant; yet with one or two exceptions, every thing asked for was granted, and even the points objected to, were not positively refused. In short, La Force obtained amnesty, approval, continuance of old privileges and rights; all decrees against him or his followers were declared null; and the rank of marshal, with a considerable sum of money, and pensions to his children were accorded by Louis, so important did it seem to his advisers, and especially the prince of Conde, to win over a protestant chieftain, and leave nothing behind him in arms in Guyenne. The articles being signed and ex-

changed, the prince of Conde and the duke d'Elboeuf took possession of the town, to prepare for the King's entry. *Mere. Franc-,* vol. viii, pp. 486—491. f ll May, 1622. *Merc. Franc.,* p. 682.— Bassompierre, vol. ii, p. 325.

The towns of Negrepelisse and Saint-Antonin were less fortunate than Ste.-Foy. The former place was taken after a short siege; and the inhabitants, without distinction of age or sex, were massacred. Some who had taken refuge in the citadel were obliged to surrender the following day, when all the men were hanged. The pretext for this severity was an accusation of the inhabitants having murdered a regiment left there in garrison by the duke of Mayenne; and the vengeance of the conquerors was completed only by the entire destruction of the town, which was set on fire in several quarters at once.-f 24 May, *Merc. Franc.,* p. 625.—Bassompierre, p. 329. 1 10 June, 1622. *Merc. Franc.,* p. 637.

The King attacked Negrepelisse professedly with a view to take revenge upon the inhabitants: there was no summons to surrender; but a general assault directly the royal army arrived. De Pontis relates that he was summoned to the King's presence to report his observations on the state of the town, he having bees appointed to take a survey. "You will attack the "place," observed the King, " on both sides at once; "and you must place something white in your hats, lest when you meet in the town you should kill one another; for I command you to give no quarter to any man, because they have irritated me, and shall be served as they treated the others." The combat lasted some hours, and the garrison made a most courageous defence; at last finding themselves overwhelmed by superior force, they asked for quarter; which being refused, they resolved to sell their lives dearly; and to a man died fighting. The sack was dreadful in the extreme: robbery and violation occurred in every house, with scarcely an exception.

St.-Antonin had soon after the fatal honour of a visit from the King, who joined his army before its walls. The siege lasted seven days; and when the garrison offered to capitulate, they were refused terms. They surrendered at discretion, in the hope of obtaining the royal clemency. Eleven of those who had been most active in the resistance were hanged on the ravelin; and among them the minister who had been a cordelier: a coincidence which gave rise to some epigrams, among the wits in the King's army.

De Pontis, Yoi. i, pp. 192—203. This work has been the subject of literary controversy, and is by some considered apocryphal; tRe author composed it after his retirement to Port-Royal, and his statement is evidently founded on fact, even supposing " dc Pontis" to be a fictitious name.

These continued misfortunes of the protestant party were followed by the abjuration of Lesdiguieres, who on a former occasion had refused the appointment of constable, on that condition. Marshal Crequi had only to announce his mission, in the presence of the parliament of Grenoble. Claude Bullion, who had already abjured, addressed this question to the marshal: "Do 44 you believe in transubstantiation?" 44 Yes!" 44 Then "you are to be constable." Lesdiguieres replied, "That he was ever obedient to the command of his "majesty," and turning to the counsellors, added: "So, now gentlemen, we'll go to mass." f This abjuration was celebrated with great pomp, and was followed by ceremonies which lasted four days. He received the sword of state from the King's hand beforeMontpellier, and Bassompierre replaced him in the list of marshals, $

The King's successes continued; and he wrote a letter to the parliament of Toulouse, announcing the prosperous results of the campaign, in which he had subdued a dozen fortified towns; and congratulating that body on the rebels of Languedoc being shut up in three places: viz. Nismes, Usez, and Montpellier, without any hope of assistance from their confederates. The siege of the latter city was already contemplated; but as a means of conciliation, the secretaryBunion was sent to offer the

King's pardon, if the town submitted. The answer he brought back was a refusal to admit the King; but that if his Majesty would retire to a distance of ten leagues, they would open their gates to the constable. This gave rise to a consultation, at which were present all the great commanders of the King's party. Bullion after making his report, explained that the severities experienced at the recent sieges, had alarmed the people of Montpellier; that they were well disposed, and would receive his capitulation as dutiful supplicants; and therefore he advised his sovereign to concede on a point of no consequence, especially as by the time so gained, he would speedily obtain the submission of Nismes and Usez. The prince of Conde could hardly suppress his impatience at this discourse; and declared that such a decision would be infamous. The King was obliged to restrain the prince's impetuosity, and insisted on his allowing every counsellor to deliver his sentiments. Many of them agreed with Bullion; but Bassompierre enlarged upon the inconsistency of a King withdrawing from one of his own towns, before his subjects would perform the ordinary homage of acknowledging his authority. Conde seconded the marshal's opinion, and Louis sent word, "that he "gave terms to his subjects, but did not receive any; "and if they did not accept his proposal, they might 4 prepare to be compelled by force." f The garrison was inflexible, and orders were given to commence the siege, which was continued with great animation until the eighth of October, when the duke de Rohan approached with a body ""of troops, to reinforce the town. The King was advised to invite the protestant commander to treat of a peace, and the constable was ordered to meet him on that business. The preliminaries being concluded, Rohan passed and repassed through the royal camp, in his visits to the town, for the purpose of persuading the inhabitants, who were obstinate in refusing to admit the King's troops. An entire week was occupied in this manner; but Rohan's perseverance and influence at last enabled him to appear before the

King with the ratification of the treaty, and the adhesion of Nismes and Usez; deputies from which places implored the King's pardon on their knees, in the name of all the protestants in France.- fThe edict of pacification and amnesty was signed on the nineteenth of October; and the following day Louis made his entry, when every thing was as tranquil as if the siege had not taken place, $ 22 Juae, 1622. *Merc. Franc.,* vol. viii, p. 648. f 24 July, 1622. *Merc. Franc.,* p. 683.— Amelot de la Houssaye *Mem. Hist.,* vol. i, p. 442. 4= 20 Aug. 1622. Bassompierre, vol. ii, p. 385.

Merc-Franc., vol. viii, p. 802. f Bassompierre. vol. ii, p. 391.

Hostilities continued some time later at Rochelle; and four successive engagements took place between the King's fleet, commanded by the count de Soissons, the duke of Guise, and M. de St.-Luc. The advantage of these encounters was decidedly in favour of the royalists; although the brave sailors of Rochelle fully sustained their old reputation. The duke of Guise having resolved to annihilate the fleet of the confederates, followed up his victories; and would have succeeded, if a violent storm had not arisen on the day fixed for his project. The hurricane lasted till the sixth of November; and in the interval intelligence was received of peace being concluded. Guiton, the protestant admiral, at first xefused to be included in the treaty; but the inevitable consequences of Guise's plan being apparent to the insurgent leaders; and their means of defence being sadly crippled by disasters, a deputation from the town announced the adhesion of the assembly to the pacification. DePontis describes the different attacks in which he was engaged; but, from the period of his being wounded, he ceases to notice the siege, and relates his conversations with two monks. The celebrated Zamet was killed by a cannon ball before this town. *Mem.,* liv. v.

f *Letlre du chancelier Sillery,* inserted in the *Mem. de Richelieu,* par Aubery, vol. i, p. 522. $ *Merc.* Franc.,vol.viii,pp. 810—844.— Bassompierre,p. 429—430.

The articles of the edict of pacification were similar to those on former occasions: Rohan, Soubise and other leaders, obtained indemnity for their losses; and fair promises were held out, that the protestants at large should be assured of their religious rights. They were however no longer in a situation to enforce their claim, having lost all their towns, except Rochelle and Montauban: many of their nobles had gone over to the court; and others, despairing of the cause, were prepared to abjure. Under such circumstances, it is not surprising that the treaty soon became a dead letter. The clergy disapproved of it, and would have preferred seeing the King follow up his advantages. The chancellor Sillery writing to his brother at Rome, deemed it necessary to justify the measure, and observed in his letter: 44 The ambassador will explain to his Holiness, "how the Huguenots have always gained by war, and "lost ground in time of peace; which it is to be hoped "will again ensue from the good conduct and piety of "his Majesty." Puysieux, the chancellor's son, did not scruple to assure the Nuncio, that peace had been made with the intention of more effectually crushing the reformed; and it was speedily seen that the stipulations of the edict would all be violated. In the first place, the fortifications of Montpellier were to be razed; but as the King's troops would not quit the town, Rohan, after several ineffectual applications to the King, declared that he should cease the demolition of the works. This instantly produced an order to Valence, who commanded for the King: but the independent spirit Rohan had manifested, did not fail to incur displeasure; and Valence went so lar as to arrest the duke, soon after he entered Montpellier, to superintend the election of protestant consuls, *f* 11 Not. 1622. Arcere, vol. ii, p. 192. *Mere. Franc.,* vol. viii, p. 865.

A similar disposition was displayed at Rochelle. The deputies, on appearing before the King at Lyons, obtained a letter ordering Arnauld, governor of Fort St.-Louis, to demolish the place within eight days, after the protestants had de-stroyed what was agreed upon by treaty. Arnauld however received counterorders at the same time; and when the inhabitants of Rochelle presented a copy of the King's letter, he replied with a smile, that the copy of the order sufficed to destroy only a copy of the fort. The original letter was then produced: he declared complete willingness to obey orders; but observed that he must have a full and perfect discharge, and would in consequence write to the court.

The letter, dated Paris, 4 Nov. 1622, is given by Aubery, vol. i, p. 522. *t* Feb. 1623. *Merc. Franc.,* vol. ix, p. 432.— Rohan, *Mem.,* p 194—8.

Arnauld entered fully into the spirit of the government; he not only kept his men actively employed in strengthening his position, but engaged an emissary to prepare for obtaining possession of the town by stratagem. The individual employed was named Vincent Yvon: he was suspected of treacherous correspondence; but proof failing, he was merely confined, as a measure of precaution. While in prison, he imagined a plan for piercing a passage through the wall to the sea, for the two-fold purpose of securing a retreat, and for admitting soldiers. His work advanced but slowly; and he made a tempting proposal to one of his gaolers to assist him. The offer met with an apparent welcome, but was received with the indignation of a patriot, whose feelings were concealed for better foiling the plan. The gaoler sent for his brother, and afterwards La Chapeliere a minister, whom he introduced to Yvon: he was exceedingly frank, and declared that in the night the soldiers from fort Louis would enter the town; and at a suitable moment open Jan. 1623. Arcere, vol. ii, p. 193.— *Mere. Frattf.,* vol. ix, p. 438. the gates to their comrades, concealed in the environs; after which all who made resistance would be killed. La Chapeliere was astonished at the scheme, and felt assured that the mayor was an accomplice. It became dangerous to speak of his discovery, but it would be criminal to conceal it. He consulted his friends: they decided on in-forming the mayor, but the proper moment had passed, for Yvon perceived that he was detected, and had effected his escape. The mayor, indignant, at the suspicion raised against him, told La Chapeliere with a menacing gest, that but for his sacred character, the outrage should be washed away with his blood. The people would have punished the gaolers as accomplices; but they were sent out of the town, and the distrust and bad feeling which arose out of this incident, did not subside for some time.

In September, a national synod was held at Charenton, in which scarcely any thing was discussed except doctrinal questions; and soon afterwards a report being circulated that the Huguenots were likely to take arms, a royal proclamation was given to tranquillize the protestants, and assure them of the King's intention to observe the edicts, *f*

In the spring of the following year, Richelieu was admitted into the cabinet. His character offers traits of decided greatness; and his situation, as minister of a weak and deceitful King, presents sufficient excuse for the duplicity and craft recorded to his prejudice. As a prince of the church of Rome, he was necessarily opposed to the Huguenots: yet state policy appears to have been his chief motive and guide; for although no considerations of humanity were ever allowed to interfere with his designs, he had too great a soul to become a mere persecutor; and the imprudent zeal of the protestant assemblies in constantly bringing their political independence under the eye of the government, could not fail to arrest the cardinal's attention, when he assumed the direction of affairs. In his opinion, no nation could be strong that permitted a variety of creeds or allowed foreign influence in its cabinet. His views were directed towards gradually realizing the former object; the latter essential he quickly obtained, by extensive changes in various departments of the state, and particularly in the list of ambassadors. The King of Spain no longer had the means of learning all that passed in the councils of France; and the Pope soon perceived an alteration in the language used to his

Nuncio.
Arcere, vol. ii, p. 195. t io Nov. 1623.
Merc. Franc., vol. ix, p. 693.

Such indications of resolution excited the apprehensions of the protestants; and their alarm was not without cause, as preparations were publicly made for blockading Rochelle, and a garrison still kept possession of Montpellier.

Soubise imagined the moment favourable for effacing the reproach of his late unfortunate expedition, and confided to his brother a project for destroying the King's ships at Blavet. Rohan agreed to second him if success appeared possible; while in case of failure, the expedition was to be disavowed. Soubise was obliged to use artifice in preparing for his enterprise; and bis intentions being discovered by the magistrates of Rochelle, they desired him to quit the isle of Rhe, and avoid compromising them. Soubise departed, and succeeded in his attempt on the port of Blavet. ƒ This good fortune however did not enable him to takeFort Louis, as the duke de Vendome hastened from Nantes, with a strong body of troops: by means of chains and cables he prevented Soubise from leaving the harbour, and greatly damaged his vessels by a destructive fire, from a newly-made battery. Soubise finding himself so much exposed, resolved to escape by night; his men, in boats, cutting the cables under a heavy discharge of musketry. Sixteen vessels escaped, but two of his ships grounded, and were taken by Vendome; he lost likewise several of the King's vessels, which had fallen into his hands, on his arrival. He succeeded in gaining Oleron, whence he sent cruisers to annoy the King's adherents. $ Rohan, *Disccurt sur la derniers Troubles,* p. 02.

The protestant deputies at Paris, alarmed at such a rash project, declared their loyalty to the crown, § and strongly disapproved of the conduct of Soubise, who was soon after proclaimed a rebel and a traitor, by royal ordonnance. The protestants in all part of France repudiated Soubise, until the success of his bold effort was known; when an attempt at conci Arcere, vol. ii, p. 206. f 17 Jan. 1625.

:fc Rohan, *Mem.,* p. 207.—*Merc. Franc.* , v. x, p. 850. § *Desadveu et Protestation des Deputes,* etc., 21 Jan. 1C25. *Merc. Franc.* liation was made, but tono purpose. It then became necessary for Rohan to support his brother's cause; and prove that a wish to restore peace had been his reason for delay, not the want of means, as his enemies published; and he took the field early in May. Marshal Themines was employed against him. The result of the campaign was unfortunate to Rohan, although no action of importance took place. The duke de Montmorency also defeated Soubise, in the isle de Rhe;-f-and a sea fight equally disastrous, was followed by the capitulation of the island. In the summer, the assembly of Milhaud attempted a pacification; and in the beginning of 1626, the King, being moved by repealed entreaties, consented to give an edict, for the restoration of peace and tranquillity, $ CHAFfER VII. SIEGE OF nOC.IIEI.LE.

From the time Richelieu became prime minister, three great projects engaged his attention. To elevate Rohan, *Mem.,* p. 211.—*Merc. Franc.,* vol. xi, p. 745. f 18 Sept. 1625.—*Merc. Franc.,ol.* xi, p. 889. % 5 Feb. 162G. *Merc. Franc.,* vol. xi, p. 119.

the regal authority, by destroying the remains of feudal independence; to raise the importance of France, by lowering the pride of Austria; and to terminate all domestic differences, by suppressing the few liberties, still enjoyed by the Huguenots. As circumstances required, he would appear to desist; but his intentions were unceasingly followed up, unto completion. Pretexts of every kind were used to cover his designs; and few would dare to counteract them, after the fate of the unfortunate Chalais, whose head paid the forfeit of abetting the King's brother in opposing the Cardinal.

However, the proceedings of the Huguenots at this period, were far from displeasing to the government; and we have the testimony of the Jesuit Daniel, that at the synod held at Castres, in July, 1626, every thing passed off quietly, and with submission to the King's will.

The correspondence of the protestant body with Spain was disavowed; and a previous vote excluding their ministers from political assemblies, was confirmed. But unfortunately the presence of emissaries for reviving insurrection in various provinces, was made known to Richelieu; and he turned his serious attention to depriving that party of the means of disturbing the kingdom.f

England was likewise suffering under a vizierate: the duke of Buckingham, celebrated for his astonishing elevation, and untimely end, swayed the councils of King Charles, without a rival. His character cannot be placed in comparison with that of Richelieu; for while the latter steadily pursued the mazy intrigues, essential to his policy, the former was immersed in pleasure; and instead of the laudable endeavour to surpass the Cardinal as a statesman, he thought only of resenting a personal humiliation, received during his recent visit to Paris, as ambassador to receive the Queen of England from her family. Buckingham had the presumption to declare his passion for the Queen of France; and in the vain supposition that his advances had been received with approbation, he returned on the conclusion of his mission; but his dream of happiness was annihilated by a peremptory order to leave the country. A war with France then became Buckingham's object, as it might afford him an opportunity to return to Paris,-j Henry de Talleyrand, marquis de Chalais, beheaded at Nantes 19 Aug. 1626. There is a *Relation,* etc., in Aubery, vol. i, p. 570 see also *Merc. Franc.,* vol. xii, p. 391. t Daniel, *Hist, de Franee,* v. xiii, p. 526.

The abbe Scaglia, agent of the duke of Savoy, and a secret enemy of the cardinal, animated the quarrel between the prime ministers; and Buckingham at his suggestion, sent away all the Queen's French attendants, $ with.the exception of one retained as chaplain; the term *confessor* being odious to the puritan party, then rising into importance. To embroil the governments yet more, Scaglia persuaded the young statesman, that the French protestants were exposed to great dangers, and that King

Charles was bound in honour, to maintain the stipulations of the treaty guaranteed by him. Soubise joined his entreaties to those of Scaglia, and Buckingham was induced to send a secret agent to the duke de Rohan, to concert some plan on behalf of the Huguenots. Count Roedercr intimates that the Queen did encourage him. *Mem: pour servir a I'Histoire de la SocieU polie*, p. 50.

f Rohan, *Mem. hist.*, p. 279. This is also stated by lord Clarendon and bishop Burnet. % July, 4626. *Merc. Franc.*, vol. xii, p. 260.

The vexations to which the Queen of England was exposed, were soon made known to her brother, who commissioned marshal Bassompierre to insist on the recall of her attendants. The marshal had not been many days in London, before he had orders to send back Sancy, a father of the Oratoire, who accompanied him as confessor. To this Bassompierre would not submit; and his refusal was accompanied with a threat, that he would quit the country. The intimation was repeated, but with no better effect; and after some prolonged discussion, the ambassador gained his point, and ultimately succeeded in his negociation respecting the Queen, f

This affair, added to the seizure of some vessels on the coast of Normandy, afforded a pretext for Buckingham to proceed on a mission to Paris: but his journey was to no purpose, for Bassompierre, who returned from London almost as the same time, was ordered by the Queen to intimate that his visit would be disagreeable, and that he must desist. Being thus frustrated in an attempt to behold the Queen, he was more than ever bent on a renewal of hostilities; and sent lord Montague to the dukes of Savoy and Rohan, successively, assuring them that thirty thousand men should be sent to support the Huguenots, if a diversion were promised at the same time, on the side of Piedmont, f Rohan, *Discours sur les derniers Troubles,* p. 104; and *Mem.,* liv. iv, p. 275.—Violart, *Hist. du Ministire d'Armand-Jean, cardinal de Richelieu,* vol. i, p. 380. This author, who

died in 1644, was bishop of Avranches. His work terminates in 1633; the remainder was suppressed.

t Bassompierre, vol. iii, p. 32 *et seq.*

An assembly of notables was at this period convoked in Paris; the sittings of which lasted the whole winter 4 The deliberations were not very important; but as a royal declaration § which arose out of a request presented by the order of nobles, announced the King's intention of bringing all his subjects into the unity of the catholic church, the protestants found cause for alarm, notwithstanding the assurance that their conversion was to be effected only by means of patience, mildness, and good example. They found that not only fort Louis, near Rochelle, was strengthened; but that Thoiras, the governor, had commenced another strong citadel at St.-Martin, in the isle of Rhe. The demolition agreed to on their side was instantly suspended; and a gentleman named St.-Blancard was sent to London, to join his efforts.to those of Soubise, and shew the inconvenience which must arise to the British government, if the liberty of Rochelle were not 22 Dec. 1626. Bassompierre, vol. iii, p. 53.

f Rohan, *Mem.,* p. 281.—Violart, vol. i, p. 383. :£ Aubery, vol. i, p. 58.—*Merc. Franf.,* vol. xii, p. 7S6.

S Dated 16 Feb. 1627.

maintained. King Charles was inclined to assist the Huguenots, Buckingham's policy as in complete unison, and a powerful armament was prepared.

The English fleet came in sight of Rochelle, in the morning of the twentieth of July 1627; and anchored before the isle of Rhe, the following day. Buckingham sent his secretary, accompanied by Soubise and St.Blancard, to communicate with the mayor and his council. The authorities were however all engaged in the devotional services of a public fast; and the interview was delayed till the morrow.

The secretary having addressed the council, presented a manifest, signed by Buckingham, and concluding in these terms. "The object of the King (of England) is to establish the churches. He feels interested in their welfare, and de-

sires to promote their happiness. In this case, if the churches wish not his assistance, the beating of these drums, the "display of these standards shall cease; and the noise of war be buried in silence. It is for your sake and "service they appear, "-j

Rochelle was then divided by two factions. The majority of the municipal authorities were for submission to the King; they had recently imprisoned two of their fellow-citizens, accused of enrolling men for the English forces; and it is doubtful whether the messengers would have been admitted, if the dowager duchess of Rohan had not gone to welcome her son: Buckingham's proposal was not therefore generally approved. The consequences of another war were to he dreaded; and even the partisans of independence were afraid to avow their sentiments without reserve. A medium decision was adopted; and a message was sent to inform the duke of Buckingham, that while they presented the grateful acknowledgments of the Rochellese to the King of Great Britain, they must defer adopting any resolution, until they had consulted the other reformed churches of France,-j Bassompierre, vol. iii, p. 61.—Leclerc, *Vie d'Armand-Jean, cardinal de Richelieu,* vol. i, p. 332.

t Mervault, *Journal,* etc., pp. 1—12.—Rohan, *Mem.,* p. 282.— *Merc. Franf.,* vol. xiii, p. 803.

When Souhise set out for the city, two resolutions had heen agreed to: first, that their operations should commence with the isle of Oleron, on account of its greater facility of conquest, no less than for the advantages which its occupation would afford; and secondly, that Buckingham should make no attempt before his colleague's return. However when St.-Blancard came to report progress to Buckingham, he found every thing completely changed; an attack on the isle of Rhe was decided upon; and every thing prepared for operations. $

The landing was met by a spirited opposition on the part of Thoiras the French governor; his resistance cost the lives of about six hundred of the assailants; and among them St.-Blancard himself who commanded a division. Buckingham succeeded in landing three thousand men; and if he had followed up his advantage when Thoiras retreated, he might have established himself in the island, and prevented the fall of Rochelle. This was urged by Soubise, who joined him the following day; but some valuable time was lost in landing guns and military stores, during which Thoiras was enabled to rally his men, and prepare for a siege in the fort St.-Martin.

Arcere, vol. ii, p. 230.

X Rohan, *Mem.,* liv. iv, p. 286.—Mervault, p. 13.

$ Ibid., liv. iv, p. 288.

Richelieu had been duly informed of Buckingham's preparations for invading France, and measures were taken for counteracting him, before he landed. The news of his being in the isle of Rhe, and the siege of Thoiras in his little fortress, caused an increase of activity in every department. Pinnaces were fitted out from all the French ports, to operate upon the coasts; and as Oleron was a position of evident importance, a strong reinforcement was sent thither immediately.f

The duke d'Angouleme was the first royalist general who approached Rochelle: he arrived before its walls on the dawn of the tenth of August; and his appearance created much alarm in the town. A deputation of the citizens was sent out to assure him, that they were loyal subjects of the King, and were not concerned in any manner, in the invasion of the English, $

Thoiras meanwhile held out firmly in the fort St.Martin. Buckingham had converted the siege into a blockade; and having taken measures for preventing the arrival of any supplies, it was calculated that in a few days the besieged would be forced to surrender. The elements were however adverse to the English: Buckingham's vessels were dispersed; his floating batteries and defences were all carried away during a stormy night; and on the following day, a dozen pinnaces entered the citadel with an ample supply of provisions.

Mervault, p. 15.—Arcere, vol. ii, p. 235.

— Rohan, *Mem.,* p. 289.—*Merc. Franc.* , vol. xiii, pp. 835 *et seq.* Bassompierre, vol. iii, p. 61.—Arcere, vol. ii, p. 236.—*Merc. Franc.,* vol. xiv, p. 3, Mervault, p. 18.

The duke d'Angouleme was at the same time endeavouring to persuade the Rochellese to submit; and Comminges the new commander of fort Louis, had an interview with some of the citizens; but the royal proclamation-f-was not heeded, although the arguments used were not entirely disregarded. The mayor declared, that if the King would frankly execute the treaty of Montpellier, and place Fort Louis in the hands of Chatillon, La Force, or La. Tremouille, the inhabitants would instantly fly to fill his Majesty's ranks, and obey his orders in repelling the English. $ The duke d'Angouleme then considered it incumbent on him to prevent the arrival of all supplies; a strong intrenchment was thrown up for that purpose; and a discharge from one of the city batteries upon the workmen, was the declaration of hostilities on the part of the town.§

During the remainder of the month, the English cruisers were successful, and captured so many vessels bound to the citadel, that at the beginning of October, Thoiras agreed to surrender, if not relieved by the eighth. Again the winds favoured the besieged: on the night of the seventh, a gale prevented the English vessels from barring the passage, and a flotilla of pinnaces carried another supply to the citadel. 7 Sept. Mervault, p. 23.—*Merc. Franc.,* vol. xiii, p. 864. -j-Dated 5 Aug.; published at Rochelle, on the 15th. £ Arcere, vol. ii, p. 246.—*Merc. Franc.,* vol. xiii, p. ail. §)0 Sept. Mervault, p. 23.—*Merc. Franc.,* p. 912.

On the first intelligence of Buckingham's intended expedition, Louis resolved on marching into Aunis with a respectable force, in order to parry the threatened blow: the intention was however frustrated by illness, which delayed his departure until late in the summer,-f-The Sovereign's presence was of the greatest importance in this age, when commanders frequently acted for their own interests; and immediately on his recovery, he proceeded to the disturbed

province. He arrived before Rochelle on the twelfth of October. The citadel of St.-Martin still held out; and orders were given for transporting troops to the isle of Rhe, for relieving Thoiras and his gallant garrison; and endeavouring to expel the English from the island, $

The position of the Huguenots was now greatly altered; as by a treaty concluded with Buckingham, they had virtually cancelled their allegiance to France; the stipulations of the convention giving them every prerogative of an independent republic, with the assurance of support from England. Louis and his discerning minister redoubled their efforts to suppress a rebellion, calculated to produce the most calamitous results; as it gave England access to the provinces, formerly subjected to that crown. Had Buckingham sincerely wished to promote the protestant cause in France, it would not have been difficult to establish an independent state in the maritime districts; and a perspective of importance in the new government, might have induced many nobles to enter zealously into the plan: but King Charles was already at variance with the presbyterians of Scotland, and found the English puritans almost beyond his controul: religious sympathy was not likely therefore to send reinforcement from the shores of Britain. The unfortunate monarch allowed his minion to embark in a scheme, fraught with ruin to the Huguenots, and deserving to be stigmatized as wanton andperfidious, if no efficient assistance were intended: but no measures appear to have been adopted for encouraging that enthusiasm, which would have produced private expeditions in favour of Bochelle; nor was any encouragement given for the departure of enthusiastic sectarians as volunteers. The public voice condemned Buckingham as frivolous and inexperienced; but Charles was obstinate in maintaining the favourite in his command.

Mervault, p. 32.—*Merc. Franc.,* vol. xiv, p. l4o. f Itohan, *Mem.,* liv. iv, p. 327. *Merc. Franc-,* vol. xiv, p. 146,—Bassompierre, vol. iii, p. 69.

On the other hand, the council of Rochelle was by no means inclined to accept the unqualified protection of England, as appears from their hesitation in admitting Soubise on Buckingham's arrival. As auxiliaries, the English were welcome; but the Huguenots were too prudent to renounce the independence of their city, as the price of foreign support; and while they desired the alliance of King Charles, they were decidedly against his domination. From the time that Buckingham discovered the existence of those sentiments, his co-operation was relaxed; his efforts in the isle of Rhe were of little value; and although he insisted upon the inhabitants selling provisions to his troops, he never reciprocated, by contributing to the city stores when he received supplies. Thus after destroying every hope of reconciliation with their natural Sovereign, they discovered that their new ally was shamefully lukewarm in their cause; and had the additional mortification of finding their own resources very much crippled by his demands.

Buckingham's expectations of taking the fort St.Martin soon grew feeble. Vessels with provisions reached the besieged citadel almost every day, and a division of twelve hundred men effected a landing on the island. Other forces were collecting, and as success would be impossible after their arrival, he decided upon making a desperate final attack, previous to re-embarking his men. Accordingly on the morning of the sixth of November, he assaulted the citadel on both sides; but with a most discouraging result, for the scaling ladders were too short, and the force was inadequate to the service; the place being defended by above fifteen hundred men, with four bastions, well furnished with every thing requisite for defence. The contest lasted two hours, when Buckingham ordered a retreat: two days afterwards he abandoned the Rohan, *Mem.*, liv. iv, p. 329.

v siege, and quitted the island. Marshal Schomberg had landed with a body of four thousand men; and had not the retreating force been well covered by a body of cavalry, the greater part of the English would have been slain or captured by the marshal. Bassompierre says

that above twelve hundred English were killed or taken prisoners.

However before the English fleet quitted the shores of Aunis, Buckingham sent a letter to the mayor and council of Rochelle, by the minister, David Vincent, and two companions. In that communication he exhorted the town to make terms with the King, who would readily grant their demands while the English force was at hand. Should they be unwilling to adopt that suggestion, he gave them the choice of two other measures: he would enter the city with two thousand men, to assist in its defence; or return to England for the purpose of procuring a sufficient reinforcement for raising the siege.-f

Buckingham well knew the distressed condition of the besieged city; yet he took away with him three hundred tons of corn, which was sold on his arrival in England, on the pretext that it was spoiling. $ The protestant agents who accompanied or followed him, at the risk of their lives, obtained splendid promises, which were followed by interminable delays. Fresh agents came over from Rochelle, braving the extreme risk, as certain death awaited them in the event of detection by the French King's authorities; and several expiated on the scaffold their zeal in the cause. The deputies in England were informed of the complete inutility of presenting any complaints against the favourite, but they solicited an audience of the King; when they implored assistance, and especially provisions, of which their city was in great need. When they concluded by displaying the overwhelming force preparing for their destruction, Charles assured them he would press the departure of an expedition for their relief; and would risk the whole force of his kingdom, rather than suffer Rochelle to fall. *Mere. Frame.,* vol. xiv, pp. 186—204.—Mervault, *in loc*—Bassompierre, vol. iii, p. 92. f 12 Nov. Mervault, p. 45. $ Rohan, *Mem.* , liv. iv, p. 332. 'Rohan, *Mim.,* liv. iv, p. 333. f Arcere, vol. ii, p. 2C7. Jan. 1628. *Merc. Franc.,* vol. xiv, pp. 587—s. *f Merc. Franc.,* vol. xiv, p. 667.

The retreat of the English force en-

abled Louis to press the city more closely, and a severe blockade was resolved on. Additional vessels were equipped, to scour the coast, and prevent the arrival of supplies. An unbroken line of fortifications, in course of time, completely sealed all communication by land; and the avant-port, or gulph of Rochelle, was barred by a strong wall or pier. Within six months from the commencement of the siege, all access or egress was absolutely impossible,-f

The population of Rochelle amounted to nearly eight and twenty thousand souls. Every one of sufficient age was a soldicr. Guiton, the mayor, displayed admirable resolution; and the energy kindled by religious feeling, increased the zeal of the citizens. Reing quite confident that the reiterated promises of Charles I would soon be followed by assistance, they refused a final proposal for adjusting their quarrel with the French King; who offered them liberty of conscience, and the personal privileges conferred by the edict of Nantes, provided they would receive his officers, and dismantle their fortifications: the besieged claimed the right of consulting with their confederates, which could not be granted; and with a resolution and boldness which seemed to partake of the characteristics of desperation, they displayed many instances of absolute heroism in several sorties, and in the conflicts which continually took place before their walls.

For a time small vessels occasionally broke through the King's ships, and brought supplies of provisions to the town; but that resource became gradually enfeebled, as the works of the mole advanced; and often the bearer of dispatches was compelled for his safety, to throw his letters into the sea, as the gibbet was inevitable if they were found upon his person by the enemy.

One instance is worthy of note, as it exemplifies the perseverance and determination of the citizens:—the bearer of a letter was arrested, and by means of the torture, compelled to confess where he had concealed it. He had swallowed a silver almond, in which it was placed; and it was discovered after an imprisonment of four days, during which interval the King's apothecary administered powerful medicines. The man was hanged; and after the surrender of the town, the silversmith who made the almond suffered the same punishment, ƒ

In February, the King set out for Paris, leaving Richelieu to command as his lieutenant. The cardinal sent a trumpeter with a letter, exhorting the people to submit; and the question was submitted to the council, but with no result. Richelieu then prepared a grand attack, which was confided to marshals Bassompierre and Schomberg: after two attempts on the night of the eleventh of March, the scheme was renounced as impracticable: the besieged set apart a day for public thanksgiving, on account of their deliverance.

A violent storm had done considerable damage to the mole, and several vessels succeeded in entering the port. The commander of an English pinnace having grounded, was fortunately able to gain the town in a small boat, when he delivered to the mayor and council a packet of letters from their deputies in England. At the ebb-tide, the Ring's troops attacked the pinnace, and another English vessel in a like predicament; but the crews defended themselves so well, that boats from the city had time to join them, and with the rising tide towed them into port. There was a cargo of corn in each; a most valuable acquisition for a famished city.f

The letters delivered on this occasion, gave a detailed account of the negociations of their agents in England, from the previous November, when Buckingham withdrew from the isle of Rhe. The deputies were Jacques David, echevin or alderman, on behalf of the corporation; Jean de Hinsse, on the part of the citizens; and Philip Vincent, a minister, who represented the consistory. Interviews with Buckingham were easily obtained; and it was not very difficult for them to have an audience of King Charles. On all which occasions they were assured that the fleet should put to sea without delay, to relieve Rochelle. Charles was remarkably earnest in his last promise; and when de Hinsse

bowed at the conclusion of the interview, he said: "Assure the Rochellese, "that I will not abandon them." The besieged were greatly encouraged by the perusal of such despatches; and they rejoiced still more when the English fleet, commanded by the earl of Denbigh, Buckingham's brother-in-law, appeared off the isle of Rhe, on the eleventh of May. The flotilla consisted of eleven ships of war; from thirty to forty small armed vessels; and as many more, laden with corn and provisions; but whether Denbigh had secret orders, or was naturally pusillanimous, he refused to attempt the chief purpose of his expedition, although requested by some French gentlemen on board. He set sail for England after remaining a week in the roads, leaving the besieged in amazement at such inexplicable conduct; and nearly reduced to despair, by the destruction of the brilliant hopes his arrival had created,-f

As Denbigh was not blamed for the disgraceful failure of his expedition, the Huguenots have accused Buckingham of wantonly deceiving them; and the "Arcere, vol, ii, p. 278.' f Arcere, vol. ii, p. 29i.
energy of desperation induced several to risk their lives in traversing the King's camp, for the purpose of making a final appeal to Charles LA gentleman of Poictou, named La Grossetierre, succeeded in the attempt, and delivered a memorial to that prince, who sent several letters with the assurance that his fleet should return in greater force; and that nothing should be spared for raising the siege, even at the cost of every one of his ships,-f-The messengers to whom these letters were entrusted, had the remarkable good fortune to pass the King's camp safely; but it is doubtful whether their failure would not have been more advantageous to the besieged Huguenots. Bassompierre had entered into preliminaries for a capitulation; and Richelieu had sent a letter to Guiton, the mayor. The cardinal gave the King's promise that the lives of the garrison and inhabitants should be spared, if the town surrendered within three days. The hollow promises of the English

monarch elated the citizens, whose religious enthusiasm imparted strength to endure sufferings and privation, almost unparalleled; and the cardinal's messenger was sent away with a reply, which could not fail of exciting irritation: "Tell the cardinal!" said Guiton to the drummer who brought the letter, " that I am his very "humble servant. " $
Meanwhile the English parliament expressed great impatience at the unskilful management of both the recent expeditions. The Huguenots also obtained an audience of Charles to remonstrate upon the slow and negligent preparations for the relief of Rochelle. The expedition was at length completed, and Buckingham proceeded to Portsmouth to take the command: he was there much engaged with Soubise, and the French gentlemen who incessantly urged the departure of the fleet, and remonstrated on every occasion at the delays, which inflicted prolonged misery upon their confederates. After one of these conversations, in which Soubise had been very animated, Buckingham was struck in the breast with a knife, and almost instantly expired. A hasty impression that the blow was given by a French hand, nearly cost the lives of Soubise and his friends, whose angry tone and gestures had been noticed, although the bystanders could not comprehend their observations. The assassin, Felton, was soon found: he made no effort to escape, and referred to a paper in his hat for an explanation of his motives; a precaution he had taken, under the conviction that he should perish in his dire attempt. Dated 18 May, 1628. Mervault, p. 117. f Letters, dated 19 and 27 May. —Mervault, p. 120. £ 7 July, Arcere, vol. ii, p. 294: 8th, according to Mervault.

This event caused a further delay; but the Rochellese manfully bore up under their trials. The earl of Lindsey succeeded Buckingham in the command; and arrived off the isle of Rhe, at the end of September. But the mole and other works were by this time so strong, that it would have been rash to attempt an attack. Another month passed off without any effort to relieve the city; and the successive preparations for attacking the mole terminated in a few exchanges of shot. At length the cravings of nature triumphed over the firmness of principle; and Richelieu having given great facilities for an adjustment, passports were sent for deputies to proceed to the King's camp, to discuss the terms of surrender. When we consider the severity shewn to many unfortunate messengers during the siege, some of whom were hanged after the reduction of the town, for the mere fact of conveying letters to or from the besieged, there is ground for surprise that the inhabitants in general were treated so leniently. Richelieu evidently discerned the advantages to be derived from humane policy; and his comprehensive views of affairs caused him to be satisfied with annihilating a little republic, which had defied the crown of France during seventy years. The gates of Rochelle were thrown open on the thirtieth of October, after a siege of nearly fifteen months; during which period the inhabitants were reduced from above twenty-seven thousand to five; and out of a company consisting of nearly six hundred Englishmen, left by Ruckingham, only sixty-two survived. 23 Aug. 1628. Vincent's *Journal,* quoted by Memult.—Violart, vol. i, p. 566—Clarendon, book i.

Perfect order was maintained on the entrance of the King's troops; and the disappointment of the vanquished was greatly soothed by their deliverance from starvation: an abundant supply of provisions being gratuitously distributed by the cardinal. He inaugurated the conquest of the protestant town, by celebrating mass with great pomp, on the festival of AH Saints.
Arcfere,vol. ii, p. 32 J.

Still there were examples of severity. The duchess of Rohan and her daughter were not named in the. capitulation, and the King's advisers excluded her from its benefits. The duke states, that his mother abstained from personal mention, to avoid the charge of having influenced the surrender. She was punished for the exertions of her sons; and was taken captive to Niort, with her daugh-

ter. "Rigour without pre"cedent," observes her son-"thataperson-ofherqua"lity, at the age of seventy, on quitting a siege on "which she and her daughter had lived for three "months on horse-flesh, and four or five ounces of "bread per day, should be held captive, deprived of "the exercises of religion, and with only one atten"dant for her service, "-j

The amnesty was limited, in its effects, to the personal liberties and property of the inhabitants. As a corporation, Rochelle was to be severely punished; and before the King's departure an ordinance was published, abrogating the rights and privileges of the city; confiscating the municipal estates, and ordering the complete destruction of the fortifications. It was even forbidden to erect a garden-wall near the town. The magistracy, on which the Rochellese had for centuries prided themselves, was abolished: and the "city of refuge" was no longer permitted to receive a *Merc. Franc.,* vol. xiv, p. 708. f Rohan, *Mem.,* liv, iv, p. 422.
foreigner without the King's permission;nor were any protestants allowed to reside there, unless they had been established prior to the arrival of Buckingham's expedition. CHAPTER VIII. CONDE'S EXPEDITION AGAINST THE INSURGENTS. — ROHAN'S TREATY WITH SPAIN.—SACK OF PRIVAS.—PACIFICATION OF 1629.— SYNOD AT CHARENTON.—DEATH OF ROHAN, MONTMORENCY, AND URBAN GRANDIER.
Conformably to the agreement between the dukes of Buckingham and Rohan, the latter had proceeded in the summer of 1627, into Languedoc; where he summoned his adherents,! and prepared to co-operate with his allies. He published a manifesto, containing his reasons for seeking the assistance of England, in support of the reformed churches of France. That declaration was circulated through all the towns in which protestants resided; and there was in Languedoc alone, a powerful party, resolved to support his Arcere, vol. ii, p. 326.
cause. An assembly was held at Uzes, to invite Rohan to resume the post of

commander-in-chief of the protestant forces; and previous to separation, the members signed an oath of union and fidelity.

The inhabitants of Milhaud protested against the assembly of Uzes; and the consuls of Montauban addressed the King, declaring their disapprobation of Rohan's treason, *f* Rut he felt confident of general support in that province; and vigorously pressed his measures for combating the prince of Conde, who was commissioned by the King to oppose his progress.

Some minute details of this expedition have been preserved, from which we may infer the dreadful degree of animosity excited against the unfortunate Huguenots, who had accepted a tempting offer from the English minister, and were now irreparably compromised. The national feeling was so much worked upon, that the protestants being charged with participating in an English invasion, were exposed to the utmost degree of hatred.

The Huguenots of the Vivarais had elected for their chieftain, a very daring and courageous man, named Rrison; and when Conde quitted Lyons, this commander was the first to call forth the prince's powers. Rrison had posted himself at Soyon, a town on the Rhone; most advantageously situated for defence, if the garrison had been at all adequate. After some heavy discharges of artillery, the besieged proposed a parley, and demanded a truce until the following day. Their proposal being rejected, they declared they would hold out, and at midnight made their escape quietly to another refuge.
11 Sept. 1627. *Merc. Franp.,* vol. xiv, p. 309.—Rohan, *Mem.,* liv. iv, p. 297. f *Merc. Franc.,* vol. xiv, p. 340. £ Commission dated Niort, 10 Oct. 1627. *Merc.Franc.,* p. 316.
Conde's subsequent behaviour was wantonly severe. The report sent to the government shews a cold, unfeeling insensibility on the part of the narrator; no less" than an excessive animosity in the prince's orders. "He set fire to the villages held by Brison, and "hanged some soldiers who had been surprised;

"among others a cordelier, newly un-frocked, whom "they found with an ar-quebuse. He gave up to "plunder the dwelling of Du Bays, first consul of '4 Nismes, in hatred of the faction to which he be"longed." f

Brison's career was soon after termi-nated. He sustained his character to the last; and surprised Vals, a town in the Vivarais. But Conde was soon delivered from an opponent who was not suffi-ciently dignified to throw a lustre on the contest; for being at Privas, within a few days afterwards, he was request-ed to hold a child of his lieutenant at the font of a neighbouring village. Mil-itary honours signalized the chieftain's presence; and a salute was fired as he left the rural temple. One of the pieces was loaded with ball, and Brison being struck, was killed on the spot. His suc-cessor in the command was Montbrun St.Andre.

12 Dec. 1627. *Merc. Franc-.* vol. xiv, p. 401. f *Relation du Voyage de Mon-sieur le Prince,* given by Aubery, vol. i, p. 604.

When the prince arrived at Toulouse, the parliament, encouraged by his pres-ence, and instigated by the dukes of Montmorency, Epernon, and Venta-dour, passed several exceedingly severe edicts against the rebels. One was per-sonally against the duke of Rohan, who was degraded from his rank and digni-ties, and condemned to be torn asunder by four horses.-fThe sentence was ex-ecuted in effigy on the fifth of Febru-ary, 1628; and if Rohan's good fortune had not preserved him from capture, he might and probably would have expiat-ed his rebellion on the scaffold. A harsh spirit prevailed; and it was very com-mon for agents and emissaries, if taken, to be hanged. This happened to a shoe-maker of Montauban, who had carried a letter to Rohan, and was returning with the answer: being arrested at Gailhac, he was taken to Toulouse, where he was condemned and forthwith executed.$

It would answer no useful purpose to describe all the movements and en-counters, between the King's forces and the protestants under Rohan. A variety of anecdotes are recorded by contempo-raries, which shew the strong feelings excited on both sides; and on perusing the chronicles of these times, the num-ber of summary executions appears aw-fully numerous.

There were three leaders in the south of France: Conde, who was striving to gain importance by serving the King; Montmorency whose aim was to be-come independent like Lesdiguieres; and Rohan, who maintained the protes-tant cause 'against them both. The mil-itary operations were on a small scale, and there were very few actions worthy of note. However Rohan's efforts prove him a more than ordinary man, when it is considered that he had to withstand the forces of several provinces; his re-sistance in Languedoc entitles him to great credit; and if the siege of Rochelle had been raised, would assuredly have procured him much renown, by the con-sequences to which it must have given rise.

4 Jan. 1628. *Merc. Franc.,* vol. xiv, p. 43. t Decree dated 29 Jan. 1628. *Merc. Franc-,* vol, xiv, p. 53. $ 16 Feb. 1628. *Merc. Franc.,* vol. xiv, p. 59.

The news of the surrender of Rochelle created great consternation, not only among Rohan's forces, but in all the protestant towns. Every confederate, from that time, felt the necessity of making the best terms in his power. And many went so far as openly to justify such intentions; alleging that as the war was undertaken with the design of sav-ing Rochelle, that town having fallen, it was incumbent upon them to make peace, without exposing their cause to extremities. Romish agents at the same time announced that promptitude was essential for all who wished to make terms, as the first submissions would be best rewarded. A royal proclamation likewise declared, that a decree of amnesty and oblivion would be granted to all individuals or communities, who in token of submission were willing to apply for the favour. is Dec. 1G28. *Merc. Franc.,* vol. xv, p. 31.— Rohan, liv. iv, p. 423.

Although the promises of Charles I had proved valueless, the Huguenots still clung to the idea of English pro-tection; and Rohan addressed that monarch, imploring his assistance. At the same time, with an inconsistency to be explained only by the desperate state of his affairs, he sent an agent to the King of Spain, to supplicate his aid: and in return for the Spanish subsidies, he engaged to keep a stipulated force in the field, to make any diversion requi-site for promoting the views and mea-sures of the Most Catholic King. Philip was highly pleased at such an oppor-tunity for annoying the French govern-ment, and concluded a treaty to this ef-fect: the duke de Rohan was to receive six hundred thousand ducats per annum, payable half yearly: he was to keep up a force of twelve thousand men, and hold himself ready to march in any direction where the Spanish government required a diversion; and he was further prohibit-ed from concluding any treaty of peace, without the consent of the King of Spain.

This treaty is disgraceful to the duke of Rohan, if its conclusion can be sub-stantiated. The text of the proposals and convention is preserved in a semi-offi-cial record;f but it does not appear af-ter all that Rohan ever received the promised subsidy although the negocia-tion can hardly be doubted; for the as-sembly of Nismes requested him to write to Cassel, his agent at Madrid, that he could not subsist without money, and that a pacification in France must speed-ily take place, unless a supply arrived shortly. This is certainly an admission of the treaty.

Letter dated Nismes, 12 March, 1629. *Merc. Franc.,* vol. xv, p. 285. f Dated Madrid, 3 May, 1629, according to *Merc Franc.,* vol. xv, p. 463.

Bernard Pels, a Dutchman, one of Ro-han's agents in Spain, was about this time arrested at Lunel, and conducted to Toulouse; where torture was used to elicit particulars on the nature of his mission, and the names of his confeder-ates. He was afterwards tried, and capi-tally condemned, as guilty of high trea-son; a sentence which it requires some ingenuity to justify, as the crown of France had not a shadow of claim to his allegiance. The severity of his punishment proves the strong apprehensions of Louis and his minister, that such a dangerous correspondence existed, between the court of Madrid and the Huguenots,-j

The'King, attended by Richelieu, quilted the capital early this year, for the purpose of raising the siege of Casal. By activity and energy at Suze, he compelled the duke of Savoy to consent to a treaty; and returned to Languedoc much earlier than could have been expected. His presence speedily produced a marked effect on the operations of his forces; and the appearance of his standard was the forerunner of success. Privas was plundered and burned, after a siege of fifteen days. $

Richelieu considered that the devastation of Privas required some palliation; and wrote a letter to the Queen, in which he represents the catastrophe, as an involuntary severity. He states that five or six hundred men who had retreated into a fort, having surrendered at discretion, the King resolved on hanging some, sending others to the galleys, and pardoning the least culpable. But as the guards entered the place, a desperate Huguenot, named Chambelan, took a lighted match, and declared to his companions, that as he would rather perish in the ruins than be hanged, he should set fire to the magazine: which he instantly effected. Many were killed on both sides; and the troops, in the fury of their vengeance, slew several of their own party. "It seems," says the cardinal, "like a particular judgment of God upon this town, "which has always been the seat of heresy in these "quarters. There was no intention of giving up the "place to pillage; but in the night it was abandoned, "and the gates thrown open for the soldiers to enter "in crowds to plunder. Every thing possible was "done to prevent its being burned; yet not a house "has escaped the flames. Orders were given to pre"vent those in the fort from "being molested by the "troops, but they violently exposed themselves to"to destruction, leaping down from their fortifica"tions, and incensing the soldiers against them, by "their desperate attempt to destroy themselves with

"theKing's followers." Rohan, *Mem.*, liv. iv, p. 444.

ƒ Pels was beheaded 16 June, 1629.— *Merc, Franc.*, vol. xv, p. 464, $ 29 May, *Merc. Franc-*, p. 479.

Many strong towns were successively surrendered to the King; and a general wish for peace was found

T Letter dated Privas, 30 May, 1629. Aubery, vol. i, p. 617.

to exist among the protestants. Rohan foresaw that the edicts would be completely annulled, if private treaties were entered into; and that a general pacification, although disadvantageous, would be less injurious to the cause.-He accordingly sent a messenger to the royal camp, requesting a few days' suspension of hostilities, with permission for the assembly at Nismes to join him at Anduze, without molestation. This after some difficulty was granted. The deputies from Nismes were rather extravagant in their pretensions, which for some time seemed likely to prevent all negotiation; but a treaty was concluded and signed at Alais on the twenty-seventh of June, ƒ The stipulations were perhaps as favourable, as the ill fortune of the protestants could have led them to expect; and while they had to lament the loss of their fortified town, they had liberty of conscience and freedom of worship again allowed them by edict. Experience had however shewn how little reliance could be placed upon such guarantees, even in the days of Henry IV; and cordiality was not established between the rival creeds. The people of Montauban would not agree to the treaty: this obstinacy gained them the empty distinction of a siege. Bassompierre invested the place; and after a few days, entered to complete Richelieu's triumph, by subduing the last town in which there remained any symptoms of revolt. Rohan, *Discours sur les derniers Troubles*, p. 112, and *Memoire$*, liv. iv, at the end. f Menard, *Histoire de Nimes*, vol. v, p. 586.— Rohan, *Memoires*, liv. iv. The edict in.favour of the duke de Rohan and the sieur de Soubise. dated Nismes, July, 1629, is given by Benoit, vol. ii *Preuves).*

No sooner was the civil war terminated,

than the princes and leading nobility discovered the immense advantages which Richelieu would derive from the circumstance, to establish himself firmly as prime minister. The court soon became a scene of extensive rivalry and dispute; and Louis was so harrassed in his domestic circle by the quarrels of his family, that he acquired a habit of considering Richelieu as indispensable to his happiness and comfort.

The Queen-mother's hatred to the cardinal was undisguised; and subsequently, when she considered it necessary to justify herself, she declared in a letter to the parliament, that she should never have resolved on quitting France, if it had not been to preserve her life from the hands of Richelieu,-j

Rut the cardinal was not the only cause of her displeasure and vexation: Gaston d'Orleans wished to marry the princess Mary de Gonzague, a measure strenuously opposed by his mother, who was desirous that he should wed her niece, a Tuscan princess. In the midst of these family disputes, an ineffectual effort was made to effect Richelieu's dismissal; $ but the failure only served to render his position stronger, while it assured his enemies of increased hostility on his part. The King's movements towards Orleans, where his brother lived in retirement, made that prince suspicious of some evil design, and in the middle of March he escaped into Lorraine.

20 Aug. 1629. *Merc. Franc., Yo.* xv,!p. 537.—Bassompierre, vol. iii, p. 222..j- Letter dated Avesnes, 27 July, 1631. Aubery, vol. ii, p. 124, $ ll Nov. 1630, commonly termed *la journee des dupes.* In July, the Queen-Mother quitted Compiegne for La Capelle, a town in Picardy, where she hoped to be joined by sufficient partisans, among the French malcontents, and Spanish mercenaries from Flanders, for resisting any effort to conduct her back to her place of confinement. However from the measures adopted on the occasion, she was compelled to change her plan, and withdrew into Flanders.

Under such circumstances, the affairs of the protestants obtained very little attention from the government. Their political importance had ceased; and the time had not yet arrived for depriving them of the rights of conscience. All Europe knew the resolution of Gustavus Adolphus, to make common cause with protestants under persecution: common prudence consequently demanded liberal treatment for them at this time. They had not been allowed to hold a synod for some years; and the King gave them permission to meet at Charenton, in September, 1631. An historian, avowedly unfavourable to them, observes, that the disputes between the King, his mother, and brother, seemed to present them with an occasion for revolting; and therefore the government endeavoured to satisfy the most reasonable of their demands, f The inquiry, instituted by the King's order, contains the most minute details: —" The Queen set out at 10 o'clock in the night of 18 July, 1631, in a coach belonging to Madame du Fresnoy, drawn by six bay horses, etc., etc. Aubery, vol. ii, p. 115. f Bernard, p. 280.

When the deputies were assembled, Gallard, the King's commissary, informed them that his Majesty would be a good father and sovereign to them, but he forbade their making protestations and remonstrances. He directed their attention to several infractions of the King's orders; such as receiving foreigners into the ministry, and French preachers going abroad. There was however, another charge, far more serious, as calculated to bring odium upon the protestant body: Beraut, minister of Montauban, had published a work, declaring that preachers had a right to take arms for the cause of religion. For this he had been prohibited by the King's order from assisting at the synod; but being questioned on the subject, he excused himself on account of the heated state of public opinion at the time he wrote, and acquiesced in the condemnation of the work. At the request of the synod, he obtained the King's permission to join the assembly.

The ministers Amirault and de Villars were deputed by the meeting, to present the statement of their grievances to the King, then staying at Compiegne. They petitioned for the right of ministers to preach in any protestant temple, whereas a recent decision had forbidden them to abandon their special charges— a cessation of proceedings instituted against some ministers of Languedoc, for preaching their avowed doctrines— admission of protestants to public charges— and the liberation of some of their brethren from the galleys. From this list of their demands, a tolerable idea may be formed of their condition at Ais epochRohan's principles were a decided obstacle to his remaining at the court of Louis XIII, although that monarch appeared willing to receive him with cordiality. The tone of his memoirs indicates a feeling of disappointment and vexation at the calumnious reports put into circulation by some, who having abjured protestantism, deemed it essential to their interests, that his motives should be assailed. In a discourse composed with the idea of justifying his conduct and character, he observes: " It is a thankless toil to serve "the public, especially a feeble and voluntary party, "for if each does not find what he anticipated, all cry "out against their leader. This I now experience—I "am blamed by the people, who have not the relief "they expected; being stimulated by false brethren, "who to increase their importance with the opposite "party, make it their business to represent me, as "they in reality are."f Benoit states that the King wished to exclude Basnage, pastor of Carentan, on account of ihe zeal he had displayed during the siege of Rochelle. *Hist, de I'Edit de Nantes,* vol. ii, p. 519.

This nobleman being grandson of Isabella d'Albret, daughter of John, King of Navarre, would have, succeeded to that crown, had Henry IY died childless. His birth entitled him to much more importance at court, than the circumstances of the time permitted; he therefore withdrew to Venice at the close of the civil wars, and was appointed generalissimo of that republic. In that capacity he had made ample preparations for repairing the disasters of some recent campaigns, when his projects were annihilated by the treaty of Cherasco, concluded in June 1631. He was afterwards sent by Louis as his ambassador to the Grisons; and was actively engaged in similar employs until March, 1637, when a treaty which he had concluded respecting the Valteline, caused considerable dissatisfaction at court; and to avoid the effects of Richelieu's animosity, he retired to Geneva. Although his conduct in the Valteline gave ample proof of his bravery and talent, he dared not return into France; being persuaded that the prime minister would make him responsible for the misfortunes attendant on an event, which had arisen entirely out of that stateman's policy. *Mfrc. Franc.,* vol. xvii, p. 723.

x Rohan, *Discours sur les derniers Troubles,* p. 97.

Grotius, in a letter to Oxenstiern, states that the court of France was alarmed at the correspondence between Rohan and Saxe-Weimar, who had great deference for his talents. Richelieu apprehended some project for reviving the protestant interest in the Cevennes. Rohan was sent to Venice with a view of drawing him away from Geneva; but he met Weimar, and instead of proceeding to Venice joined his army. While charging at the head of a body of troops, at the battle of Rhinfeldt, he received a wound, which ultimately proved fatal.f The King wrote Rohan a letter of thanks for the victory he had been instrumental in gaining; bdt it w£s generally supposed; that Richelieu's satisfaction at the defeat of the Imperialists, was inferior to his pleasure on being freed from a powerful enemy. D'Avrigny, *Mim. chronologiques,* vol. i, p. 308.

f He was wounded 28 Feb., and died 13 April, 1638, *Je.* 59. His body was carried to Geneva and buried with great honours. Levassor, liv. xliii.

Hehry, duke of Rohan, was by general admission, one of the greatest men of his age. His opinions On military. tactics have been highly prized, especially on questions relating to mountain warfare. It has been said of him, that he followed the traces of Sertorius, and became the model of Catinat. He had great talent as a writer; and Voltaire has passed some high encomiums on his account of the Valteline wars. He detested avarice, and spared no expense for spies, whom he termed the eyes of an army.-f-An idea obtained circulation, that he was in treaty with the Porte, for the purchase of Cyprus, in order to establish a free government, where the persecuted protestants might find a refuge. The project failed in consequence of the death of the patriarch Cyril, who had promoted the negociation. $

The remainder of the reign of Louis XIII presents very few incidents, claiming notice in this work. Richelieu was firm, he was even severe; but his enemies must admit he possessed greatness of mind; and his advice tempered and neutralized the tendency to cruelty and bigotry, which corroded the weak monarch's breast.

Leclerc, *Fie de Richelieu,* vol. ii, p. 331.
f Levassor, liv. Ixiii. 4= Amelot de la Houssaye, *Mem. Hist.,* vol. ii, p. 80.

The fate of Montmorency will always be a stigma upon the cardinal's government. That nobleman's sentence was as strictly just, as marshal Marillac's was legally iniquitous; but Montmorency had rendered great assistance in consolidating the throne; for which Louis had many times expressed his gratitude; indeed it is doubtful whether Richelieu could have suppressed the Huguenot party in Languedoc, without his cooperation. His name was moreover popular; and his character stood very high for social excellence; those circumstances combined have thrown a halo around his name, and probably ensured his fate; for his insurrection might have been pardoned; if Richelieu's plan of government had not required the sacrifice of every rival.

Marillac's sentence is, by all, admitted to be odious in the extreme; but Richelieu's apologises contend, that the marshal was guilty of the basest ingratitude, in conspiring against his benefactor; and thus divert a portion of the odium from the statesman, whose firm administration excited much discontent, and provoked continual plots against his person. He was therefore, in self-de-

fence, compelled to adopt tyrannical measures; and a long catalogue of victims is displayed in the annals of this reign. The Huguenots were not however the objects of his judicial rigour; and on one occasion when two students of Saumur were convicted of mingling, in a frolic, with the faithful at the midnight mass, on which occasion they irreverently received the sacrament of the Eucharist, the sentence was free from the cruelty which had long characterised such judgments. They were banished from Paris for three years, from Saumur for ever; were fined twelve hundred livres; and the punishment of death was threatened if the offence were repeated. Montmorency was beheaded at Toulouse, 30 Oct., 1632: Marillac at Paris, in May of the same year.

Urban Grandier, a priest, is among the names rendered famous by a melancholy fate. The Ursuline convent at Loudon was disturbed by apparitions; and subsequentlythe nuns displayed all the symptoms of demoniacal possession; which facts were related in the *proces-verbaux* of three consecutive ceremonials for exorcising.the place.-f-Grandier wa§ a man of considerable talents, and had written a treatise condemning the celibacy of the clergy; for which it is however probable he would never have been molested, had he not published a satyrical libel upon Richelieu. He was accused of having bewitched the Ursuline nuns; and writers in the cardinal's employ have asserted, that his simulated apparitions Avere only covers for effecting his impure designs. It was believed at court that he was the cause of the demoniacal possession, and to doubt it became a state offence. Grandier was arrested in December, 1633; and as the sentence which condemned him to be burned alive, was not given till August following, it would appear that he defended himself with ability. *t* was however in vain; for Laubardemont, one of Richelieu's, creatures, and the Jesuit Lactance, who was there tQ exorcise the nuns, condemned him for magic, sorcery, impiety, etc. Grandier endured a long martyrdom, being tortured for some time

with in.geujous. devices. To inspire the public with a hatred of his memory, father Lactance held a *heated* iron crucifix to Grandier's lips: the sufferer drew bck with the pain, and the Jesuit pointed out to the by-standers, how the heretic abhorred the symbol of redemption. *JrrU du parlement de Paris,* 17 Feb., 1632.—*Merc. Franc.* vol. xviii, p. 26.
f 7 Oct., 14 Nov., and 4 Dec, 1632.—*Merc) Franc.,* vol. xx, pp: 487—764.

The count de Lude exposed the infamous imposture, which wa.s continued after Grandier had expired in the flauies. Pretending to. have a choice relic in a casket, he expressed a desire to test the reality of the possession, by holding it near to one of those suffering from the demon. The nun in consequence threw herself intp violent convulsions, directly the holy relic was near her; and 3 tremendous outcry was raised against the count, when. he opened his box, and displayed a bunch of hair and some feathers,-f-The deception was then evident; and the exorcists lost the gratuity allowed them by the government.

From this tinie the affairs of France assumed an entirely different character: R(chelieu interfered in the general concerns of Europe; and the military operations in Germany, by engagingattention,and occupying the active spirits of the age, completely finished the

"Hisl. des Diables de Loudon.—Merc. Franc., vol. xx. t *Arcana GalHca,* p. 96.
civil wars; and introduced a new system of policy, more hostile to the power and influence of the nobles, and for a time severe towards all classes: it was however requisite, after so many years of anarchy, to pass under the ordeal of tyranny, as the price of restored order.

Ere we quit this era of the Huguenot annals, there remains only to allude;to the death of Sully, whose patriotism and loyalty were made to harmonise with his religious principles, in attachment to which he remained unchanged until his death. We have found him, even while suffering a species of vexatious banishment, forget his injuries, and act as mediator before the walls of Montauban;

for which service he was subsequently rewarded with the marshal's baton.

It is related that notwithstanding Sully's firm and uncompromising views upon his religious tenets, he entertained great partiality for some Gapucins, by whom he was visited; and that a short time before his death, he wished to converse with them, but the duchess refused them admittance, and threatened to have them thrown into the moat, unless they retired. That lady was an exceedingly zealous protestant; and her daughter, the duchess of Rohan, followed her example; they washed with their own hands, the linen of the com Yet,according to Benoit, his conduct at the religious services was very irreverent; he kept the congregation waiting for his appearance, remained covered,and played with a favourite dog during the sermon. *Hist, de I'Edit de Nantes,* vol. ii, p. 536.

amnion table: but with that single exception, all Sully's children embraced the Romish faith. CHAPTER IX. MAZARINES ADMINISTRATION.—ENCROACHMENTS ON THE EDICTS BY LOUIS XIV.—MADAME DE MAINTENON'S INFLUENCE.— COMMENCEMENT OF THE DRAGONNADES.

From the pacification of 1629, until 1661, when Louis XIV assumed the direction of affairs, the general history of the Huguenots presents few important incidents. There were from time to time, individual cases of complaint, and isolated instances of hostility; for the spirit of the League was not extinct, and the more zealous partisans of Rome were only restrained from urging their favourite measure by the commanding genius of the celebrated cardinals, who successively administered the affairs of France. Popular prejudice would frequently burst forth in an access of animosity, under the garb of zeal for religion; and whenever, through some technical irregularity, the protecting clauses of the edict of Nantes could be evaded or infringed, the circumstance was regarded as a victory over heresy. Unfortunately for the protestants, no effort was made by them, to appease the hostile opinion of the people; they repeat-edly asserted in their discussions and publications, that the Pope was Antichrist; and that the church of Rome was signified in Scripture by Babylon. The catholic clergy became more and more animated in the quarrel; and from the superior advantages of the Romish religion, the result could not be doubtful. The church, as a powerful body in the state, was enabled to conferva service on the crown, in voting grants, termed *dons graiuits* or free gifts. The protestants on the other hand, were poor; nearly all the noble members of their community had been seduced into abjuration, by the hopes of lucrative employs and honorable distinctions. And as the votes of each assembly of the clergy was accompanied by some request for edicts against the protestants, it is rather a cause for surprise, that the edict of Nantes should have remained in force so long, than that it was ultimately revoked. The high ecclesiastical rank of Richelieu and Mazarin doubtless enabled them to repel the successive demands of the clergy, while a layman enjoying the sovereign's confidence in the same degree, could hardly have escaped the suspicion of secretly favouring heresy; but as princes of the church, they were able to postpone nearly every project against freedom of conscience; and as they both gave the most liberal recompenses to encourage desertion from the Huguenot cause, no complaint could consistently be raised against their policy.

Supplement aux Memoires de Sully, par l'abbe de l'JEcluse.

Richelieu was magnificent in his projects, and elevated in his ideas. His disposition led him to patronize literature and the fine arts. He was a generous friend, but an implacable enemy; and having succeeded in restoring the regal authority, he swayed it conformable to his own caprices and feelings. He was both hated and feared by the King, whose councils he directed; and would have been speedily removed from his exalted situation, if Louis had been more vigorous, or the kingdom less agitated. Being well served by father Joseph, he firmly established his author-ity; and every effort to overthrow him, recoiled upon his rivals and adversaries.

Louis XIII soon followed his minister to the grave: his character appears in a most disadvantageous light, on account of the severe examples to which the disorganised state of society gave rise. He was inclined to piety, but under the influence of injudicious or crafty advisers, he became so infatuated, that he wrote to the Pope in 1631, declaring his readiness to break the existing treaties with his northern allies, provided the King of Spain would join him in extirpating protestantism. *f* His domestic misfortunes arose principally from his readiness to receive impressions of distrust *i* the inevitable consequence was a series of family feuds, which never failed to kindle political troubles. After making every allowance for his weakness, and placing upon his advisers, the responsibility of many unjust condemnations during his reign, his name and character are very far from commanding the respect of posterity, Richelieu died 4 Dec. , 1642; Louis XIII, 14 May, 164a. f lyAvrigny, *Mem. chron.,* vol. i, p. 365.

Mazarin's government appears to have been destined to form a contrast with that of his predecessor. The predominant feeling of the public against Richelieu, was hatred; against Mazarin, it was contempt; yet both succeeded in completely subjugating all orders of the state. Each excelled in crafty manoeuvre; but although Mazarin was the object of avowed jealousy, and exposed to the efforts of open hostilities, he never sought his revenge by means of the scaffold. His besetting weakness was a love of money; and the success of his schemes was probably the true cause of the enmity to which he was exposed. His talent is admitted by his enemies. His plans were less gigantic than those of Richelieu; hut much better arranged and digested. He was less inclined to shine in forming new alliances and combinations, than to follow up the measures begun by his predecessor. With Conde and Turenne to command the forces; and, on the other hand, finding the nobles greatly humbled by the augmented stability of the monarchy, it was to be naturally expected that the results of his administration would be more extensive than those produced by Richelieu, upon whose foundation his political edifice was raised.

In his foreign negociations, he had to assume an attitude altogether different. The power of France had made great advances; Spain was considerably weaker; the peace of Westphalia had changed the tactics of several cabinets; and the rise of Cromwell completely altered the aspect of French diplomacy with England. To this last reason may be probably ascribed Mazarin's tenderness for the protestants. He prized Cromwell's alliance; and was aware of the strong feeling of sympathy and brotherhood existing between the British presbyterians and the Huguenots, The protector was solicited to form an alliance with the prince of Conde, who even offered to become a protestant; and Cromwell sent an agent privately, to notice the state of the reformed in France. He reported that they were well treated, because Mazarin caused the edicts to be carefully observed; and stated, in addition, that Conde was not much esteemed by the Huguenots.

An inclination to tolerance has exposed Mazarin to some severe animadversions, from the more violent writers among the French clergy. One, particularly noted for his acrimony against the protestants, after representing as a riot what was merely a display of feeling, on account of a protestant youth being induced to turn romanist, complains of the cardinal's truckling to the Huguenots. Mazarin's letter to the consistory ofNismes, where it occurred, is thus estimated: "It contains expressions as unworthy of the purple, "and of his ministerial character, as it is conformable "to.the supple and dissembling spirit which sustained, "and may be said to have glided him to the end of "a difficult and thwarted administration. "-f Burnet, *Hist, of his own Times,* vol. i, p. 42. f Cavcirac, *Apologie de Louis XIF,* p. 203.

During the troubles of the Fronde, the cardinal's enemies endeavoured, but in vain, to enrol the Huguenots among their partisans. Conde's friends seized some forts at Rochelle; and the prince hoped, by establishing himself in that port, to secure a communication with foreign countries. But the loyal spirit of the inhabitants enabled the King's general, d'Estissac, to regain possession, after a siege of three days. Conde had, by that time, advanced to Muron, within six leagues of Rochelle: but on learning that the forts had surrendered, he precipitately withdrew his forces into Saintonge. The count de Daugnion, Conde's chief agent in the enterprise, maintained himself at Brouage, which place was for some time the centre of a most daring system of insurrectionary warfare; his soldiers infested the surrounding country; and vessels, under his flag, annoyed the commerce of that coast. He had even the audacity to solicit aid from Cromwell, who promised to send him ten thousand infantry and three thousand cavalry. That assistance never came; and a Spanish naval expedition, with which he was to co-operate, was completely defeated by the duke de Vendome. Still Daugnion was determined to defend his desperate cause; and the court considering it better to win, than to have the trouble of subduing so desperate a man, sent the bishop of Saintes to treat with him: his submission was purchased with a marshal's baton and five hundred thousand livres.

Having failed at Rochelle, Conde proceeded to MontaubaH, still relying oil the insurrectionary disposition attributed to the protestants. There he had some grounds for anticipating success for his overtures, as the parliament of Toulouse had lately passed decrees condemning Mazarin'S conduct: and that body was prevented from declaring openly for the prince, solely through fear of the Huguenots who were in the Ring's party. On presenting himself before the town, a trumpeter was sent Id call oft the people to submit; appealing to the services rendered by Conde's ancestors to the protestant cause; and promising; oft his part, the maintenance of their liberties, if they embraced his interests. But his offers Were unanimously rejected; and St.-Luc, the King's general; who after a recent defeat by the prince, had taken shelter there, finding himself so well supported, sent back the trumpeter, with a message thatjhe town was prepared to resist his attack. The prince" had not materials for carrying on a siege, and withdrew to Moissac, a small town af a distance of three leagues: whence a body of troops from Montauban soon after dislodged him. Never were circumstances more favourable for the Huguenots, to make an attempt for regaining their lost advantages, than during the civil wars of the Fronde, which lasted from 1649 to 1653; but there appears to have existed no such desire in that body. Conde's project for seizing Rochelle was in 1651; and we have Mazarin's testimony to the quiet disposition of the protestants. He is represented to have said concerning Arceie,vol. ii,p.34l. His edict of amnesty is dated (8 March, 1633. t Coste, *Hist, de Louis de Bourbon, prime de Condi,* p. 298.

them: "I have no reason to complain of the Utile flock; if they brouze upon bad herbs, at least they do not go astray." For their encouragemeht, the King published a declaration,-f-in which positive proofs of their fidelity and affection were recorded, and confirming the various edicts in their favour, notwithstanding any judgments or decrees given against them. Louis likewise wrote a letter to the consistory of Montauban, thanking its members for the marks of their attachment to his service, and permitting them to restore the fortifications of their town. $ A comparison of the above dates will sufficiently prove, that the royal promise was not given with a view to future advantage in the civil war; because the declaration was not made until most of the partisans of the Fronde had submitted; still it is maliciously recorded by an apologist and flatterer of Louis XIV, that he gave the declaration in order to prevent the protestants from joining the malcontents; and because it was given from no other motive, the request of the clergy procured its revocation in 1656. §

This reversal of a declaration, which

should have been deemed sacred and irrevocable, caused much apprehension among the protestants. For some years, the attention of many eminent persons in the church and among the offices of parliament, had been directed towards the most efficacious means for delivering France from the presence of heresy. Various measures were proposed for hastening the general conversion of the Huguenots; and the plan first adopted, corruption, was attended with great success; however the middle and lower classes could not be bribed by such inducements. Men of high birth were dazzled with the perspective of rank and honours; but the peaceable manufacturers and tradesmen continued steadfast in the reformed faith. A notion as ridiculous as it is tyrannical, had been extensively adopted. "That it was essential for all the subjects of a sovereign to have the same creed." This was maintained by Paul Hay du Chatelet, an advocate-general, who suffered imprisonment for nobly refusing to join in the iniquitous judgment of marshal Marillac. In the dispensation of justice, that magistrate was alive to its first principles; but in discussing the rights of conscience, he was lost amid the subtilties of the Romish doctrines; and seems to have been insensible to the value of quiet, orderly conduct in a numerous body of men, unless they concurred with the state authorities on religious opinions. In his remarks upon the protestants, he assumes that they cherish feelings of hatred to public order; and are ever ready for revolt, confusion, and anarchy. These general accusations were however unimportant, compared with his demand for repealing the edict of Nantes, which he observes' "was "exacted by violence, and in arms; and which was, "after all, only a temporary measure, to await their "being instructed in the truth for which they have "had sufficient time., When the edict was Rulhiere, *Eclaircissemens hiitoriques,* vol. i, p. 19.

f Dated Saint-Germain, 21 May, 1652. :£ Coste, p. 303.

§ Soulier, *Hist, du Calvinisme,* p. 552.

"given, the happiness of France was promoted by it; "and if the same motive now demands its revocation, "there needs no hesitation, it must be repealed or "set aside." He then proposes *fifteen* methods for inducing a general conversion; by which.the protestant religion might be made to disappear, without resorting to open persecution; one of these methods will suffice to exemplify the spirit, in which the whole are conceived: it consists in suing the protestants for their common debts, and thus obtain decrees of seizure and sale of their temples, which cannot be admitted as in mortmain.

Such sentiments being avowed, every decision of the parliaments against the protestants, appeared as an evidence that the suggestions were being acted upon. For the Huguenots under such circumstances to prepare for the coming storm, was no more than common sense would induce any one to expect. And when their lawful sovereign could so far despise the obligations of honour, as to revoke the declaration of 1652 merely because the reasons for making it no longer existed; when this wanton breach of faith is considered, there is great excuse to be made for the Huguenots seeking for foreign assistance in case of need. An act is said to have been signed at the synod of Montpazier, in 1659; it was presented to the King in 1677 by a minister named Mounier, who had embraced the Romish religion; and who in order to *Traii de la politique de France,* ch. Hi.

prove his sincerity, endeavoured to injure his late companions. This act contains, among other clauses, that their *brethren* in England would come to their assistance, on condition that the towns and places at their disposal should be given up to them. When the document was published, it was declared a calumny and a fabrication; and protestant writers impugned and criticised it with severity. The charge was unquestionably serious; yet the convention appears intended to be acted upon, only in the event of anticipated persecution. Admitting the authenticity of the piece, it was not with the English gov-

ernment, but with private individuals they treated; and it proves that the English negociators merely made a stipulation to preserve themselves from a repetition of the treacheries committed by Huguenot commanders, in former civil Wars; when it frequently happened that a chieftain being offered advantageous terms by the court, would conclude a separate treaty, and abandon his confederates. And on this head even the grandson of Coligny was not exempt from blame.

When Louis took into his own hands the reins of government the protestants were entitled to some very valuable rights; and that their conduct proved they deserved them, we have the testimony of that Monarch himself, who at a later period of his reign dictated memoirs for the instruction of his son. Mazarin's unpopularity called for some explanation, why an obnoxious minister Was allowed to exerci e au

"Soulier,-p. 553.

thority, after he had attained his majority; and Louis XIV justifies himself by enumerating the commotions at the commencement of his reign. The prince of Conde at the head of the malcontents; the parliament inclined to infringe upon the rcyal prerogatives; and much interested feeling among the nobility, formed a serious combination, by subduing which Mazarin gained his esteem and gratitude. Surely, if the protestants had given him apprehension, their discontent would have been included among the causes which had combined to direct his policy. To borrow the expression of one who had" devoted much time and labour to researches on this epoch: "He com"plains of the clergy, the Jansenists, the nobility, "the courtiers, the magistrates, the financiers; and "does not make the slightest mention of the Galvin"ists." And in reviewing the characters of those selected to fill the various departments of the state, the King observes: "La Vrilliere and Duplessis were "worthy men; but with intelligence merely propor"tioned to the exercise of their charges, which em"braced *nothing important."* f The affairs of the protestants especially occupied La Vrilliere, and the preceding remark upon his abilities, is an additional proof that no charge of disaffection could at that timo be brought against the Huguenots.

'Rulhiere, vol. i, p. 30. This author is not qiute justified in his assertion; for the *Memoires* do mention the protestants, though not complainingly: "L'on m'avait dit que dans le faubourg St.-Germain "ils'etait fait par eux quelques assemblies, et que l'on y pretendait "etablir des ecoles de cette secte; mais je fis si bien entendre que je "ne voulois pas souffrir ces nouveautes, qu'elles *cesseret inconti"tient." Mem.*, vol. i, p. 31. The King himself thus testifies fheir ready submissipn.

f *Memoires de Louis XIV, ecrits par lui-meme,* Vol. i, p. «.

In further corroboration may be cited a letter from Louis to the duke de St.-Aignan: "You have acted "very prudently, in not precipitating any thing, "upon the information sent you respecting some in"habitants of Havre, of the pretended reformed reli"gion. Those who profess it, being *no less jaithful* "to me than my other subjects, they must not be "treated with less attention and kindness." f

It must not, however, be supposed, that the efforts of the intolerant party were laid aside at this period. A polemical fever tormented the whole nation; and there are many instances of individuals having changed their religion, who afterwards returned to their first faith. $ As the conversions were mostly from protestantism to popery, every powerful interest leading in that direction, the clergy endeavoured to obtain a law for preventing relapse after abjuration. The bishops of Languedoc had attempted it in 1638; Richelieu however refused to confirm the provisional decrees, given by the authorities of the province. In 1660, the assembly of the clergy renewed the application, but Mazarin withstood their demand; and after his death, the new administration and a change *fi* policy, encouraged them to make another effort. A decree of the intendant of Rochelle, was confirmed; and the ordinance was afterwards converted into a general law. Its disposi-

tions were very severe; for a relapse into heresy exposed the individual to perpetual banishment. But its remote consequences were still more oppressive; for the protestant ministers were forbidden to expostulate with, or exhort their converted brethren; and the presence of such at their preachings, was a sufficient cause for closing a temple and dispersing a flock. Remorse frequently led there some, who in an unguarded moment, had been induced to abjure; they usually manifested contrition on witnessing their brethren and friends engaged in a form of worship which they had vowed to renounce and condemn; the pastor's feelings naturally led him to revive, if possible, the penitent's former sentiments; and most of the protestant churches coming in this manner under the penalty of the law, their numbers. were rapidly reduced in consequence.

Rulhiere, vol. i, p. 31. *if* Letter dated St.-Gerroain, 1 April, 1666. La Beaumellc, vol. vi, p. 216.

Among others, Bayle.

In 1666 the Catholic clergy made another step towards the subversion of religious liberty. There had been many cases before the courts, entirely new in their nature; and the interpretation of the law had often required a declaratory decree. Impartial decisions had sometimes been given; but for the greater part, those decrees were favourable to the state religion. The clergy demanded and obtained that those decisions should be embodied in a general law. The protestants then apprehended a design for their complete ruin; and within a few years, numbers abandoned their country, to seek in other lands that equal protection of the laws, which they could not hope to enjoy in France. An edict against emigration was issued in 1669. The tyrannical enactments on this subject, afford materials for extensive commentary. Edict followed edict in rapid succession; and the degree of penalty proceeded in an awful gradation from fine to imprisonment, galleys, and death.

The adverse feeling of the judicial authorities may be gathered from an incident which occurred in May, 1CC2. The

minister Amyrault was concerned in a cause before the court of *Aides:* the procureur-general demanded, and the court decreed, that he should not style himself D.D., nor allude to his *wife.* Benoit, vol. iii, p. 453.

Colbert's influence was still in favour of the protestants, and the threatened storm was for a time postponed; but the revocation of the edict of Nantes was certainly contemplated in 1669; f during which year, a royal proclamation forbade the synods from censuring parents or guardians who sent their children to catholic schools; and enjoined the closing of shops on festivals, with a number of regulations, highly, vexatious to the protestants. $

Circumstances however combined to postpone the evil day: the King was favoured with a series of brilliant successes, almost unparalleled in history; the Jesuits were engaged in a long dispute with the Jansenists; and some speculative theologians proposed a scheme for uniting the differing creeds, by certain concessions from the Pope, on matters of form. The last measure was more than once entered upon seriously; and was under consideration about three years. Turenne, who had recently abjured, was in its favour; and the scheme was not entirely renounced until 1673, when the synod of Charenton declared it impracticable,-j Registered in parliament 13 Aug., 1669.

t *Rapport du baron de Breleuil,* given at length by Rulhiere, vol. ii, pp. 49 *et seq.* It is generally thought that Rulhiere himself drew up this document, as he was the baron's secretary. 4= *Declaration du Roy,* dated Paris, t Feb., 466D. The jubilee of 1676 revived in the King's bosom that fervent zeal for the Romish religion, which had been laid aside in the transports of his passion for Madame de Montespan. Even at his most voluptuous periods, that monarch was observant of devotional forms; and it is said that during his whole life he never missed hearing daily mass, excepting on two occasions, when engaged in military affairs. % His qualm of conscience caused him to dismiss, for a time, his fascinating mistress; and without accusing him of hypocrisy, the religious exercises enjoined at this period produced.such an effect upon his mind, that he imagined he could meet the late object of his unlawful love, on terms of pure friendship. Bossuet was deceived—less by the King, than by his own confidence in a religion of formalities. His opinion was asked, whether Madame de Montespan should be allowed to appear at court. She had been as exemplary in fasting, praying and confessing, as her royal seducer; and it was declared that as she had vanquished her own heart, she could live at court, consistently with her altered Grotius had proposed a measure of this kind in 1631.

t Rulhiere, vol. i, p. 122. *Souvenirs de Madame de Cay his,* p. 37. character. It was decided that their first intervieV-should be in public. They met—the King conversed with her in the recess of a window: they sighed, they wept, they withdrew; and their intercourse was completely renewed.

In the confessional, Louis was taught the necessity of expiating his fault; and a large sum was added to the existing grant, for promoting the conversion of protestants. The direction of this undertaking was entrusted to Pellisspn, a converted protectant; very much celebrated as an elegant writer, but whose character is tarnished by repeated instances of interestedness. His accounts were left at his death, in great disorder; and although he took orders in the church of Rome, to be qualified for holding the abbey of Gimont, and the priory of St. -Orens,-f-it is doubtful whether he did not die professing the faith he had abjured. $

Many of the conversions effected by money, were the result of momentary necessities or accidental circumstances, acting upon irresolution; and to prevent backsliding, the proclamation against relapsed heretics was renewed. § On the other hand, children were, very soon after, allowed to renounce Calvinism at the early age of seven years; a period of infancy, when a toy would suffice to lead a child to assent to any opinion, however abstruse and unintelligible;

while no child was allowed to make a public profession of 'protestantism under fourteen years of age for boys, and twelve for girls,-f Caylus, p. 39.

f Abbe d'Olivet, *Hist, de VAcadimie Francaise. .$;* Rulhiere, *Eclaircissements,* etc., vol. i, p. 148.

§ The declaration, dated 13 March, 1670, awards the *amende honorable,* banishment, and confiscation, as the punishment; stating, as a reason, that banishment alone had proved too mild a punishment to deter the converts.

At this time, Madame de Maintenon began to exercise great influence upon the King's mind. Her letters prove, that she already contributed essentially to the triumph of the Romish clergy. In one we find: "The "King has passed two hours in my cabinet: he is "the most amiable man in his kingdom. I spoke to "him of Bourdaloue, and he listened with attention. "Perhaps he is not so far from thinking of his salva'4 tion, as the court imagines. He has good sentiments, "and frequent returns towards God."$ In another letter she observes: " The King is imbued with good "sentiments; he sometimes reads the Scriptures, and "deems it the finest of all books. He confesses his "weaknesses; he admits his faults. We must wait "the operation of grace. He thinks seriously about "the conversion of the heretics; and in a short time, "that will be attended to in earnest."§

It appears almost incredible, that the grandchild of Theodore-Agrippa d'Aubigne could have penned such sentiments. Had her father, Constant d'Aubigne, superintended her education, that circumstance would have been a sufficient explanation: his disposition and character were bad in the extreme; and he detested his father's faith, which he openly abjured. But an aunt, Madame de Villetle, a lady of irreproachable character, had removed her in infancy, from a state of destitution, caused by her father's imprudence; and by that kind relative, those principles were imparted, which would have obtained the approbation of the venerable d'Aubigne. Indeed, so fervent was the child in her attachment to Calvinism,

that she felt a degree of horror at her father's apostacy; and manifested mucb ardour on behalf of theprotestant religion. Many interesting anecdotes are recorded of her Grmness in defending her opinions, when successively assailed by priests and nuns at a convent of Niort, where she was placed for completing her education: a measure commanded by the government, at the request of her mother, a rigid catholic. To detail them here would be superfluous; but they were viewed as an earnest of liberal views, which unfortunately did not appear, when Francoise d'Aubigne became Marchioness de Main tenon.

Declaration dated 17 June, 1681. *t. t* Edict of 1 Feb., 1669, art. 39. *f $ Lettre a la comtesse de Sl.-Geran,* 19 April, 1679. $ Letter to the same, 28 Oct., 1679.

Yet her ideas of tolerance did not cease immediately after her change of religion. A letter to her brother then governor of Amersfort, contains the following censure: "I have complaints on your account, which "are not to your honour. You ill treat the Hugue"nots; you seek the means, you create the occasions: "thaft-is unlike a man of quality. Have pity on people more unhappy than culpable: they are in "the errors wherein we ourselves were; and from "which violence would never have removed us/'

A conviction that her calvinistic education might diminish the King's respect for her opinions, and destroy the effect of her exhortations, made her desirous of removing every trace of heresy from among her relations. She hegan by endeavouring to convert her cousin, the Marquis de la Villette. Bossuet wasemployed to convince him, but to no purpose; and Bourdaloue's eloquence produced no result. The King sent him orders to be converted; Villette asked for time, which was granted. But when Madame de Maintenon pressed him to fix a period, he replied: "It will require a hundred years — ten at least, to "believe in the infallibility of a body of men; twenty "to be accustomed to transubstantiation, etc." His cousin did not anticipate such obstinacy; and as he was in the navy, she had him ordered upon a long voyage, that he might not frustrate her views for sav» ing his children, f

The dispute between the Jesuit and Jansenist parties menaced the church of Rome with another schism. Louis, who had become a confirmed devotee,. was strongly inclined to favour the former party; and was enslaved by illiberal, narrow views to such a degree, that while Duquesne and Turenne were treated with distinction, although protestants, he would not allow the appointment of a Jansenist to any command. The rival sects were both ambitious of the honour of directing the great measure, for bringing back the lost sheep to the Romish church; and each presented a scheme for effecting that object, drawn up in form of a memorial. And it is worthy of remark, that neither of these plans embraced the revocation of the edict of Nantes; on the contrary, its strict and literal observance was demanded by both. The Jansenists founded their hopes of success upon reiterated instruc'tions by the clergy, and the good example of their conduct r the Jesuits insisted on the firm and unceasing action of the royal authority. The principles of Port-Royal *f* were tolerant; for according to the Jansenist views, it was better to remain separate from the church, than to join it without sincere convictions. The Jesuits on the contrary were violent in their zeal they were impatient to stifle heresy, rather than conTert the heretics; they considered the support of the military far preferable to the influence of the bishops; and called for the expulsion of protestants from every government employ. *Lettre au comte d'Aubigne,* 1 Oct., 1672. f LaBeaumelle, *Mem. de Maintenon,* vol. ii, p. 202.—Auger, *Vit de Madame de Maintenon,* vol. ii, p. 77.—Caylus, p. 15. This prejudice increased with the King's age. In 1706, the duke of Orleans, on setting out for Italy, wished to be accompanied by Augrand de Fontpertuis, a decided libertine. Louis sent for him, and expressed his displeasure that he should have selected a Jansenist. "He a Jansenist?" said the duke, doubtingly. "Is he not," replied Louis," the son of that mad woman who

ran after Arnaud?" "I "know nothing of his mother," the duke answered, " but with "repect to the son, far from being a Jansenist, I doubt whether he "believes in a God." "ThenI have been deceived," observed Louis, who allowed Fontpertuis to accompany the duke. Duclos, *M4m.dk Louis XIV,* vol. i, p. 133. *f* The abbey of Port-Royal was the cradle of Jansenism; and, so far as corporate existence was concerned, it was also its grave: but the doctrines taught by the fathers can never be eradicated—unfortunately, the clergy were not impressed with their liberal views.

Probably the natural feelings of Louis XIV would have inclined him to adopt the milder recommendations of the Jansenists, but his soul was enslaved by the Jesuits. La Chaise, his confessor, had for some time refused him the sacraments, on account of his adultery with Madame de Montespan, a married woman. His passion was now fixed upon Mademoiselle de Fontanges; the illicit connexion was more susceptible of palliation, and the confessor's complaisance opened a field for sarcasm. The voluptuous monarch was admitted to the sacrament at Whitsuntide, in 1680; and the consolation thus afforded, was recompensed by several hostile edicts against the protestants.

Hitherto the collection of the revenue had been chiefly confided to Huguenots; and the absence of all complaint against them, affords an inference, greatly in their favour. Satyrical publications abounded, in which courtiers and magistrates were severely handled; but the *fermiers* are passed by in silence. Their successors by a system of unblushing peculation, attracted the shafts of censure, and converted the previous silence into an absolute eulogy.

The misfortune of Louis consisted in his judging men in general, by the conduct of those who breathed the atmosphere of his court. As he beheld continual sacrifices of honour and principle for selfish considerations, it was natural for him to be persuaded that it would be easy to seduce the Huguenots from their err6neous religion, by rendering their interests subservient to the change. A

base spirit of flattery made every functionary throughout the kingdom ambitious to imitate the King's devout career; and suggestions were constantly forwarded to court, for promoting the pious design.

They were excluded from such employs by *Arret du Conseil,* dated 17 Aug., 1680.

Ordinances were continually published, forbidding or enjoining some particular, of minor importance in itself; but serious in its application, as it became exceedingly difficult for the protestants to avoid the contravention of some of those numerous enactments; and a conviction of the slightest infringement was immediately followed by the suppression of the temple, wherein it occurred.

From these attacks upon their public worship, the hostility of the intolerant party was directed to personal annoyance: no seats were allowed in the temples, that the audience might be disgusted with attendance, f Often the consequences of one evil became a ready indicator for its more extensive application. A notary who had become catholic, found that he had lost the confidence of his former friends: to secure his professional gains, the protestants were declared incapable of exercising the charge of notary. For similar reasons they were successively prohibited from acting in any branch of the legal profession;-f-and according to the preamble of another spoliatory edict, it "was "represented that most of the young men of the said "religion, would decide upon studying medicine, to "take degrees, on finding themselves excluded from "other functions:" protestants were in consequence debarred from following the medical professions. The same excluding system pervaded every line of life: and the callings of apothecaries, grocers, booksellers, and printers, were forbidden to them. While no protestant of any trade, was allowed to have an appentice even a catholic. § But all these inducements combined, failed to effect conversions sufficiently rapid, to satisfy the enemies of religious liberty; as a premium for abjuration, converts had been already allowed a delay of three years for the payment of their debts; and at an interval of nearly five years from" this dishonest measure, a fresh enactment was issued against surgeons, who are charged with preventing conversions, under the pretence of visiting patients.

Rulhiere, vol. i, p. 181.—*Mem. de Noailles* vol. i, p. 14. f Bayle, in a letter to his brother, dated 16 May, 1679, states that the decree was executed with such severity at Rouen, that not a seat was allowed, even to the members of the Consistory. *Arrit du Conseil,* 6 April, 168!. f Idem, 6 April, 1682.—*Declaration du Hoy,* 15 June, 1682.

£ *Declaration du Roy,* 6 Aug., 1685. The spirit of these tyrannical enactments is admirably ppurtrayed by Rabaut St.-Etienne, in a tale, entitled *Le vieux Cevenol, ou anecdotes de la vie d'Ambroise Borely.*

§ In the MSS. of M. de la Reynie, lieutenant-general of police, there are lists of protestants made out at various periods; the number described as *marchands de vin* is remarkable: but almost every other calling was debarred them.

II *Arret du Conseil,* 18 Nov., 1080. J Idem, 15 Sept., 1685. *Madame de Maintenon & Madame de Villette,* 5 April, 1681.

It would appear that at court, the most sanguine expectations were raised upon the edicts just alluded to, since the following remark is preserved in a private letter: "If God spares the King, there will not be a "single Huguenot in twenty years."

At length arrived the commencement of positive persecution, by the invasion of private dwellings, under the pretext of quartering soldiers. This cruel method of annoyance has been termed the *dragonnade* and *mission bottee.* The following extract of a letter addressed by Louvois to Marillac, intendant of Poictou, will convey some idea of the malicious calculation, on which those expeditions were based. "His "Majesty has learned with much joy, the great "number of persons converted in your district. His "Majesty appreciates your endeavours to increase the "number,

and desires you will continue your exer44 tions; using the same means which have hitherto "succeeded. M. Colbert has been charged to exa"mine what can be done, in reducing the taxes for "those who are converted, in order to diminish the "numbers of that religion. His Majesty has com"manded me to send, at the beginning of next No"vember, a regiment of cavalry into Poictou, which "will be lodged in the places you will be mindful to "propose, before that time; and his Majesty will "deem it right, that the greater part of the officers "and horsemen should be lodged with protestants: 44 but he does not think that *ail* should be lodged with "them. That is to say, that when by a strict distri"bution the protestants would support *ten,* you can "send *twenty;* and put them upon the richest among "the protestants, *assigning as a pretext,* that when "the troops are not sufficiently numerous for all to be "charged with them, it is but just the poor should "be spared, and the rich have the burden."

This letter was accompanied by an ordinance, exempting converts from receiving soldiers in their houses, for two years. That was afterwards decreed as a general law,f and although published as a recompense for those who had been converted, it became a most terrible instrument for harrassing the steadfast Louvois was well seconded by his father, Michel Le Tellier, keeper of the seals. In describing his persecuting zeal, the testimony of a catholic, as violent as himself, shall be adduced. "He had such an ardent "desire to see Huguenotism terminated in this "kingdom, and to behold the King's subjects united "in the same faith, that he favoured the interest of "the church on all occasions; and particularly when "the weakening of that party, or the destruction of "their temples was in question." The same writer adds: "Whenever the accusation against a consistory "failed, and the continuance of the worship was "permitted, he was nearly overcome; and his "countenance on leaving the council, sufficiently an-" "nounced the disappointment to his friends." Rulhiere, vol. i, p. 203.

f *Ordonnance du Roi,* 11 April, 1681.

Soulier, *Hut. du Calvinisme,* p. 814.

The ruin of the protestants was now resolved on. Madame de Maintenon thus writes on the subject: "The King begins to think seriously of his salvation, "and of that of his subjects. If God spares him, "there will be only one religion in his kingdom. "That is the sentiment of M. de Louvois; and I "believe him more readily than M. Colbert, who "thinks only of his finances, and rarely of religion.

The infatuation which dictated the foregoing may be pitied, as arising out of a subjugation of the writer's mind to some strong passion. There is however so %nuch sordid feeling in another letter from the same lady, written shortly after, that the pretence of anxiety for the salvation of the people, becomes an awful mockery. The count d'Aubigne was a notorious spendthrift; and nothing short of his sister's power, could have saved him from ruin on several occasions. In writing to announce a royal gratuity, she states: "T hegrant of a hundred thousand livres, which you "are to receive, affords me pleasure; ybu cannot do "better than to buy lands in Poictou; they will be '4 bad there for a mere nothing on account of the flight." of the Sluguenots."f

The persecution which lasted for several years subse quent to 1681, surpasses in cold blooded malignity, lhat of the sixteenth century; for the undisguised hostility of the last kings of the house of Valois, although barbarous, was frank: their object was avowed and the conflicting interests were openly hostile. But the Jesuits, who now swayed the royal councils, were crafty: insidious-enactments rendered it almost impossible to avoid contravention; and liberty of worship was in feet destroyed, even while the edict of Nantes was still in force.

Lettre a la comtesse de St.-Geran, 20 Aug., 1681. -j-Dated 22 Oct., 1681. This letter, which is quoted as genuine by Rulhiere, vol. i, p. 212, is suppressed by Auger, *Fie de Madame de Maintenon.*

Yet the principal actors in this persecution were evidently ashamed of their proceedings; although they have applauded the wisdom and piety of the infatuated King, whose services to the church are compared to the abolition of paganism by Constantine. Every detail of the transaction has been carefully excluded from publications under the control of the French authorities; and the narratives of the fugitives, published in England and Holland, are in general sneeringly treated as libels. Pellisson has already been alluded to, as an able and industrious writer; and his letters form a valuable journal of the court, for a long period. He was employed in gaining conversions by means of corruption; and must necessarily have alluded to the progress of the great work, in his continued correspondence: yet from 1681 until the close of 1688, there is a blank; those letters which mentioned the events of intervening years being suppressed, f Many of the reports forwarded by the provincial authorities are missing from the public ar-$ chives; yet enough remains to prove the violence of the persecution, independent of the flight of many thousand industrious families; there is moreover, strong corroborative evidence in the ill-judged panegyrics of the Romish clergy, who in the ardour of adulation have presented materials for decided censure.

JVAvrigny, *Mem. dogmatiques,* vol. iii, p. 247. + I have found several of the year 1084, in vol. iv of the MSS. *de la Reynie;* they all allude either to the *bonne ceuvre,* or recompenses for conversions. In one, dated 19 May, 1684, is this observation, "La nommée Pingard a reçu trois fois plus qu'elle ne Tous dit; et "beaucoup plus qu'elle ne devoit espérer."

A book was published, under the *sanction of the King's advisers,* which completely establishes the fact of severity being exercised towards the protestants, by justifying the measure as completely similar to the means used for suppressing the doaatist heresy in the fifth century. The condition of the Huguenots; their peaceable demeanour, and admitted loyalty; for 'it was unimpeached at the time, though subsequent accusations have been put forward to justify what

had taken place—all these circumstances combine to shew that state policy was *not* the cause, as some apologists pretend, and as many are willing to believe, *f* It was an odious breaking forth of intolerance and bigotry; *Conformité de la conduite de l'Église de France, pour ramener les Protestons avec celle de l'Eglise d'Afrique, pour ramener les Donatistes à l'Eglise catholique,* Paris, 1685. The following is from the preface: " Ceux qui ont la principale part à la confiance du Roy, "sur ce qui regarde les affaires de l'église, et à la conduite du grand "dessein qui s'exécute si heureusement, ont jugé à propos de faire "imprimer à part quelques-unes de ces lettres" (de St-Augustin).

f The author was inclined to that sentiment until his researches for this volume convinced him of his error. and in the preface of the work just alluded to, it is declared, "that St.-Augustin was at first of opinion, "that the force of truth should alone be used to bring "back the heretics; but experience caused him to "alter his views, and the success of the salutary seve"rity employed for converting the Donatists, con"vinced him that it would be hostile to the salvation "of many souls, who would perish miserably, not to "wish to force them to join the church, which is "justified in punishing its faithless members, although "in the event of successful resistance, any violence on "their part, is impious." The advance of civilisation forbade a renewal of capital punishments for heretical opinions, but the disposition to inflict it, was evidentlyunchanged. CHAPTER X. LETTERS OF CHRISTINA, EX-QUEEN OF SWEDEN.—SUFFERINGS OF JEAN MIGAULT.—GENERAL PERSECUTION OF THE HUGUENOTS.—FORCED CONVERSIONS.

Although it might appear superfluous to present a complete list of the atrocities, practised at this time under a pretext of religion, some of them must be recorded; and their real motives placed beyond doubt, or the forbearance which would dictate the exclusion of such painful scenes, may be considered an accusation of all preceding statements. More detail will therefore be necessary in

treating of this period, than when other circumstances were under consideration; and where the more important events alone claimed description, those of minor consequence frequentlyobtaining no more than a passing allusion. The narrative of one who suffered greatly in this persecution will afford means for estimating the general conduct of the oppressors. With respect to the value of its testimony, it must not be confounded with the published accounts of the time, which the court of France sweepingly denounced as libels, composed in a spirit of revenge. This however was never intended for publicity; and the manuscript remained neglected and forgotten among the records of the family, until the author's descendants had become blended with another nation. The account it contains is moreover amply corroborated by contemporary writers; and the description harmonises completely with the views given in the correspondence of eminent persons, who cannot be suspected of exaggeration on behalf of the Huguenots. *Narrative of the Sufferings of a French Protestant Family,* etc., by John Migault, London, 1824. *Le Journal de Jean Migault* was published at Paris, in 1825, and at Berlin in 1827. Although the French copy has been chiefly consulted, the pages refer lo the London edition, for the convenience of the English reader.

Of such the foremost is Christina, ex-Queen of Sweden, who was so decidedly attached to popery, that the propositions of the clergy of France, at their assembly in 1682, amounted in her view, to a scandal nearly allied to rebellion. And subsequently when her declared sympathy was held up by Bayle, as a remnant of protestantism, she wrote to him, complaining severely of his injustice, in doubting the sincerity of her conversion.--Her letter to the chevalier de Terlon, the French ambassador at Stockholm, contains the following passages: "I will frankly avow, "that I am not quite persuaded of the success of this "great design; and that I cannot rejoice at it, as an "affair very advantageous to our holy religion. "Military men are strange apostles. I consider them "more likely to kill, to ravish and to plunder, than "to persuade: and in fact, accounts beyond doubt "inform us, that they fulfil the mission entirely in "their mode. I pity the people abandoned to their 44 discretion: I sympathise with so many ruined fami"lies, so many respectable persons reduced to beg"gary; and I cannot look upon what is now passing "in France, without compassion." £ The four celebrated articles for restraining the papal authority— drawn up by Bossuet, who, by his eloquence, secured their adoption. The Jesuit d'Avrigny looks upon the proceeding as one of the rudest blows which had been given to the court of Rome for ages. De Burigny, *Vie de Bossuet,* p. 262.—Tabaraud, *Histoire de I'Assemblee generale du Clerge, en* 1G8 2, p. 94.

f Letter dated Reme, 14 Dec, 1686. *Letires de Bayle,* vol. i, p. 247.

£ Ibid., 2 Feb., 1686. *Nouvelles de la Republique des Letires,* May, 1686.

Another letter to cardinal Azolino is in a similar strain: " I am overwhelmed with grief when I think "of all the innocent blood, which a blind fanaticism "causes daily to flow. France exercises, without re"morse or fear, the most barbarous persecution, upon "the dearest and most industrious portion of her "people., Every time I contemplate the atro

"cious torments, which have been inflicted upon the "protestants, my heart throbs, and my eyes are filled "with tears."

The admission of one of the most abject flatterers of Louis XIV, being added to Christina's testimony, will suffice to remove every doubt, as to the reality of the persecution: " But if the King has been obliged "to use some severity, and to send soldiers into the "houses of the most obstinate, to bring them back "into the pale of the church, we have reason to hope, "that like the Donatists, they will rejoice that this "holy and salutary violence has been adopted, for "withdrawing them from the lethargy into which "the misfortune of their birth had thrown them/'-f

One more proof shall be adduced.

The baron de Breteuil, in an official report to Louis XVI, makes the following assertion: " The very minutes of all the or"ders sent into the provinces, forelfecting conversions "by quartering soldiers, are preserved in the archives "ofthe war-office.";..

Dated Hamburgh, 1686. *Leltres secretes de Christine,* p. 170. Geneva, 1761. f Soulier, p. 623. This seems to be a favourite phrase, as the author uses it on more than one occasion.

Having premised these corroborating statements, the sufferings of John Migault and his family will be more readily credited. That victim of tyranny exercised the profession of notary until 1681, when a royal decree disqualified protestants from such functions. Sympathy for his numerous family, and respect for his character, induced the consistory of Mougon to offer him the situation of reader and registrar of the temple in that place: but his quiet occupation did not last long. Louvois had informed Marillac, intendant of Poictou, that a body of dragoons should be sent there in November; the design of the court was however hastened, and the warlike missionaries entered that province in the summer. The terror inspired by their approach, will be appreciated by the fact of a soldier casually exhibiting some slips of paper, as billets for quartering his comrades; and within two hours, three of the first families in the place abjured,-j

"We were not exposed to the fury of the storm," observes Migault, " until Tuesday the twenty-second "of. August, 1681. In the morning, as we quitted "the church where we had just offered up our ac"customed prayers, we beheld a troop of cavalry, "commanded by M. de la Brique, advance towards "us at a gallop, take their station around the ceme"tery, and by their demonstrations strike terror into "the stoutest hearts. I had scarcely entered my "house, when the quartermaster appeared, holding "in his hand a billet. Without dismounting, he de"manded most peremptorily, if it was our intention "to become catholics? Such was the method in "which these *convertisseurs* were accustomed to

pro"ceed. On the solemn assurance given him by your "excellent mother and myself, that we would not "change our religion, he turned his horse and went "away." Uulhiere, vol. ii, p. 71. f Migault, p. 26.

The appearance of the dragoons, in many cases sufficed to make an entire village embrace the Romish religion; but when the acquiescence was only partial, the burden was proportionately aggravated for the more steadfast Huguenots. The system was one of absolute plunder; for the soldiers levied contributions on their hosts, and if the amount demanded was not punctually paid, their furniture, cattle, and even their apparel were sold to raise the money. Those sales afforded great facilities for the Roman catholics to obtain property on very easy terms, of which they frequently availed themselves, f

Migault had fifteen soldiers quartered upon him: they behaved brutally, and made the most insolent demands. It was necessary to send to Niort, in order to supply their table; and because the forage for their horses did-not please them, they used the grossest imprecations. As it was indispensable to dispatch a messenger to Niort for supplies, Migault was allowed to leave the house; and while absent from his home, he learned from some catholic friends, that his complete ruin was intended; and that it arose from the instigations of the cure, whose suggestions included a plan for dragging him forcibly to the catholic church, when, if violent measures were not used to induce his abjuration, it would at all events be declared that he had made a formal recantation, and joined in the Romish rites. This is known to have been done in other places, in order to swell the reports upon the progress of conversion. . ' Migault, p. 29. This circumstantial journal was addressed by the author to his children, f Migault, p. 27.

By the advice of his kind neighbours, the unfortunate man remained concealed in their house; and when the dragoons perceived that he had escaped from their grasp, they directed their malevolence against his wife,: whom they threatened to burn, un less she abjured. In vain did some ladies intercede: the commander disregarded the appeal, and the poor woman would probably have perished, if an unexpected deliverer had not appeared in the person of M. Billon, the vicar, an excellent man and a friend of the family. He heard of the treatment to which Madame Migault was exposed, and removed her out of the power of her persecutors; but not before he had promised to restore her, if his arguments failed to effect her conversion. The ladies being left alone with the sufferer, led her to a place of concealment, and the.... '.-.. '...-.:..'..... '' '.. .'..; Migault, pp. 30 *et seq.* vicar was too humane to regret the involuntary breach of his engagement; he retired to his own house, without noticing the dragoons.

The next day every protestant in the village abjured, with the exception of about twenty families, who had quitted their homes on the approach of the troops. The dwellings of the absentees were stripped of every thing; and when it was ascertained that no further mischief could be accomplished at Mougon, the dragoons were marched to Souche, where all the protestants experienced their severities,-j

A similar scene passed in the adjoining parish of Thorigne, chiefly inhabited by protestants; and as the first visit of the troops effected very little conversion, the cure was incensed, and instigated the soldiers tooppression and wanton cruelty, far surpassing their former exploits. The people however displayed great constancy and patience; very few recantations occurred; and the forest was again crowded with miserable wanderers. Tbis naturally led to an extensiveemigration; the protestants left the kingdom by thousands for England, Holland, and the new settlements of North America; the hospitable reception afforded the fugitives, was amply rewarded by the advantages which resulted from the intelligence and industry of the exiles. $

Migault's young family was a serious impediment to his flight. The cure, his old enemy, continued to urge. the persecution against him; and after.every

thing saleable in his house had been removed, the rest was destroyed; even the doors and windows. And to aggravate the unhappy man's misfortunes, one of his children died; on which occasion the cruel priest strenuously exerted his influence with the husband of the child's nurse, to have the infant's body thrown to the dogs. The man was not so lost to a sense of humanity as to consent; and the child was interred in the protestant burial ground,-f Migault, p. 39. f Ibid., p. 44.

-f *Declaration du Roy,* dated 14 July, 1682, forbids emigration, and cancels all sales of properly made within a year of departure.

The persecution continued during the month of November, 1681; and more severe than at the commencement, because at this time the bare fact of persisting in the reformed faith, authorized the seizure of every thing. What the military did not consume, was sold or destroyed; and the losses were rendered more painful by the animosity of some converts, who being animated in the work of spoliation against their late brethren, acted as informers, and shared in the pillage. $

Migault then removed to Mauze, a small town in Aunis, where he established a school, which afforded him the means of living comfortably, until March, 1683, when the Ring published a declaration forbidding protestant schoolmasters from receiving boarders into their houses. § The provisions of that tyrannical decree were evaded by the scholars being placed in neighbouring houses, but one blow was no sooner parried, than another was struck. A schoolmaster who had abjured, denounced Migault to the authorities, for infringing the ordonnance, by permitting his pupils to sing psalms. A technical objection saved the unfortunate man on this occasion; but within a few months, the dragoons were again on the march to complete the ruin of those families, who had withstood the ravages of 1681. We were apprized (Migault relates) of the iniquitous and arbitrary proceedings of the *cours souveraines,* and of the intendants of provinces, re-

cently invested with authority for pronouncing definitively, and without appeal, on any charge preferred against our churches. If no charge existed one was invented, and thus all the reformed churches, not only of Porctou but throughout the kingdom, were soon destroyed or. interdicted. The temple at Mauze was however spared, amid the wide spread desolation; a circumstance graiefully attributed to the influence of the duchess of BrunswicL-Lunenburgh, who left no means untried for warding off the impending rigours; or at least for delaying their execution; and for that purpose she employed all the resources of her credit at the French court, and interceded on behalf-of the protestants with the King himself.-J-.-.'.'-..

Migault, p. 51. *f* Ibid., p. 54. $ Ibid.p. 56. § Ibid., p. 67.

The duke de Noailles, who 'commanded in Languedoc, allowed his desire to please Louis, to supersede every other consideration. Soon after his appointment, he addressed the monarch to this effect: " It "suffices that your Majesty's orders be known, to "ensure their immediate execution." Unhappily the bigoted designs of the court rendered this otherwise humane nobleman, a minister of wrath to the Huguenots.

Cours souveraines, under the old regime, were the courts in which the King was supposed to be present, and where the decrees were given in his name. f Migault, p. 72.....

Conformably to instructions from court, the parliament of Toulouse had, in 1682, forbidden the protestant worship, and ordered the demolition of the temple, on pretext of infractions of the laws. The bishop of the diocese having demanded permission to use the. temple as a church, Chateauneuf, secretary of state, wrote to Noailles, that it would have more effect to execute the decree fully, as it would destroy all hope of its recovery by the *religionnaives.* f The protestants on their side, pressed Noailles with solicitations on behalf of religious liberty; and when two ministers declared, that even the fear of death should not deter them from discharging their duty, the duke confined them in his house, as the most effectual reply.

Noailles had sufficient force to carry the decree of the parliament into execution; and by impartial severity maintained order, at a moment when insurrection appeared imminent: he punished some catholics for insulting the Huguenots; and issued a proclamation to enjoin good fellowship, and avoid anything calculated to irritate, by word or writing. The ministers remained in confinement until after the following Sunday, when they were released, and sent away from that town.

Noailles, vol. i, p. ij...... f 23 Nov., 1682. Noailles, vol. i, p. 15.

The success which had attended the plan for abolishing the protestant worship at Montpellier, induced a similar proceeding against Montauban and other places; but the government being informed of the irritation arising from the apprehensions of the Huguenots, Chateauneuf wrote to suspend the execution, "as they should not put too much fuel on the fire, at "one time."f

D'Aguesseau about the same time wrote to urge the necessity of instructing the people, in preference to the adopted methods of fear and corruption. There does not appear to have existed a corresponding desire on the part of the executive; to enforce submission to the King's will, was the aim of all functionaries; and the public mind was inflamed to a degree, which rendered an insurrection probable.

The ministers encouraged their followers to brave the King's orders, and obtain the crown reserved for martyrs. As the danger became more evident, the enthusiasm increased; and at last the troops under the command of St.-Ruth, were ordered into the province in the summer of 1683. $ The presence of those formidable missionaries intimidated the protestants, who manifested a readiness to submit. An amnesty was offered under certain conditions: the terms were however too severe, and the protestants resumed their arms. They were attacked in a favourable position selected for their head quarters, near Pierregourde, in the Vivarais. A part of the royal army maintained some skir-

mishes, to engage their attention, while the main body was engaged in surrounding them. Their defence was well conducted; but their assailants' force overwhelmed them, and under cover of the adjoining wood most of them escaped. Yet numbers were killed by the dragoons; and of the prisoners thirteen were selected: twelve were hanged at once-upon the spot, their companion being compelled to act as executioner. Noaillcs, vol. i, p. 20. t 7 Dec. Ibid., vol. i, p. 21.

$ Ibid., p. 36.

This victory wasnaturally followed by the destruction of several temples; and in some places, they found the inhabitants had all fled. The expedition caused great terror, as none were spared, who fell into the hands of the troops. The duke de Noailles in his letters observes: " These wretches went to the gibbet, "with the firm assurance of dying as martyrs; and "demanded no other favour, than that they might be "quickly executed. They begged pardon of the sol"diers; but not one of them would ask it of the "King."f

Noailles was an advocate for severe measures; by forming an erroneous estimate of the consequences of former rigour, he felt encouraged to continue; and the recent insurrection produced still more severe orders from Louvois, than he had hitherto received. "His "Majesty desires you will order M. de St.-Ruth to 44 place troops in all the places you deem it necessary; "to support them at the expence of the country; "to seize the culpable, and hand them over to "M. d'Aguesseau for judgment; to destroy the houses "of those killed in arms. You will give orders for "demolishing ten of the principal temples of the Vi"varais; and in a word, to cause such a desolation in "the country, that the example may keep the other "religion-naires within bounds, and teach them how "dangerous it is to revolt against the Ring."

The Huguenots of the Cevennes, still undaunted by.the defeat of their brethren, sent a deputation to.Nismes: they presented a request to Noailles, that he would obtain from the King's

goodness and justice, a general amnesty; the right of worship; and the revocation of the edicts contrary to their liberties. Noailles astonished at the boldness of men, whom he calls *pauvres miserables,* instantly sent them as prisoners to the citadel of Saint-Esprit. Their proceeding was too extravagant to deserve such treatment: for even their brethren viewed the deputation as an act of madness; and the consistory of Nismes disavowed thena.f

Circumstances were very adverse to the Huguenots of Languedoc; yet they perseveringly asserted the rights of conscience, while Noailles was equally firm and decided in his efforts to bring under subjection men whom he viewed as rebels. His superior force enabled him to disperse their assemblies; but they collected again in other parts; and as the most effectual means of straitening their resources, orders were given to seize all arms in the possession of protestants: a considerable quantity was found in Nismes. Noailles, p. 47. f Ibid. , vol. i, p. 50.

Many of the protestant ministers had been arrested; their exhortations had supported the energy of the insurgents; and they were viewed as the chief instigators of the public troubles. Audoyer and Homel were both condemned to death: the former was respited, but the latter was broken upon the wheel, after enduring the rack. His head was exposed at Chalencon, and his body at Beauchatel; at both of which places he had been conspicuous in his exertions. Hoguier, another minister of *the sect,* to use the expression of the abbe Millot, cut his throat in prison: f an assertion which demands some proof, before posterity will credit a statement at variance with probability; for the fear of condemnation and public execution could have had no weight with men who preached the glory of martyrdom: it is far more reasonable to conclude, that his enemies killed him secretly, from a dread of his example.

As the want of instruction had so frequently been urged upon the notice of the government, the abbe Herve, with twelve missionaries, was sent into

Languedoc. Hispreachingwassupportedandstrengthened by liberal distributions of money, to all who would declare themselves convinced. He was very successful, but not equal to his wishes or expectations; and demanded further funds to supply his proselytes. Noailles, in a letter full of commendation, states: "The King's money appears to me so well employed "for this purpose, that economy would be pernicious; "for they are subjects gained both for God and his "Majesty." Noaillcs, v. i., p. 57. t Ibid., p. 58

While Herve pursued his persuasions, the troops continued their career of severity. The ministers of Languedoc had in consequence, withdrawn into Switzerland, where they joined a Swiss synod, in which it was resolved tt receive all who fled from France, on account of their religion; and to address the protestant governments on behalf of the French calvinists. This gave rise to a hostile demonstration by the states of Languedoc, who demanded fresh severities against them; and with some trifling modifications, the suggestions were adopted by the court,-f

The notorious Basville $ had succeeded Marillac, as intendant of Poictou, in 1682. On his arrival in that province, he found that thirty-four thousand conversions had taken place; and within three years, he had the gratification of announcing above twelve thousand more, resulting from what an apologist styles " measures replete with mildness.";§ Noailles, vol. i, p. 60. f Ibid., p. 66.

$ Nicolas deLamoignon, seigneur de Basville, born in 1648, fifth son of the president of the same name. $ " Par ces mcmes voyes, pleines de douceur." Soulier, p. 65.

Every day confirmed the general apprehension of the protestants, that a crisis in their affairs was at hand; in consequence, some regulations were drawn up for the guidance of both ministers and people, in the event of the congregations being dispersed. The project comprised eighteen articles, and was adopted in May, 1683, at Toulouse; where deputies had assembled from all

parts, under pretexts of busuiess. A day was fixed for a general fast; but with that exception, the decisions were far from being calculated to give umbrage to the government. It has been asserted however, that this was in reality, a conspiracy formed on an understanding with the antipapist party in England, which made great preparations at the same time, for a general insurrection. And as the protestants mutually exhorted each other to sustain persecution with firmness, their conduct is condemned, because forsooth, the primitive Christians acted otherwise; they were contented with secret assemblings, and never revolted to obtain theright of public worship. Happy indeed the Huguenots would have been, to feel secure in the secret exercise of religious worship, or if even the right of private opinion had been permitted them. The course of this history will however show, that the suspicion of calvinistic sentiments exposed the party to molestation, while he lived; and indignity to his remains at his decease.

An idea was prevalent among the protestants, that Louis was not aware of the cruelties excercised towards them; he was not in fact made acquainted with the naked truth. His ministers presented numerous lists of conversions and abjurations; but made no mention of the violence by which they were effected. A request was therefore drawn up in the most submissive terms, yet with a forcible appeal to the monarch's feelings. It contained a pathetic statement of their sufferings; and was presented to the King by the marquis de Ruvigny, their deputy-general, in March, 1684. Soulier, pp. 589—94.

When the marquis had concluded his address, the King replied that he believed all he had stated of the prejudice it might cause to his affairs, only he thought it would not extend to bloodshed: but he said he felt so indispensably bound to attempt the conversion of all his subjects and the extirpation of heresy, that if the doing it required that with one hand he should cut off the other, he would submit. Ruvigny warned his friends of the threatened danger; and

some were for preparing in earnest against a civil war. The aged nobleman however dissuaded them, as he knew they could not rely on England for support. The statementof the Huguenots' grievances merits examination.

After expressing a conviction, that the violations of the edicts in their favour were unknown to their Sovereign, they reminded Louis of his declaration of 1669, which was openly violated in every part of the kingdom. One of its articles prohibited all attempts to remove children from their protestant parents, in order to convert them, under fourteen years of age; but every day, those of the tenderest age were taken from their families, and placed in convents or prisons, where cruel treatment was resorted to for effecting their renunciation of the reformed religion; while there was no possibility of obtaining access to the retreats, in which the laws were so outrageously violated. The magistrates., instead of censuring such conduct, openly encouraged it; and the clergy defended the measure, on the grounds that the King's orders could not withdraw from the authority of the church, those who are its members without distinction of age.
Burnet, vol. i, p. 362.

Another article protected the protestants against exclusion from practising any art or trade; but their apprentices were refused admittance into the most inferior kinds of handicraft, and the protestant artisans were completely deprived of the means of earning their livelihood.

A third grievance was the prohibition against publishing any work respecting their religion; that privilege had been conferred by revoking an ordonnance, obtained by their enemies in 1666. But a decree of the council, given in November, 1670, was permitted to nullify the royal declaration, no less than one of the articles of the edict of Nantes.

Not only public charges, the legitimate reward of merit, were denied to the protestants; they were interdicted from exercising any honourable profession. They could not become advocates or physicians; and as if under a mark of infamy, were thus declared unworthy to serve the public in any manner. The request is given at length by de Limiers, *Hist, de Louis XIV,* vol. iv, pp. 135—152.

This appeal to the King's humanity produced no good result. To judge from the measures which almost immediately followed its presentation, it would appear that by exposing their complaints, the protestants only rendered their enemies more eager to hasten their entire destruction. Even their charitable intentions were viewed in an odious light; and the sick and infirm poor were forbidden, under a penalty of five hundred livres, to receive an asylum in private houses;. in order that a compulsory residence in the hospitals might produce conversions. Madame de Maintenon thus alludes to the King's intentions in a letter to the countess de Saint-Geran:-f-"He proposes to labour "for the entire conversion of the heretics; he has fre"quent conferences on that subject with Le Tellier "and Chateauneuf; at which they persuade me, that "my presence would not be unwelcome. M. de Cha,4 teauneuf has proposed measures, which are not "suitable. The business must not be precipitated. "It must be conversion, not persecution. M. de Lou"vois wishes for mildness; which does not agree with "his disposition, and his desire to finish the affair. The "King is ready to do whatever may be deemed most "useful for the advancement of religion. This under"taking will cover him with glory in the eyes of God "and men. He will have brought back all his sub"jects into the bosom of the church; and destroyed "the heresy, which none of his predecessors could "vanquish."

It is however due to the memory of Louis, to dedare that much of what passed was concealed from him. From the period of his marriage with Madame de Maintenon, that lady had the means of keeping back many communications and reports. She was herself deceived by fallacious statements; and her grand object was to ward off every thing calculated to disturb the King's tranquillity. The charms of her society lulled him into a blind confidence; and after a time,

he was confirmed in a wish to repose from publiccares. Louis left the means of execution to his ministers, whose anticipations of success were most sanguine; the conversions already obtained by fear, made them calculate upon still greater results; and while poets sang, and historians recorded the monarch's absolute power, the vital interests of the nation were at the mercy of an ardent triumvirate; who flattered their prince that his views were promoted, while in reality, he was merely the instrument of their purposes. Madame de Maintenon and the Jesuit La Chaise were decidedly influenced by religious zeal; but Louvois acquiesced in their views, as the surest means of maintaining himself at the headof affairs.
Arrit du Cornell, t Sept., 1684. f Dated is Aug., 1684.

In confirmation of this view, we have the testimony of Madame de Caylus. "The King yielded, against his "own convictions and his natural inclination, which "always dispased him to mildness. His orders were "exceeded, unknown to him; and cruelties were com"mitted, which he would have prevented, had he "been informed of them; but Louvois contented him"self with saying every day: So many persons are "converted, as I had told your Majesty it would be "at the mere appearance of your troops."

There is no necessity to consult the complaints of protestant refugees, for finding the materials of accusation against the bigoted government of France: the eulogy of a priest is sufficiently condemnatory. 44 While "the King's council was striving to suppress the pro"testant academies, and overthrow their temples, es"tablished contrary to the edict of Nantes, the bi"shops, the parliaments, the governors, and even the "inferior authorities did each their best, to second 4' the King's designs. So that the temples, which the "council could not condemn, as not being contrary "to the edict, were demolished or closed on account "of infractions, made by ministers and consistories "upon his Majesty's declarations; and by this means, "most of the

provinces where Huguenotism was for"merly very flourishing, were reduced to the priva"tionof public worship."-j

In March, 1685, Louis contemplated a renewalof the *dragonnades,* when the march of an army into Bearn, preparatory to an irruption into Spain, hastened the execution of the grand scheme. Foucault, intendant of Bearn, moved by his own zealous feelings, or probably excited by some Jesuitical influence, availed himself of the presence of such a force, to declare that the King would no longer allow more than one religion in his dominions. This man, like his father and grandfather, was remarkable for his hatred towards the protestants; a quality quite incompatible with his character for erudition, which gave rise to a singular incident; for he discovered and published *Lactanlius de morlibus persecutorum.* The horrors which occurred in his ill-fated province are scarcely credible: they will form the subject of another chapter, along with the events of Languedoc and the Vivarais. The whole kingdom presented a uniform scene of desolation. Edicts were hastily given, at the officious suggestions of the clerical courtiers; who proposed plans for terminating a state of affairs, which all felt to be disgraceful. "Twenty-eight decrees," observes the Jesuit d'Avrigny, "were given in quick succession; "Louis XIV steadfastly following his plan, continued "to publish declarations and ordonnances, according," as the clergy deemed it necessary, for gradually pre"paring the revocation of the edict of Nantes."-j *Souvenirs de Madame de Caylus,* p. It. *f* Soulier, p. 598, Rulhiere, *Eclaircissements,* etc., vol. i, p. 289. f D'Avrigny, *M6m. dogmaliques,* vol. iii, p. 96.

CHAPTER XI. REVOCATION OF THE EDICT OF NANTES.

Lest it should be supposed that the materials for these pages are drawn from hostile sources, a panegyrist of Louis XIV shall supply the account of a most odious persecution commenced in Bearn, during the spring of 1685, above six months before the legal right of protestant worship was abolished. "It was "believed," observes the abbe Soulier, "that the "calvinists being reduced to have very few *exercices* "*publics,* would more willingly listen to the instruc- "tions which the prelates gave in their dioceses, in "order to draw them from error; and that the money "which the King distributed on all sides to assist the "new converts, would induce the followers of that "religion to enter almost voluntarily into the bosom 44 of the church; but as these mild means had not all "the effect which was expected; and as it appeared 44 on the contrary, that the calvinists, far from listening "to the missionaries became more obstinate, his Ma"jesty deemed it necessary to use stronger remedies "to draw them from that lethargy into which the "misfortune of their birth had thrown them. It *Vide antea,* p. 200 of Ihis vol.

"was then resolved that the King's troops should be "employed to co-operate with the missionaries, for "effecting in other provinces what Marillac had done '4 in Poictou, where in a short time he subjugated near "forty thousand." The example of St.-Augustin is then quoted as a precedent; and some instances of violence, on the part of the calvinists, appealed to as a justification.

The account of Foucault's success in making converts, drawn up for the King's perusal, is one of the most barefaced impostures ever written-According to this statement the protestants of Oleron were summoned in the King's name to be instructed in the doctrines of the catholic church: they demanded fifteen days for reflection, and at the expiration of that delay, declared their readiness to abjure, *f* But without referring to the complaints of the sufferers, it will suffice toadduce another narrative, mentionedby Rulhiere, who observes thereon: "Whatever can be imagined of '4 military licentiousness was exercised in Bear n against "the calvinists. It is attributed tothis intendant "(Foucault) that he improved upon more than one "kind of torture: invention was employed to discover "torments, which might be painful without being "mortal; and cause the unhappy victims to under-

go "the utmost which the human body can sustain with"out expiring." \$ Soulier, *Hist, du Calvinisme,* pp. 598 — 9. This work was printed at Paris in 1686, before the importance of its admissions could be appreciated.

f Soulier, p. 600. % Rulhiere, vol. i, p. 291.

What more than this is stated in the complaints of the refugees? Greater detail is given; but the accusation is no stronger. There we find accounts of the victims being suspended by the hair, or by the feet, and nearly suffocated by damp straw being burned in the places where they were tied up: the hairs of their head and beard were plucked out: they were plunged repeatedly into deep water, and drawn out by a rope fastened under their arms, only in time to prevent their being drowned. Sometimes an unfortunate creature was drenched with wine by means of a funnel; and when intoxicated, taken to church, where his presence was deemed equivalent to abjuration. A similar method was adopted with individuals overcome with bodily pain. In some cases the Huguenots were prevented from sleeping for an entire week, by sentinels continually rousing them; and when any protestant was confined to his bed by illness, a dozen drummers were sent to beat under his window, without intermission, until the sick man promised to be converted: with a long catalogue of other diabolical suggestions for subduing the firmness of the protestants.

"Burnet, vol. i, p. 393.—Benoit,vol. iv.—Claude,*Plaintes des Protestans,* pp. 42 *et seq.*—Limiers, *Hist, de Louis XIV,o.* vt.—*Manifestedes habitans desCevennessur leur prise d'armes,* inserted *inMem. deLamberty,* vol. ii, p. 527. In addition to the above accounts, which, though attacked, are not disproved, the author has been favoured with a MS. addressed by one Salcedo to the secretary of State, which completely corroborates the published narratives, and manfully urges a change of policy, on the grounds of national advantage. Although riot dated, allusions to the anticipated dispute on the Spanish succession indicate the time when it was writ-

ten.

Among the documents of this period which have come to light, is a letter from Louvois to marshal Boufflers, commanding the army assembled in Bearn. After stating that the Spanish expedition was abandoned, the minister observes, that his majesty has thought proper to make use of the troops, to diminish as much as possible the great number of *religionnaires* in the generalities of Bordeaux and Montauban. The marshal was to confer with the intendants, in order to learn in what places the protestants were most numerous. "In executing his Majesty's orders," continues Louvois, "You will send into each com." munity the number of cavalry and infantry which "may be concerted upon with the intendant. You 44 will lodge them entirely in the houses of the reli"gionnaires, withdrawing them from each individual." as he is converted: and you will remove the troops "from the community to send them to another, when "all the religionnaires, or even the principal part are "converted; postponing until another time, the con"version of the remainder, as will be hereafter ex"" plained." It was enjoined on the marshal to maintain good conduct and discipline among the soldiers, and severely punish any infraction of that order. This-provision was a complete mockery, because no attempt was made to restrain the excesses of the military. Subsequent letters from Louvois repeated the King's wishes, that no stress should be laid upon the entire 'conversion of a place; but that without making efforts to gain individuals of importance by their fortune or character, he was to swell the list of conversions to the utmost. The letter, dated 31 July, 1685, is given at length by Rulhiere, vol. i,p. 295.

The compilers of the official accounts which were submitted to the King, being aware of his desire, obsequiously related every thing in a manner calculated to gratify his feelings, and confirm his resolutions. Bergerac was looked upon as the Geneva of Lower Guyenne, and Montauban was unquestionably the protestant head-quarters of the upper province: the general conversion of those places is represented as a spontaneous movement arising from conviction, and resulting from argument and persuasion; but in the complacency of success, the author already often cited, admits that the inhabitants of Bergerac " may have had apprehensions of ill treatment from the soldiers." f

In describing the theological victory at Montauban, the avowal is still more important; inasmuch as it corroborates the accusing cry raised against the persecutions of Bearn. "A report was spread in Montauban, that the battalion of Bouvincourt which was in Bear n (where it had favoured the conversions of those of the pretended reformed religion) was soon to arrive in that town; every one was persuaded that it came with the same orders as were given in Bearn, and many of the *religionnaires* began to manifest a design of joining the Catholic, Apostolic and Boman Church." Here is a decided admission of fear, in consequence of the cruelty exercised in the neighbouring province. There was however a delay in the appearance of the military, which caused a change of sentiment, and the protestants informed the intendant, that they were ever willing to obey God and the King, *according to their conscience.* The intendant then wrote to Boufflers to hasten the march of his troops. The readiness to be converted again displayed itself; and the abjurations were so numerous, lhat the soldiers were obliged to leave the quarters in which thev were but just before installed, and camp for the night. Many abjured with a view to gain time and facilitate their escape; indeed the sincerity of scarcely any of these conversions could be expected; but Louvois was enraptured at the illusory success, and in the beginning of September wrote to inform his aged father, Le Tellier, that sixty thousand conversions had taken place in the generality of Bordeaux, and twenty thousand in that of Montauban.-f Rulhiere, p. 302.-j-Soulier, p. 603.

The duke de Noailles commanded in Languedoc, and pursued his missionary career in a similar manner. After relating in his Report the forced conversion of Nismes, Uzes and other towns, he adds: "I am pre"paring to go through the Cevennes, and hope that 4' by the end of this month, not a Huguenot will 44 remain." $ He was afterwards obliged to intercede with the King, for a remission of the taxes levied in his province, all the protestant districts being ruined by supporting the soldiers. Soulier, p. 604. This occurred in August, 1685. f Rulhiere, vol. i, p. 304.

:£ Noailles, vol. i, p. 80. The abbe Millot, compiler of these memoirs, admits the compulsory measures adopted.

Louis was certainly misled by the exaggerated and deceptive accounts. Madame de Maintenon thus writes to her confessor: "The King is well; every "courier brings him great cause for joy; that is to "say, news of conversions by thousands."-f-The Jesuit La Chaise and Louvois both assured the monarch, that his glorious achievement would be completed without bloodshed; and he gave a finishing stroke to the persecution, by revoking what remained of the edict of Nantes. Frittered away, as that statute had been, it still sanctioned liberty of conscience, and the right of protestant worship. The edict of revocation was signed at Fontainebleau on the eighteenth of October, 1685. The following judgment is passed upon this measure by the duke de Saint-Simon: although young at this period, his opinion has weight from his subsequent experience; and above all from the facilities he enjoyed for appreciating any causes, not generally known, which might justify the proceeding. "The revocation of the edict of Nantes, without the least pretext or necessity; and the various proscriptions, rather than proclamations, which followed it, were the fruits of this dreadful plot which depopulated one fourth of the kingdom, ruined trade in all its branches, placed it so long under the public avowed pillage of the dragoons, and authorized torments and executions, in which thousands of innocent persons of both sexes perished.'' After reciting a long list of attendant ills, he adds: "Such was the general abomination produced by flattery and cruelty." Noailles, vol. i, p. 98. h f Letter to the abbe" Gobelin, dated Chambord, 26 Sept., 1684.

The chancellor Le Tellier terminated his career by sealing the document, so fatal to the interests of France, so disgraceful for the King and his ministers; his soul had been absorbed in the chimerical project of legislating for the conscience. In his view, the edict of Nantes alone prevented the realisation of that grand desideratum — one fold under one shepherd. And when he had signed the abolition of the heretics' charter, he sang the *Nunc dimittis* in token of his joy. He died ten days after, at Chaville near Sevres. Bossuet and Flechier exerted their eloquence to describe him as a saint, and model of excellence: his character is however given differently by other hands. He is said to have notoriously abused the influence of his position, for injuring those who had displeased him; and the count de Grammont perceiving him quit the King's cabinet, after a private audience, observed: "1 "picture to myself a polecat, who has just killed some "fowls, and is licking his jaws yet stained with their "blood." f

Madame de Maintenon thus writes a few days after the edict of revocation; "The King is very well pleased "at having completed the great work of bringing the "heretics back to the church. Father La Chaise has "promised that it shall not cost one drop of blood, "and M. de Louvois says the same. I am glad those "of Paris have been brought to reason. Claude was 44 a seditious man, who confirmed them in their errors: "since they have lost him, they are more docile. I "think with you, that all these conversions are not "sincere; but at least their children will be catho"lies." *QEuvres computes de Louis de Saint-Simon,* vol. ii, p. 43. f Voltaire and *U* Beaumelle, conflicting authorities' concur in admitting this anecdote as veracious.

The count de Bussy Rabutin, alluding to the same subject, observes: " I admire the King's plan for ruin"ing the Huguenots: the wars carried on formerly "against them, and the St.

Bartholomew, have mul"tiplied and given vigour to this sect. His Majesty "has gradually undermined it; and the edict he has "just given, supported by dragoons and Bourdaloue, "has been the *coup de (jrdce."-*

But in spite of the eulogies of the clergy, and the flattery of courtiers, the revocation of the edict of Nantes will ever be deemed a cruel and disgraceful act of authority: it contains in its own text, proofs of the treachery used in preparing its enactments; as likewise of the duplicity and fear, common to all instigators of tyrannical measures. The following are its principal features.

The preamble declares that as the greater part of the protestants had embraced the catholic religion, the edict of Nantes was useless. The three first clauses revoke, in consequence, the said edict, with every

„ *Letter to the countess de Saint-Geran,* dated 25 Oct., 1685. f 14 Nov., 1685. *Letlres de Bussy-Rafoitin,* vol. ii, p. 47.

royal declaration in favour of the pretended reformed religion, and prohibit protestant worship under severe penalties. Art. 4 orders all ministers refusing to be converted, to quit the kingdom within fifteen days, and Ho abstain from preaching and exhortation under pain of condemnation to the galleys. Art. 7 forbids schools for the instruction of protestant children. The ninth article invites the return of fugitives; and the tenth forbids emigration, under penalty of the galleys and confiscation of property. The law against relapsed heretics is maintained in the eleventh article; while the twelfth hypocritically offers protection to the obstinate, in the anticipation of their future conversion. They might continue their trade, and enjoy their property, without being troubled under pretext of their religion, on condition only of abstaining from worship.

The faint semblance of toleration contained in the last clause, gave umbrage to the zealous supporters of the revocation. Several memoirs were addressed to Louvois, complaining of the encouragement given to the obstinate by that provision; and as many conver-

sions had taken place, entirely on account of the King's declared will, that there should be only *one* religion in France, it was to be feared that multitudes would relapse, f In the *Recueil des Edits,* etc., it is thus entitled: " Edit du Roy "du mois d'octobre 1685, portant revocation de celui de Nantes; et "defenses de faire aucun exercice public de la R. P. R. dans son "royaume."

'J-Noailles, vol. i,p. 92.

Spies were employed to ascertain whether any French subjects attended worship at the chapels of the Danish, Swedish, and Dutch ambassadors. The official papers of M. de la Reynie abound with reports made by the agents employed.

The conduct of the government amply proves that the preamble of the edict of revocation was known to be false. A complete extirpation of religious freedom could alone satisfy the King's advisers; and the treacherous character of the concluding article was manifested immediately after the edict was given. The demolition of the temple at Charenton, and the disdainful expulsion of M. Claude, were in harmony with its purposes; but no sophistry can justify the conduct of the Parisian authorities towards the lay Huguenots. The attorney-general and other magistrates having summoned the protestant heads of families, immediately after the edict was published, informed them that the King's intention was absolutely that they should change their religion: they were no more than their fellow subjects, and if they did not consent, the King would make use of means at his command for compelling them. The elders of the consistory and some protestants of known firmness, were at the same time imprisoned by *tettres de cachet.*

These measures however failing to produce the effect anticipated, the secretary of state, Seignelay, took the business in hand. He collected in his hotel above a hundred protestants of the mercantile class; and having closed the gates, presented an act ot abjuration for their signature; declaring at the same time, that none should leave until they had signed it. This act set forth, not only

their renunciation of heresy, but their return to the catholic church; and further, that they signed it freely and without being constrained. It was in vain that several exclaimed against the proceeding, and appealed to the last clause of the edict of revocation: they were haughtily told that there was nothing to dispute upon, for they *must obey.-ln* short, all signed the paper. This was violence; but other cases followed, in which cruelty was mingled. Separation of families, and imprisonment were general; besides the spoliatory practice of quartering soldiers, and selling the furniture for their supply.

Vide Appendix, No. II.

Claude received orders to quit Paris, within twentyfour hours; one of the King's valets was charged by special ordinance, to conduct him to the frontier,- jOther ministers were less harshly treated: they had two days allowed them; and a few obtained their liberty on parole. But even the tender mercies of the wicked are cruel. Those ministers who were best treated, could not dispose of their effects; and their books were seized as consistorial property, their enemies hoping by that method, to cripple their controversial powers. And in their banishment they were not permitted to have the company of any relative; although many among them had blind and aged parents, entirely dependent upon them for support. The rigour in enforcing the law against emigration, was carried so far as to compel the abandonment of their children, above the age of seven years. The horrible spirit of persecution was not however satisfied with that extent of vengeance against the preachers of the reformed religion; some of the ministers who had set out for their exile, in compliance with the edict, were arrested at the frontier, and imprisoned under various pretexts. In some cases they were called upon to prove their identity; in others to shew that no criminal accusation had been preferred against them, or that they did not carry away any thing belonging to their late flocks; and after being thus litigiously detained, it was contended in some instances, that the delay of fifteen days having expired, they were no longer at liberty to depart, and must go to the galleys. The severities enforced for preventing the departure of lay protestants equalled those for compelling the exile of the preachers: a measure unparalleled in history, as all previous proscriptions permitted self-banishment. The precautions were so multiplied, that commercial intercourse with neighbouring countries was impeded. Every stranger seen at a seaport was arrested; guard-boats were stationed on the coast; half the property of the fugitives was awarded to those who denounced them; and a succession of edicts were issued awarding fine, imprisonment, galleys, and finally death, as the penalty for aiding the escape of protestants.-f Limiers, vol. iv, pp. 180, 181. f Vide Appendix.

Limicrs, vol. iv, p. 177.—Claude, *Plaintes des Prolestans,* p. 50. t The principal enactments on this subject are dated 31 May, 20 Aug., and 20 Nov., 1685; 26 April and 7 May, 1686; and 12 Oct., 1687.

The capital seemed likely to afford some protection against violence in matters of conscience; concealment being so much easier among a crowded population; but the wily directors of the persecution had provided a remedy. An ordinance issued a few days before that of revocation, enjoins all protestants, arrived in Paris or the suburbs within a year, to retire to their homes in the delay of four days, under a penalty of a thousand livres.

The persecution was general. Even the independent principality of Orange was visited by the dragoons, and the same violence exercised there as in the French King's territory. The correspondence of Louvois will give an idea of the feeling which then pervaded the authorities. Soon after the edict of revocation, he wrote to the duke de Noailles: "His Ma"jesty wishes the most severe rigours to be inflicted "on those, who will not follow *his* religion; they "who desire the stupid glory of being the last to "convert, must be pressed to extremities, "f

Poictou was exposed to a third drag-

onnade in September, 1685, when the inflictions of the former visits were surpassed. The narrative already quoted on several occasions, describes the devastation at Mauze, where the author's house was plundered, and nothing left but the bare walls. $ The inhabitants took shelter where it could be had; a difficult affair, as none dared receive a fugitive into their houses. "Every body," observes Migault, "was under the influence of terror; "a brother scarcely durst receive a brother. In the "course of this month, I passed three days with "mine; and it is impossible to imagine the continual "alarm which tormented him, lest I should bedisco"vered in his house." Ordinance dated 25 Oct., 1685. t Letter dated 5 Nov., 1685. Rulhiere, vol. i,p. 344.—De Larrey, *Hist, de Louis XIV,* vol. v, p. 180.' .$. Migault, p. 77. After wandering about the country; at one time taking refuge in a cave, at others escaping as if by miracle from the dragoons, he proceeded to Rochelle with a view to prepare for leaving France. As a stranger in that town, his movements were closely watched: he was arrested, and the treatment he endured at length overcame his resolution—he consented to sign an act of abjuration.-f-From that time all his efforts were directed towards an eternal abandonment of the land, which had witnessed what he felt as a disgrace of the foulest die; but so many difficulties intervened, that his escape with his family was not effected until April, 1688.

Although it was declared a capital crime to worship the Almighty according to the pro testa nt form, numbers continued to assemble in retired places, ready to submit to death rather than swerve from their duty. On one occasion, the intendant of Poictou having surprised an assembly at worship in a sequestered field, fiercely charged upon them with his dragoons. Many perished on the scaffold, for no other cause than their perseverance in following the dictates of conscience; and three whose names are recorded by Migault, suffered at St.-Maixent. Migault, p. 80. f Feb. 1686. Migault, pp. 94 *etseq.* $ Ibid., p. 159.

Never was oppression more cruel than that endured by the unfortunate Huguenots at this period—harrassed and tormented if they remained in the kingdom, yet punished as malefactors if they attempted to escape. And still this horrid persecution has apologists. The pious zeal of Louis XIV was eulogised in the pulpits; and every publication in France was replete with bold denials of the naked truth, or with miserable arguments based upon unwarrantable surmises, for justifying what had passed. The official instructions, issued by Louvois, embody frequent recommendations of mildness in the proceedings; and the vindicators of the measure refer to these studied documents, as sufficient to repel and confute the complaints of the sufferers. But even the excess of eulogy has in several instances borne testimony to the truth of the broad charge of persecution; and without noticing the numerous writers, who emulously strove to exceed each other in praising the monarch's sublime design, the following extract will suffice for an example: it is taken from the work of a Barnabite monk, who lived in the succeeding reign; and the tenacity with which he justifies the measure, is an additional proof that the revocation of the edict of Nantes was in reality, more of a theological than of a political nature; because at the time he wrote, personal feeling had subsided, the authors and promoters of the measure had ceased to exist, and the feehle remnant of the Huguenot party had become objects of general compassion. "The "compulsory conversions," he observes, "mustnotbe "placed to his (the King's) account, any more than to that of the bishops and governors of provinces. If their orders were not always punctually executed, it would be difficult to indicate even one which was dictated by a'spirit of unjust and tyrannical intolerance; for that is the matter in question; and the *dragonnades,* the *missionnaires bottes,* against which so much has been said, were not *every where equally odious.* There were innocent Calvinists; but for one such, there were a hundred criminals." Thomas Marclie, James Guerin, and

Peter Rousseau

After this admission that odious proceedings had taken place in some parts, the Barnabite, in a warm strain of partisanship, adds the following remark: But I have said, and cannot too often repeat it, the church employs none but spiritual arms. The penalties it imposes are not murderous in their nature; it does not direct those which are borrowed from the temporal authority, and which should fall only upon crimes, hurtful to the state." *f* What a hollow subterfuge! it resembles that of the Inquisition, which in handing over a victim to the *Auto-da-fe,* pretends that the church is no party to the execution.

In the revocation of the edict of Nantes, Louis XIV Mirasson, *Hist, des Troubles de Beam,* p. 345. f Ibid., p. 349.

found the limits of his power. It was a superfluous measure, inasmuch as the persecution had preceded the enactment. It failed of converting the steadfast; and supplementary decrees were published in rapid succession, some of which contained provisions so monstrous, as to render execution impracticable. Among others, an edict which authorized the separation of all children from protestant parents: the space requisite for their reception, and the expense attendant on their maintenance, rendered the edict a dead letter.

There were some very severe enactments to deter preachers from attempting to return to France. The penalty of death was awarded to any minister who should be found in the kingdom: all persons receiving or assisting them to be sent, the men to the galleys for life, the women to be shaved and imprisoned; with confiscation of property in either case. A reward of five thousand five hundred livres was promised to any one giving information, by which a minister could be arrested; and the penalty of death for any one discovered preaching, or exercising other worship than the Roman Catholic, f In executing this law, Basville was dreadfully severe Twenty protestants were soon after put to death in Languedoc; and an active pursuit was set on foot for seizing the fugitive ministers, who defied the haughty Monarch's edicts, and returned clandestinely among their flocks. $ Registered in parliament. 12 Jan., 1686. t Declaration du Roy, dated 1 July, 1686. Registered in parliament 12 July. $ Noailles, vol. i, p. ill.

The readiness with which they were every where received, supported, and warned of danger, added to the ingenuity of their disguises, enabled them to baffle the vigilance of the government. Sometimes they passed as pilgrims, or dealers in images and rosaries; sometimes as soldiers. In all cases they were joyfully hailed by their brethren, and crowds attended their preaching in caverns and secret places. The worship of the desert became very general, notwithstanding the dangers to which it was exposed; and when the protestants were prevented by the presence of troops from acting as they would, they still refused to attend mass, on to send their children to the catholic schools; and disregarded every practice commanded by the church of Rome, f

Emigration continued in defiance of the laws for preventing it, and in spite of the encouragement given to impede the departure of fugitives, whose clothes and others effects were distributed among the captors. $ There were repeated instances of converts returning to the faith they had consented to abjure, when pressed by violence: others at the point of death, would spurn the Romish sacraments. These symptoms caused much alarm among the zealots, who obtained an edict, by which all those who refused the sacraments during their illness, should after their death be drawn upon hurdles; and in the event of their recovery, the men were condemned to the galleys for life, the women to confinement, with confiscation of property. Rulhiere, Toi. i, p. 348.
f Noailles, vol. i, p. H2.

£ Ordonnance du 26 avril 168C.

In pursuance of this edict, the troops received orders in some provinces, to ascertain whether the new converts were regular in their attendance at mass; and if they constantly practised the duties enjoined by the Romish church. The King perceived that his advisers had persuaded him virtually to establish an inquisition; and the orders were revoked, although secretly, lest obstinate protestants might infer from the circumstance, a change in his own principles. He had been assured that the edict was merely a threat, to complete the general conversion: but in many towns the disgusting scene of its literal execution took place. Priests, attended by magistrates, would beset a dying man; and unless he yielded to their invitations, his remains were no sooner cold, than the populace was regaled with the barbarous spectacle decreed by the edict.

The intendants were informed by a circular, that as the law had not produced all the advantages which had been hoped for, whenever converted Huguenots endeavoured to make a display of their obstinacy, the edict might be rigourously executed; but when it arose purely from conviction, and the relatives expressed their disapprobation, the circumstance should not be noticed; and to that end, " his Majesty deems "it right, that ecclesiastics should not be so ready to "call in the magistrates as witnesses, so that they "may not be obliged to carry the declaration into "effect." Declaration du 29 avril 1686.

However some years after, the bishop of Nismes addressing the secretary of state, observes: "I have 44 desired my curates, according to his Majesty's orders, "to watch the new converts who are ill: they find "many who refuse to listen to them, declaring they "will die in the religion in which they were born. "The judges are called in, after the priest has done his "utmost to bring them back."-j

Marshal Vauban, with the generosity allied to true courage, presented a memorial to Louvois, deploring the injury which his ruinous measures inflicted on the country, and demanding a retractation of all that had been done during the preceding nine years. The following expression is remarkable: "Compulsory con"version has inspired a general horror of the conduct "of the ecclesiastics."

At the death of Louvois in 1691, the royal council was swayed by Beauvilliers, Pontchartrain, and Pompone; men favourably disposed towards the Jansenists. That party at length succeeded in allaying the King's ardour for compelling all his subjects to adopt his faith. Their principles throughout had been uniform; and a compulsory participation in the sacraments, was ever regarded by them as a profanation. But they were disliked by Louis, whose conscience was in the care of the Jesuits; and their efforts were unavailing, until Fenelon and d'Aguesseau by their arguments, convinced Madame de Maintenon of the dangers attendant upon the King's policy. Soon after those eminent men had joined the court, the persecution slackened, and the dragonnades ceased; but the laws against emigration remained.

S Feb., 1637. Rulhiere, vol. i, pp. 350—357. .J-4 June, 1699. Flechier, *Lettres,* etc., vol. i, p. 137. % Rulhiere, vol. i, p. 380.

These results might have-been obtained much earlier, but for the extravagant praises bestowed upon Louis, and which he had sanctioned by lavish remuneration. Numbers of his subjects were rendered legally and civilly dead, with the anomalous tyranny of maintaining a claim upon their loyalty and obedience. Spoliation, beyond all precedent, had spread poverty and desolation far and wide; yet the church had gained a victory, and the modern Constantine's praises were proclaimed in orations and poems; by monuments and addresses. Madame de Maintenon might well write, "How can he renounce an enter44 prise, upon which he has permitted such praise to be "offered him?"f In 1689, the Dey of Algiers made a distinction between the Huguenots and the Catholics who fell into his power. When a French ship was sent to claim captives, he surrendered the latter: bu t refused to deliver the protestants, who, he said, were no longer the King's subjects, since he had expelled them from his kingdom. —*Balance de la Religion et de la Politique,* p. 184. Hague, 1695.

f In a Memoir written in 1690 or 1691, at which period the restoration of the edict of Nantes was regarded as probable. This piece is given at length by La Beaumclle, vol. vi. *.f* CHAPTER XII. TROUBLES IN THE VIVARAIS.—NOTICE OF CLAUDE BROUSSON. — SEVERITIES AT ORANGE.—REMARKS ON THE INTENDANT BASVILLE, AND ON THE EMIGRATION OF THE HUGUENOTS.

The publication of a mystical work in 1686, which announced the speedy overthrow of popery, and promised in glowing terms the triumph of true religion over error, gave rise to a movement in the Vivarais, which for a time threatened serious consequences. The book in question was composed by Jurieu, a protestant writer of some eminence; but his treatise was severely censured by his fellow ministers,and condemned by several synods for its visionary tendencies. Most probably its chief defect in the estimation of the exiled theologians, caused its importance among the Huguenots, still groaning under persecution. How eould they refrain from consoling themselves with the hope that its predictions would be fulfilled? They would naturally cherish views so favourable to their circumstances; and the vicinity of Geneva enabled preachers and partisans to raise the hopes and expectations of the simple-hearted mountaineers, by whom the bordering districts were peopled; and in whose opinion, *De I'accomplissement des Propheties.* See Bayle, *Lettre d M. Minutoli,* 6 Oct., 169 2. the compulsory abjurations had produced no other effect, than a more determined hatred of Romanism.

At the close of 1688 circumstances combined to favour Jurieu's system of interpretation. The dethronement of James II, and the League formed against Louis XIV, revived the hopes of/ the Huguenots so much, that in a short time sanguine expectations were elevated into a general conflding enthusiasm, not unfrequently producing extravagance. Sad indeed was the disappointment of the protestants of Dauphiny: a few months sufficed to annihilate their dreams of restored liberty; and the severity inflicted upon the principal actors, was an unequivocal lesson for a population noted for tenacity in religious views, and obnoxious on account of the difficulty experienced in forcing their conversion. That was their chief crime—a fault far less pardonable than joining in this effervescence, which did not deserve the name of an insurrection.

Geneva at this period teemed with protestant refugees, and especially ministers. They perceived the effect produced upon the public by the prevalent notions, and warmly promoted the sentiment, with the view of effecting a change in the situation of the Huguenots. Much talent, hitherto latent, was now drawn out into activity: every capacity was brought into play; even if the service was merely to convey communications, or to serve as guides to the proscribed preachers.

Du Serre, a glass-maker of Dieu-le-Fit, promulgated the doctrines in Dauphiny. Meetings were frequently held in secret; consisting of few persons, but most obnoxious in their nature, as the constant themes of discussion were the antichristian character of the papacy, appeals to repent of abjuration, and severe criticisms on the mass. Brueys, *Hist, du Fanatisme,* vol. i, p. 97. Utrecht, 1737, t Jmo.

According to the statements of the stronger party, Tvhich are deeply tinged with a sentiment of hatred, two leaders were conspicuous above all others, by the parts they assumed: Gabriel As tier, a young man of Clien in Dauphiny, and a shepherdess of Crest, named Isabeau Vincent; known, it is stated, as the Fair Isabeau. f After preaching for some time in the streets and public places of Grenoble, she was arrested with several companions: she manifested great firmness in her interrogatories, professing contempt of death, and declaring her conviction that others would rise up to supply her place, and surpass her powers. Her resolution was not put to the test; for during her imprisonment she yielded to persuasion, and embraced the Romish religion. £

Astier, who had chosen the Vivarais for the scene of his exertions, was greatly encouraged by the success of his preaching. His relatives and connexions joined in the work, and spread his tenets throughout the country; which being difficult for the passage of troops, was comparatively secure for the preachers; while the rustic simplicity of the inhabitants, and the recollections of the late persecution combined to give force to their sermons. At the outset the congregations assembled in barns; but their confidence augmented with their numbers; and Astier was in the frequent habit of preaching on the hills to meetings of several thousands. They were accompanied,. according to the bishop of Nismes, "by two prophe"tesses, equally mad, and of debauched lives."-j

Fléchier (Relation des Fanatiques) calls Du Serre gentilhomme verrier. Bishop Fléchier is beside himself on this subject; with him no terms are too harsh or too gross for obstinate heretics. See his Letires, Recit fictile, etc.
f Brueys", vol. i, p. 116..;. $ Ibid., pp. 124 and 134.

The magistrates and military chiefs of the province did not remain idle during such bold infringements of the King's decrees; and a regiment was sent to disperse the assemblies. Some Huguenots were killed by a detachment; upon which their companions attacked the troops so furiously with stones, that the captain and nine of his men were slain. The assembly celebrated their victory by singing a psalm on the ruins of a temple, and then dispersed; but. it was to collect again in other places. $ The attack tended only to irritate the party and increase their numbers.

The count de Broglie, lieutenant-general of the forces in Languedoc, and Basville, intendant of the province, then proceeded to stay the sedition. § They quitted Montpellier for the Vivarais, and by great exertions a considerable force was soon collected for restoring order. Colonel Folville had sent for dragoons, militia, and other reinforcements from the surrounding parts: he had learned by experience, the inutility of merely dispersing them, as the military force in Dauphiny was inadequate to prevent their reassembling. While undecided as to the point he should select

for his first operation, some loud shoutings from a mountain determined his movement. He found a numerous assemblage, so full of determination that although they had ample time to escape, they continued their devotions and refused to listen to an offer of pardon. Folville having barred most of the issues, then charged upon them. Very few had fire-arms, and the soldiers were assailed with stones and other missiles; but when they were at close quarters, the swords and bayonets proved irresistible, and the rustics endeavoured to escape among the precipices and woods, where they could not be followed without danger and difficulty. Between three and four hundred were killed; fifty were made prisoners, and the remainder were scattered among the surrounding hills and forests,-j-Another meeting was surprised at Privas: they were attacked; observes Flechier, in the midst of their prophetic declamations; twelve were killed, and the house they met in was burned. $ Brueys, vol. i, p. 145.

.j-Fleshier, Recit fidele, etc. This opuscule is printed with his Lettres choisies.
% Fleshier, Recit fidele, etc., p. 387.
§ In a manifest, subsequently published by the inhabitants of the Cevennes, it is stated that Broglie was Basville's brother-in-law. ' Dated t5 March, 1703, and preserved by Lamberty, vol. ii, p. 527.
17 Feb., 1689. Brueys, vol. i, p. 171."
t Brueys, vol. i, p. 183. Fleshier, Becit (idele, elc, p. 394. $ Jtecit fidile, p. 397.
Similar scenes occurred at Besset, Pourcheres, and other places, where a refusal to disperse was followed by a charge of the military. Viviers, bishop of.Lodeve, followed the troops, in order to use his clerical authority and influence, for the conversion of the mountaineers; while Basville dispensed the severities of the law, with the diligence for which he is celebrated. He condemned the leaders to capital punishment, and gave milder judgments against their companions; exempting those only, whose ignorance proved them incapable of any thing more than submission to the powerful influence of their preachers.

The assemblies soon after ceased; but the authorities would not desist from the pursuit of Gabriel Astier. He had not been found among the killed or captives; and his portrait was extensively distributed, for assisting his arrest. He was at length discovered in the ranks of a regiment at Montpellier, having enlisted as the best means of escaping. Basville condemned him, to death, and he was hanged at Bays on the second of April, 1689.

From this time until the conclusion of the peace of Byswick, nothing of importance occurred. Edicts and proclamations against emigration were repeatedly issued, and many preachers were victims to their resolution, in visiting the country from which they were for ever banished. The constancy of these martyrs is almost incredible; and if an individual case is selected for example, it is less on account of his superior firmness, than from the malignity which has pursued his memory, and given publicity to an unfounded accusation.
Brueys, vol, i, p. 195.

Claude Brousson was originally an advocate of Nismes; he was afterwards employed in the mixed chamber at Castres, and followed that court, hen it was incorporated with the parliament of Toulouse. He presided at an assembly held in that city, in 1685, for consulting upon the general interests of the protestants under the threatening aspect of affairs; and as the increasing difficulties deterred some from entering upon the ministerial office, he devoted himself to the ecclesiastical service of the reformed church. His sermons, which have been printed, display much pious zeal and scriptural erudition; they likewise prove uncommon facility on his part; as he was constantly a wanderer, and preached by stealth in caves and barns. He was arrested at Oloron, and executed at Montpellier on the fourth of November, 1698.

His character is maliciously portrayed by Brueys, who describes him as "a gloomy splenetic, with a "very ordinary genius, and inflated with pride; hav"ing a slight knowledge of Scripture, affecting mo"deration, but meditating insurrection."-f-He had a colleague named Francois Vivens, who is represented by the same writer, as a "libertine and thief, with "the hardihood of a rascal, rather than real courage." He is stated to have ordained Brousson in 1689, but as much that has been advanced concerning the character of the latter has been disproved, this may also be unfounded. At all events the assumption affords Brueys an opportunity for invective. "Thus a public assas"sin laid his bloody hands upon a seditious visionary, "and declared him a minister of the Gospel." *La Manne du Desert, or Sermons,* by Claude Brousson, 3 vols. 12mo. Utrecht, 1695. f Brueys, vol. i, p. 208.

Vivens does not appear to have been highly esteemed as a preacher, or his character would most probably have been vindicated from such accusations. Indeed if the current accounts respecting his end, are well founded, he was better qualified for conducting a partisan warfare than to impart religious instruction. In the spring of 1692 he was surprised in a cavern, between Anduze and Alais; and his desperate defence almost deterred his assailants from the perilous task of his capture. Two companions loaded his piece, while he fired on the soldiers, several of whom were slain; and he was at length killed by an officer of militia, while levelling his musket at the commander of the detachment. His death was immediately followed by the surrender of his comrades, who were hanged at Alais.-j

Brousson has been accused, conjointly with Vivens, of forming a project for raising an insurrection; and an intercepted letter addressed to count Schomberg, inviting a foreign invasion, has been alleged and argued upon, to justify his condemnation and blacken his character. This version has been adopted by Voltaire, and as a matter of course by all popish writers; yet his judges must have been satisfied that he was not so guilty, or his punishment would hardly have been commuted. His conference with Basville after condemnation was kept secret: he was sentenced to be broken alive after being tortured; but was spared such suffering, as the rack was remitted; and he was strangled before his body was placed upon the wheel. Interment was also permitted; and no reply was made to the publications of his friends, who refuted the charges brought against him, within a month after his execution,-j

Brueys, Toi. i, p. 221. t Ibid., vol. i, p. 201.

The persecuted Huguenots had vainly hoped that their interests would have been attended to in the negociation for the treaty of Ryswick; but they discovered to their cost, that the cessation of foreign disputes only served to revive the efforts of domestic tyranny. $ It was no longer sufficient to prevent assemblies for worship: violence was again resorted to for compelling a change of religion, and the law against relapsed heretics was severely enforced. Even Orange, an independent principality in the centre of the Vaucluse, was exposed to the despotism of a monarch who had no claim on its allegiance. § Relying on the privileges inferred from the preliminary negociations, the inhabitants re-opened their temples, and the ministers resumed their functions. By degrees the protestants of the neighbouring districts proceeded there, to join in the religious services; and the vicelegate of Avignon perceiving his inability,to prevent their attendance, withdrew the guards posted at the bridges and passes. This removal of restraint increased the confidence of the country people, who then attended in greater numbers.

Steele de Louis XIV, ch. xxxvi. .' De Larrey, vol. vii, p. 75. % There is much curious and interesting information on this subject in a work, entitled *Relation de tout ce qui s'est fait dans les affaires de la Religion reformee et pour ses interns, depuis le commencement de la paix de Reswick.* Rotterdam, 1698.
§ This territory had been treated in a most hostile manner at the revocation, which is attributed by Puffendorff to a hatred of the prince. August, 1697. The treaty was concluded 20 Sept.

However, when it was ascertained, that above seven thousand protestants were assembled, the vicelegate sent troops, under pretext that the Catholics were exposed to insult; and informed the populace that if they would fall upon the Huguenots and plunder them, the spoil should be their own. The unsuspecting protestants were in consequence assailed, robbed, and even stripped, as they were returning home in small parties; and numbers were led as prisoners to Roquemaure. Basville being informed of what had occurred, sent orders for them to be conducted to Montpellier: they were tied together two by two, to the number of ninety-seven men, and thirty-eight women.,

A party of forty was retiring into Dauphiny; and in order to escape a similar disaster, had avoided all the towns and villages. They were attacked at Porteclaire, in the district of Orange. A body of peasants well armed fell upon them, induced by the promise of their spoils. The protestants having no means of defence, were an easy prey; and the female captives were stripped quite naked. Some of the parly escaped into the woods, and one unfortunate man being seized, was stripped and tied to a tree, to die of cold and starvation. On the third day of his agony, an Irishman passing by, was moved with pity, and cut the cords which bound him; but immediately four men rushed forward, declaring that the Huguenot should die in that manner; and that he should have similar treatment if he interlered. The brutality exercised on this occasion is almost incredible. Females were found with their noses cut off, and their eyes put out; and the bodies of the slain were left at the laystalls.

The readiness to resume protestantism, manifested by the concourse at Orange, was sufficient to convince Louis, that he had incurred great odium to little purpose. If persecution was slackened, the assemblies were numerously attended; and on the other hand, if the penal edicts were enforced, emigration recommenced. The government complained of the libels composed by the fugitives in England and Holland; but no publication is more injurious to the King's character, than the collection of his own edicts; which awarded confiscation, the galleys, and even. death as the penalty for infractions of previous laws, so monstruous in their character, that their observance could not be expected.

Limiers, vol. v, pp. 243—247. A declaration was soon after published forbidding all persons from settling at Orange, and awarding death as the penalty for proceeding there to contract marriage, or perform any religious act. Dated Versailles, 23 Nov., 1697.

In 1697, the King ordered a succinct return of the state of the country, in all its bearings— military, civil, ecclesiastical and productive; and in consequence, each intendant drew up a memoir, from which some details might he fairly expected concerning the condition of the Huguenots, after the revocation of the edict of Nantes. But the duties and responsibility of the intendants prevented them from dispassionately reporting the truth, and in general the existence of protestants is but slightly alluded to. The office of intendant was a modern invention: one of those measures by which the last traces of seignorial independence were obliterated, in the establishment of absolute monarchy; and the common people soon discovered that additional chains were thus forged for their oppression. "They learned," observes a judicious writer, "that these new magistrates were to be the immediate "instruments of their misery; that their lives, their "properties, and their families, would be at their "disposal/ Masters of their children, by forced en"rolments; of their property, by depriving them of "their sustenance; and of their lives, by the prison, "the gibbet or the wheel."

Lefevre d'Ormesson, intendant of Riom, gives a specimen of the value of these official accounts. He reports that the province had the happiness to be scarcely infected with heresy, as there were not more than ten Huguenot families at the publication of the edict of revocation; which he declares " the most glorious of the King's acts, the most advantageous to religion, most beneficial to the state." Yet he subsequently confesses that two towns in his generali-

ty continue very much impoverished by the retreat of the Huguenots.

Boulainvilliers, *Etat de la France,* preface, p. 39.

Basville, intendant of Languedoc was the most eminent of these functionaries. His plan was to strike terror into the minds of those, whom he knew to be rankling under oppression. Anticipating a period of resistance, he prepared measures for aiding the movement of troops, by opening roads and constructing forts. The new converts found themselves as much the objects of suspicion, as the staunch Huguenots; *f* and persecution drove many to the desperate resolution of professing their first faith, although it exposed them to the worst consequences, as relapsed heretics. This intendant's memoir was much better composed than any which were presented; and Louis is said to have perused it with satisfaction. Basville unfolds the services he has rendered the crown, but of course conceals the fact, that an insurrection was to be apprehended from his excessive rigour. 44 Insensible to the misery of which he was the author, and to the death of several thousand persons, sacrificed to maintain his sway, he speaks only of the necessity of obedience. Can we," observes the writer before quoted, "avoid considering him as one of the most cruel instruments of the public suffering, and as the most dangerous seducer of our Prince's piety?" In commenting upon the memoir of this intendant, the same author declares: "One hundred thousand persons were sacrificed to justify the conduct of M. de" Basville; and of that number, the tenth part perished in the flames, by the gibbet, or on the wheel." *f* Boulainvilliers, *Discours sur le Memoire de Mom.*

'j-" Peu sont reellement catholiques: ils conservent presque tous "leur mauvaise religion dans leur coeur, dans l'espoir d'un change"ment." Basville, *Mem. pour servir d I'Hist. de Languedoc,* p. 79. Amsterdam, 1734.

The apologists of this persecution have attempted to shew that the number of victims has been much exaggerated, and especially in the extent to which emigration was carried. None of the

statements published by the refugees, can be received as altogether correct; but there is a wide difference between the deductions to be made on account of erroneous impressions, and the hardy denial of any injury being sustained by France, through the loss of so many industrious subjects. It was on that point that the French government was most exposed to positive, specific censure: hireling writers therefore directed their efforts to ward off the expected attacks, and vindicate the policy of their patrons in the eyes of posterity. There is strong evidence of the extent of emigration in the persons of their descendants, numerous at the present day, in every protestant state; and a letter from the StatesGeneral to the King of Sweden $ establishes the fact that their numbers were so great in Holland, that the country could support no more; his Swedish Majesty was in consequence, etreated to locate them in his German provinces.

Boulainvilliers, preface, p. 56. .' Ibid, *Discours sur le Memoire de Languedoc.* % " Nostra quidem terra tam angustis circumscribitur limitibus,

Besides which, it may be asked, for what reason were so many severe edicts issued against emigration during half a century, if the preference shewn for a state of exile had not menaced the prosperity of France, while it proved the unhappy condition of a numerous class of its inhabitants. But the unprecedented severity of the law did not deter the Huguenots from making an effort to escape. Every day fugitives passed the frontier in defiance of the proclamations, and Bayle relates, in a letter to a friend, that thirty persons from Caen with their children, had reached Rotterdam in a small vessel, with a hundred others from different pro vinces.

A contemporary statement mentions eleven English regiments, composed *entirely* of refugees, besides others enrolled among the troops of the line. There were in London twenty-two French churches, supported by the government; about three thousand refugees were maintained by public subscription; many

"totque repleta est ex Gallia religionis

causft profugis, ut *plures*

"*alere nequeat* quapropter si sub imperio regis majestatis

"vestra, praesertim in provinciis ejus Germanicis, major daretur "opportunitas,Regiam majestatem vestram enixe rogamus,velithuic "genti afflictae, vel parti eorum, terras ubi domicilium statuant "largiri." The letter, dated Hague, 6 Nov. 1698, is given at length by Lamberty. *Mem. pour servir a VHist. du* I8 *Siicle,* vol. i, p. 35. f Letter to M. Janicon, dated 8 Oct., 1699.

received grants from the crown; and a great number lived by their own industry. Some of the nobility were naturalised and obtained high rank; among others Ruvigny, son of the marquis, was made earl of Galway, and Schomberg received the dignity of duke. CHAPTER XIII. COMMENCEMENT OF THE CAMISARD WARS UNDER THE COUNT DE BROGUE.

The cruelties exercised by Basville were, for a long period, patiently endured by the Huguenots of Languedoc. Their constancy in meeting for prayer and religious exercises, exposed them to frequent attacks, invariably followed by the condemnation of those who were unfortunately seized. Many were hanged; preachers were broken on the wheel, or burnt alive; and numbers, convicted merely of being present, were sent to the galleys. To detail these revolting spectacles woiild be impossible; but the following instance will suffice to establish the Tiolenoe and extent of the persecution, some years after Louis had been congratulated on the extinction of heresy in his dominions; and at a period when the court affected to deny the existence of any protestants in France. Indeed whenever an edict was issued against them, they were uniformly termed *new converts. Memoires et observations faitts par un F"oyageur en Angleterre,* l2mo. La Haye, 1698, p. 362.

Some protestants had assembled at le Creux de Vaie in the Vivarais, when a body of soldiers fired upon them, killing many and wounding more; the remainder were nearly all secured. Basville condemned five of the prisoners to be

hanged—four men and agirl: they were each executed in a different town. Five others were sentenced to the galleys, and among them were three brothers named Marlie. Their father was one of those who suffered capitally; another brother was wounded by the soldiers, and died in prison; their family dwelling was destroyed, and all their property confiscated.-f-Thus an entire family was cut off, for no other cause than a perseverance in their religious duties.

The mountaineers of the Cevennes and the Vivarais, had for ages cherished the Scriptural doctrines embodied in the tenets of protestantism. This is clearly proved by the conduct of the Vaudois and Albigenses, n Sept., teas, f *Mercure Mstorique,* Nov., lt98, quoted by Court. — *Hist, des Troubles des Cevennes ou de la Guerre des Camisards,* vol. i, p. 11. This author was an inhabitant of Nismes, and drew much of his information from actors in the scenes which he describes.

in the twelfth century; by the revival of the sacred flame among their descendants, immediately after Luther's preaching was made known; and by the firmness with which they resisted the tyranny of Basville and his associates. Even to the present day, their descendants remain steadfastly attached to the faith for which their forefathers suffered so much; and there are many families lineally descended from Basville's victims, among whom the profession of protestantism has never ceased.

Basville was actively seconded in his rigours by the abbeDu Chaila, whose disposition had attracted the intendant's notice in 1687. His zeal and severity, with other qualities so well calculated for the suppression of heresy, had procured him the office of *inspector of missions,* in the Cevennes; and in the fulfilment of the duties which thus devolved upon him, no means were too violent for his adoption. He would accompany the troops searching for assemblies engaged in secret worship; and the prisoners who fell into his hands, were treated with cruelty almost surpassing credibility.. Whenever his tortures failed of effecting abjuration, or extorting some

statement to assist his search for other victims, he would confine his captives in narrow cells, called *ceps,* where the impossibility of moving caused terrible torments. His obduracy at length brought down upon himself, a severe retribution; and his death was the signal for an insurrection, almost unparalleled in history.

Louvreleuil *(Le Fanatisme renouveU)* quoted by Court, vol. i, p. 33. Louvreleuil was a priest: his work was published in 1704, and a continuation in 1706.

In July 1702 a guide named Massip, was arrested at Pont-de-Montvert, as he was conducting a party of fugitive protestants to Geneva. Du Chaila had been informed by his spies of the projected evasion; and placed the whole party in the *ceps,* to await judgment. Great interest was made to move the inexorable abbe in favour of some young ladies, who for security were travelling in male attire; bui in vain. And as a warm appeal was addressed to some assembled Huguenots, that an effort should be made for their rescue, the abbe declared that on his return to Pont-de-Montvert, he would order Massip to be executed. The Huguenots re-assembled, nearly fifty in number; and after prayer, proceeded in a body to that village, armed chiefly with swords, old halberts and scythes; only a few had fire-arms. They entered the place at night fall: as they chaunted a psalm on their march, the abbe, who was already there, imagined a religious assembly was being held; and accordingly ordered some soldiers to fall upon them. Almost immediately the house he lodged in was surrounded, and numerous voices claimed the enlargement of his captives. Du Chaila gave orders to fire; and one of the liberators being killed, his comrades forced open the door. While some proceeded to free the prisoners, others sought the abbe, who was barricaded in his chamber. An invitation to surrender was answered by a discharge of fire-arms; and the enraged assailants at once decided on setting fire to the house. The progress of the flames compelled the abbe to retreat. Aided by a servant, he descended to the garden, by tying his sheets together. In the attempt, he fell and broke his leg; yet with his servant's assistance, he sought concealment among the shrubs and bushes, where the light of the conflagration caused his detection. The Huguenots at once reproached him with his cruelty, to which he replied by abjectly begging his life. He was almost instantly pierced with nearly fifty wounds, every blow being accompanied by expressions to this effect: "That is for your violence towards my father! "That for sending my brother to the galleys!" etc. Several residents in the house were killed with him; but a soldier and one servant were spared; as the liberated prisoners spoke in their favour,-j-This energetic proceeding gave rise to the war of the *Camisards. $* Court assures that he conversed frequently with Massip, and had from his lips full particulars of this event, his imprisonment, and the ill-treatment he received from Du Chaila; as well as the circumstances of the abbe's death. Vol. i, p. 43.

A deed of such enormity was no sooner committed, than the perpetrators perceived the severe pursuit which must follow; for however the circumstances might claim and find palliation, in the odious cruelty by which it was provoked, that consideration would have no weight with their enemies, armed with every description of authority, and doubly incensed against them for this demonstration. Their case became desperate; they decided on retreating into the forests, and there defend themselves to the utmost; and in their excitement, took revenge upon several priests, and other persons who had been active in the persecution.

Brueys says that his life would have been spared, had he changed his religion and consented to become their minister—an absurdity. *Hist, du Fanaiisme,* vol. i, pp. 296. 301.
'J-Court, vol. i, p. 44.
4: There are several opinions as to the origin of this word: the most probable derivation is a corruption of *camisade,* a nocturnal attack.
The clergy were greatly alarmed, and

the count de Broglie mustered the nobility and militia, to pursue the insurgents. He was for some days uninformed of the route they had taken; and under the impression that they bad retired to their respective homes, he dismissed his forces, and returned to Montpellier; leaving small detachments in the different towns, under the command of Captain Poul, an officer notorious for his severity. He soon discovered the retreat of the insurgents; and falling upon them suddenly, captured Esprit Seguier, chief of the band, with two others.

It is related that while Poul was conducting his prisoners to Florae, he thus addressed their chief: "Well! wretched man, how dost thou expect to be treated?'' To which Seguier replied haughtily: As I would have treated thee, hadst thou fallen into my hands." Brueys, vol. i, p. 318. It is also mentioned by the anonymous author of *Hist, des Camisaris,* printed 1744, vol. i, p. 132. This writer has evidently compiled his account from oral statements,.there is a confusion in the dates which lessens its historical value yel, as a corroborating testimony, it is worth consulting.

Basville with all possible dispatch, sent a chamber of Justice from Nismes,. to condemn the prisoners. Seguier was sentenced to have his hand cut off, and to be burnt alive at Pont-de-Montvert; his companions were condemned to be broken on the wheel; one at Deveze, the other at St.-Andre, those being the principal scenes of their violence. Seguier died with such firmness, that the spectators were astonished: his composure was undisturbed by the flames; and he declared to the last, that he gloried in having given the first blow to the abbe Du Chaila.

A scene of desolation succeeded this severity: parties of soldiers scoured the country, and the information of a priest was sufficient to have any one arrested—his condemnation ensued as a matter of course,and to spread the intimidation, the executions took place in different towns. The murder of the abbe,, and the outrages which followed, were deeds meriting condign punishment; and if none but the actors in those tragic

scenes had been executed, no complaint could have been raised against the intendant Basville: but he assumed that it was the result of a conspiracy, in which all the protestants and new converts were concerned. An ordinance was subsequently published, rendering every township responsible for all acts committed within it; and lists were made of every protestant absent from his dwelling,-fThe malcontents were then joined by many, who in despair saw no safety in their homes; and who if they failed to better their condition, were convinced that nothing could render it worse.
Court, vol, i, p. 6S. t Ordinance dated 19 Oct., 1702.—Court, vol. i, p. 104.—Brueys, Toi. i, p. 371.

One project of the insurgents was to leave the country in a body; another for each to find a retreat separately, as he best could. In their dilemma, they were harangued by one of their number, named Laporte.—He had some military experience; and by his appeal, induced them to proceed in their dangerous undertaking, to deliver the captives, punish their persecutors, and claim the right of worship by force of arms. "They might and probably would perish," said Laporte, "but it was more glorious to fall in "arms, than to die tamely, under the hands of the "executioner." He was forthwith elected their chief; and proceeded to instruct his companions in military tactics, *f* His efforts were encouraged by the success of Castanet, and Roland or Rolland, £ who at the same time formed each a corps, composed of protestants who felt themselves obnoxious to the authorities, on account of their religious sentiments. These bodies were soon augmented by recruits, when their early successes were known, and their means of arming were increased.

"Brueys says he was *un fameux teeli-rat,* a preacher, and a disciple of Vivens: he confounds him with a minister of the same name, executed at Montpellier in 1696.
.J-Court, vol. i, p. 72. .*$* Andre" Castanet was originally a forest-keeper; though uneducated, he became a

preacher of note in the mountains. Rolland was Laporte's nephew; he had served in the army, and was also an energetic preacher.

"It was thought," observes Brueys, "that the terrible execution, just made of the most atrocious, would have deterred others from imitating them; but one had to deal with madmen, on whom example produced no effect; whom neither the gibbet, the wheel, nor the stake, could render reasonable. It was evident by the result, that the evil was irritated instead of being cured."

The operations of the three insurgent leaders, were to a certain extent in concert; but each command was distinct. Their most pressing necessity was for arms. It was useless to seek them among the protestants; as every weapon in their possession had long been seized. The priests were in general the depositories of such confiscations; and as force alone could remove them from such keeping, the Camisards combined their operations of vengeance, with the effort to obtain the means of effecting it.

Laporte soon became celebrated in the province, and Poul was earnestly bent upon his capture. Stratagem and corruption were both tried, but in vain. At length it was known where the rebel chief was to sleep: Poul took his measures for preventing escape; and on the alarm being given, the Camisards prepared for defence. A heavy shower rendered their muskets almost useless: only three pieces were discharged at the first volley, but each dispatched an enemy. The soldiers then rushed upon the insurgents, who were retreating among the rocks, when their leader was

'Brueys, vol. i, p. 3S8.

struck by a musket ball. The Camisards lost nine of their number, whose heads were cut off, and exposed in the towns, along with those of the soldiers who fell, and who thus contributed to swell their commander's triumph. ,

Meanwhile a new company was formed by a youth, who became subsequently the chief of the insurrection. Jean Cavalier, a native of Ribaute, near Anduze, at that time only twenty-one years of age. He had for some time as-

sisted a shepherd, and afterwards served a baker of Anduze, from which place he withdrew to Geneva, to escape persecution. He was there when he heard of the movements in the Cevennes; and felt a conviction that he was called by heaven to assist his brethren. Being at an assembly in his native village, he proposed to the young men to take arms, and either join their friends in theCevennes,or create a diversion in their favour. He represented with energy, that it was disgraceful to remain quiet, and allow their brethren to be massacred, without an effort on their behalf; that they ought equally to aim at the liberation of their captive kinsmen; and that as religion should be more precious in their estimation than existence, they were bound to risk their lives in order to obtain liberty of worship. The discourse found an echo in the bosoms of the hearers, and they met the following day, eighteen in number. But their means corresponded little with their resolution: among the whole party, there were no other arms, than one musket and two old swords; while none but Cavalier had the least notion of military exercise, and his instruction was limited to seeing the manoeuvres of the town guards at Geneva. Their enthusiasm was not however damped by their scanty resources: they were well versed in the Scriptures; and descanting upon the examples of Moses and Gideon, they proceeded to the residence of the prior of St.-Martin, where they were certain of finding a supply. Their route lay through Anduze, where they beheld the heads of Laporte and his companions, fixed upon the bridge: instead of terrifying them, it doubled their desire to enter upon their campaign. Cavalier's expectation was justified on reaching the prior's house: that ecclesiastic was well known for the mildness of his character; and confiding in his own reputation, he had remained at home, when all other priests were terrorstruck, and fled to the towns on account of the revoltHe received the troops with serenity; and on learning that they required arms, he allowed them to carry away the recent spoils of neighbouring protestants, suf-

ficient to equip twenty men. 12 Oct., 1702. Court, vol. i, p. H2.

This commencement was a good omen; but Cavalier took other measures for advancing his cause. He held religious assemblies, and preached with fluency and force. The protestants with joy beheld his rising importance: some compared him to Gideon and Macchabeus, others to Zisca and Ragotzi. ƒ There was nothing in his person to impress beholders. On the contrary, he is represented as' small in stature; the head large, and sunk upon the shoulders; with a broad red face and light hair. His countenance did not bespeak intelligence; but his career proves that he was well endowed.

Court, vol. i, pp. 107 et 115. f Menard, vol. vi, p. 381. 15 Nov., 1702.

The count de Broglie being informed of his holding a meeting at Aigues-Vives, immediately proceeded there. Having summoned the entire community, without troubling himself with investigation, he selected sixteen persons as objects of the legal vindict. Four of them were hanged at the church door, and twelve Were sent to the galleys: the town was further assessed with a fine of a thousand livres, to defray the expenses. This act of flagrant injustice was generally condemned, and was one of the causes of Broglie's recall,-j

Cavalier's troop continued to increase: every day added to his supply of arms; and as he was soon joined by several other companies, it was considered necessary to invest him regularly with authority, as commander-in-chief. He represented that several among them were more competent; but the general voice wasin his favour, and he accepted the command, on condition that he should have power of life and death over the troop, without calling a council of war. Theinsurgents consented; but it does not appear that Cavalier ever abused that prerogative, $

From the time their force was organized, they regularly performed divine worship, administered the Lord's Supper, and celebrated marriages and baptisms, in every town. Their numbers included some who had great talent for preaching; and the romantic hazardous life they led, contributed so much to promote their enthusiasm, that several believed themselves inspired. Their motive for taking arms was to enjoy the right of worship; and in the woods and caverns they were constantly engaged in devotional exercises: especially on Sundays, for the convenience-of the country labourers, who flocked to hear them; and it was their invariable custom before they marched, to pray for divine guidance, and on halting, to offer public thanksgiving. Need we then wonder at the energy they manifested, their contempt of death, and the admirable order which prevailed among them: they were supported by the courage, which religious conviction can alone impart.

ƒ Court, vol. i, p. 121. $ lbid- vol. i, p. 135.

It is not precisely known what was the largest force the Camisards mustered: they were never all collected, and prudence compelled them to conceal their numbers. The general sympathy in their favour brought them recruits, even while they were engaged. This occurred at the battle of Martignargues, when several villages sounded the tocsin during the combat, so that Cavalier's force was greatly augmented by the peasantry, ƒ At one period this chieftain was accompanied by two thousand men; but there were strong detachments in various parts of the Cevennes; and their plan of operating in small bodies, over a wide extent of country, prevented the concentration of the royal troops. Yet they must have been numerous; for "with few exceptions, all the rustic population was with them; and these hardy uneducated mountaineers, inured to peril and constantly exposed to an ignominious death, were kept in habits of good order and fellowship. There were no quarrels nor slanderings among them; oaths and obscenity were unknown; their goods and provisions were in common; and they addressed their chief as *brother.* In the accounts given by their enemies, it is insinuated that great debauchery was practised among them; and the presence of women found among their slain, has been adduced as

a proof. But all the inhabitants of the Cevennes well knew why women and girls were sometimes seized in their company, and not unfrequently killed by their side. They were the wives and daughters of Camisards who carried them provisions, or were bearers of communications from friends in the towns; and as the military looked keenly after all persons connected with the insurgents, their female relations often remained among them for safety.

Court, vol. i, p. 179. t *Mem. du due deFillars,* vol. ii, p. 152. l2mo., La Haye, 1758.

For their sustenance they received contributions from the protestants, who joyfully aided in supporting their brethren; and when an ordinance decreed the punishment of death, against any who gave them provisions, the Camisards formed stores in caverns, which they replenished at the expense of the Catholic clergy, and from the houses of gentlemen who had promoted the persecution. The want of shoes was their.greatest inconvenience, as the rugged paths they traversed, quickly used their stock; but that deficiency was partly supplied by taking those worn by the soldiers they killed; partly by purchases in the towns. The country abounds with chesnut trees, presenting a supply of food in the immediate vicinity of their retreats.

They found it almost impossible to obtain ammunition in sufficient quantities, on account of the severe orders given by the intendant: they accordingly persevered in making it for their own use. The leads of churches supplied them with bullets, and the pewter utensils of an abbe, were often melted for that purpose: it was found, that soldiers wounded by pewter balls rarely recovered; and a malignant rumour was circulated, that their bullets had been steeped in poison. The Camisards also endeavoured to cast cannon; for they are accused of stealing eighteen church bells, to be converted into culverines; in which they were assisted by an agent of the duke of Savoy, -ƒ

It sometimes happened that emissaries joined them, or the temptatio of a large bribe would induce a weak broth-

er to denounce their movements. These dangers were however warded off by means, which though they may appear visionary, were quite consistent with the character and objects of the Camisards. The leaders declared themselves informed by *inspiration,* of the presence of traitors. On one occasion Claris (whose functions resembled the commissariat department) announced to the assembly, that the treason of two men had been revealed to him. Cavalier instantly ordered those under arms to surround the meeting, and Claris seized by the arm, one whom he charged with a design to betray them: his confederate then rushed forward, threw himself at Cavalier's feet, confessed his crime, and implored mercy. The names of the traitors are preserved by a highly esteemed writer, who was satisfied that the incident did so occur, and has related a most extravagant scene which followed. There existed at the time a strong impression of miraculous interposition, which is recorded with gravity by one party, and ridiculed by other; but the force of conscience in the traitors, on being challenged, and strong discernment in Claris, are quite sufficient to explain the detection.

Court, vol. i,p. 185. f Villars, vol. ii, p. 145

A brief notice of the leading Camisards may assist the reader: in addition to those already mentioned, were Abdias Morel, surnamed Catinat, who had served under the marshal of that name; he commanded the cavalry, and was the most feared of all the insurgents. —Nicholas Joany, who also had served in the army, and frequently distinguished himself in this war—and Ravanel, who yielded to none of his party in courage and energy: the latter was Cavalier's lieutenant. Sa-lomon Couderc, one of those who contributed to the death of the abbe Du Chaila—he was not only formidable as a chieftain, but had great influence as a preacher; he was believed to have the gift of inspiration, and is frequently termed the prophet Salomon, by contemporaries. He had a relative of the same name, who was designated La Fleur; one of the abbe's prisoners at the time of his murder. Esperandieu was another Camisard of eminence; he was killed in one of their earliest victories. Cavalier and Joany alone survived the wars; Rolland and Esperandieu died in arms; the other chiefs all perished at the stake or on the wheel.

Court, vol. i, p. 438.

These details were requisite to explain how a small force, without a single officer or person of distinction, could have resisted a strong body of troops for the space of eighteen months, under one marshal; while his successor in the command, of the same rank, could appease the revolt only by a formal treaty with Cavalier.

The military movements during this insurrection were carried on by small bodies of men, as the designs of the Camisards were to occupy their enemies in every direction: the encounters were consequently very numerous; and what in ordinary warfare would be scarcely worth mention, or at most be alluded to as a mere skirmish, in this struggle acquired the importance of a battle. Thirty-four such engagements are described by historians; and in a very great proportion the Camisards had the advantage. The more important can alone be mentioned here; but they will fully exhibit the determined courage of the mountaineers.

The count de Broglie, who had impatiently sought an opportunity to attack the insurgents, overtook them at Val-de-Bane, on the twelfth of January, 1703. There were not above two hundred Camisards assembled, and Cavalier being absent, the command had devolved upon Ravanel. The approach of the troops did not move the resolute band, who continued singing a psalm, with one knee on the ground, until they had received the first volley; when they replied with such effect, that their enemies retreated. Poul the officer already mentioned, was thrown from his saddle, struck by a stone which a lad aimed at his head. The stripling killed Poul with his own sword, and mounted his horse to join in pursuing the routed troops. Broglie found it impossible to rally his men, and withdrew to Bernis.f The defeat caused great consternation in Nismes, of which Cavalier availed himself: he had entered the city in disguise, for the purpose of procuring powder; and the pretext of preparing for the defence of the town, was advanced by his friends, who under other circumstances would not have dared to apply for the prohibited article. £ The sixty-eighth, thus versified:

Que Dieu se montre settlement,
Et l'on verra dans le moment
Abandonner la place; Le camp des ennemis epars, Epouvante de toutes parts, Fuira devant sa face, etc. f Court, vol. i, p. S05.—Brueys states that Poul was killed by a musket ball, vol. ii, p. 205.—The author of *Hisl. des Camisards* says he received a pistol shot, and that his head was cleft by a sabre as he endeavoured to rise, vol. ii, p. 11. $ *Memoirs of Cavalier,* London, 1726; quoted by Court *ut supra.* Fleshier, *Letlres choisies,* 3 Joen., and i Oct., 1703; 9 Feb. , 1704.

JBasville's administration of Languedoc unfolds a scene of cruelty and severity, scarcely equalled, certainly never surpassed in any country. The revolt of the Gamisards was sufficient to inspire terror; but the chief ground of the alarm was the consciousness of incessant and unprovoked persecution. However, the instruments of the King's bigotry, unwilling to confess its injustice, represented the evil as the natural consequence of heresy, the source of every bad passion. Even the bishop of Nismes is open to much censure on this head; though his character is held up, with that of Fenelon, as a sufficient reply to all detractors of the Romish clergy. In his letters no expressions are too harsh to be applied to the insurgents, on whom he lavishes the terms wretch and fanatic, and to whom he imputes the commission of every crime. In the same feeling he complains of the lukewarmness of the authorities; and expresses his astonishment that so many enormities have been committed, *without reprisals* being adopted.

It was hoped and indeed expected, that winter would put an end to the excursions of the Camisards; and when Basville discovered that the severity of the season gave him no relief, he summoned the principal officers of Languedoc ., to consider the most efficacious means for terminating the insurrection. Among other measures, it was proposed to kill all the protestants of the province, and burn every town suspected of favouring the revolt. Awful as it was, that project was supported in the council, on the grounds " that it was "doing nothing to kill the Camisards found in arms; "because the country being infected, supplied others, "and in greater number." Happily Basville reflected upon the injury his reputation would sustain, from the ruin which must follow such a measure; he adopted a comparatively lenient plan—that of pursuing the insurgents without relaxation.

The Camisards being hunted like wild beasts, embraced every opportunity of revenge. A garrison placed in the castle of St.-Felix soon experienced their fury. Holland commenced his attack, by setting fire to some barns dependant on the castle; sending information to the governor, who sallied forth with a body of men to seize the assailants. Rolland meanwhile advanced to the castle, and promised to spare the lives of those who opened the gates: two yielded, the others were all killed, and the castle was fired, after the assailants had taken away forty-five muskets, a barrel of powder, and some provisions. The governor perceiving the flames of his castle, hastened back, and was attacked so fiercely by Rolland's men, that he escaped with difficulty, after losing the greater part of his detachment,-j-Similar expeditions were entered on by Cavalier and other chiefs, but they were loudly condemned by the protestants; a Swiss Synod addressed a letter to the Camisards, severely reprimanding their violence; and this intervention is admitted to have saved the lives of several priests who fell into their power. Brueys, vol. ii, p. 29.

f?7 Jan., 1703. Court, vol. i,p. jifi.

About the same period, the count du Roure wrote to Cavalier, demanding his motives for taking arms. The Camisard replied "that it was in self defence: that the cruel persecution to which they had been exposed for twenty years, and which daily increased, had constrained him and his friends; who preferred death to the relinquishment of a religion they considered good, or to attend mass and prostrate themselves before images of wood and stone, against the light of their conscience. They were ready to lay down their arms, and employ their lives and property for the lung's service, whenever they had obtained liberty of conscience; the liberation of their brethren, emprisoned. for religion; and a cessation of cruel and ignominious punishments for the protestants."-f

Cavalier then made an attempt to penetrate intothe Vivarais; where he expected to find an addition to his force among the protestants of that district; but. the passages of the Ardeche were so well guarded,, that he renounced the project: his return gave rise totwo encounters of some importance. A marshal-decamp, named Julien, commanded the troops stationed, on that quarter; he was a converted protestant, and had been page to the prince of Orange: a disappointment induced him to apply for employment in the French army, and his desire to prove the sincerity of his abjuration, led to acts of extreme barbarity. He gave no quarter, and obtained much approbation from the bishops and clergy. Although his language was outrageously blasphemous, his bigotry carried him into a senseless extreme, in the punctual observance of Romish discipline; and another converted protestant, who cherished feelings equally violent, gives his panegyric in these terms: "His great services convinced every body, that a better choice could not have been made."-j Brueys, vol. ii, p. 30.
t Cavalier, quoted by Court, vol. i, p. 226..

One of his regiments overtook Cavalier at Vagnas, a small town not far from the Ardeche. The count du Roure and the baron de la Gorce, each with a body of militia, co-operated in the plan ordered by Julien, who hoped to surround the insurgents, and make a general capture. Notwithstanding the extreme disparity of their force, the Camisards

awaited the attack with composure. They received the first volley without stirring; and then fired with such precision, that the assailants were completely routed. Five captains, including the baron de la Gorce, several subalterns, and a considerable number of soldiers were slain on the side of the troops; on the part of the Camisards, Esperandieu alone was killed, and a few were wounded, $

The count du Roure sent immediate intelligence to Julien, who hastened to repair the disaster; marching all night, although the roads were a foot deep in snow. His reinforcement greatly increased the chances of victory; but Cavalier awaited him with resolution at Barjac. Julien aware of the invincible courage of his opponents, prepared an ambuscade. The action passed off in the same manner as on the previous day; lut when the Camisards pursued their advantage, they found themselves exposed to the attack of fresh troops, and were compelled to retreat into the woods. The amount of their loss was published by their enemies, as three hundred: Cavalier however states in his own memoirs, that on reviewing his forces, he found the number of missing between fifty and sixty; some of whom were drowned in the river Ceze: he considers his own escape on this occasion, as almost miraculous.-f Aygalier, quoted by Court, vol. i, p. 198.
--Brucys, vol. ii, p. 2G. $ Court, vol. i, p, 228.—Brueys, vol. ii, p. 57.
It would be tedious to detail the operations of the chiefs, during Cavalier's absence. The unfortunate town of Genouillac was taken and retaken three different times, by the contending parties; and both parties experienced in turn, the effects of vengeance. Julien finally gave up the place to plunder and massacre. $

The unsettled state of the country occasioned disorders on every side; but some catholic partisans appear to have aimed at surpassing the exploits of the Camisards; and as their ravages were frequently attributed to the protestants, the latter were doubly injured. They spared neither property nor person;

killed indiscriminately, men, women and children; were active in burning houses, and most rapacious in pillage. At first these bandits were called Florentines, as the company was formed at St.-Florent: afterwards, others imitated their example, and they received the general appellation of *Cadets de la Croix.* They had four commanders, the most celebrated of whom was a retired military officer, named La Fayole. Through remorse from a life of debauchery, he had withdrawn to a hermitage; whence he emerged, in the cause of his religion, under the name of brother Gabriel: he had a corps of three hundred men, paid by contributions levied upon the new converts,-f Bishop Flechier has thought proper to eulogize this man, in one of his epistles: "We must cheer brother Gabriel—Endea44 vours are made to decry him and his troop; *we* have 44 well supported him. I know not what he is destined "to; but should be glad that he effected something of Brueys, vol. ii, p. 70. f Court, vol. i, p. 230.
$ 23 Feb., 1703. Court, vol. ii, p. 233.
"importance," $

Brueys admits that these bands were contrary to the precepts of the Gospel, but apologizes for the injudicious zeal of the catholics, by alleging in excuse 44 their.4 churches burned, their curates massacred, and their "families destroyed. "§ In good policy, this writer should have abstained from such an extenuation; because the same arguments, with a hundred fold greater force, may be urged on the adverse side. The justification was moreover misplaced; because those bands had ample authority in the bull issued by Clement XI, who enjoined a crusade against the "accursed and mi"serable race," which he assimilated to the ancient Albigenses: and granted absolute and general pardon for every sin, to those who might be killed in effecting their extermination. Brueys calls him La Sagiote, and says he took arms because his hermitage had been pillaged; on which occasion he consulted the bishop of Nismes, who approved of his resolution, praised his design, and recommended him. to marshal Mon-

trevel, vol. ii, p. 243.
f Court, vol. i, p. 347. $ Flechier, *Lettrcs,* 9 fe"v. 1704. % Krueys, vol. ii, p 77.

The serious character of the insurrection, after Broglie's defeat, caused great alarm at court. Marshal Montrevel succeeded him in the command, with an increased force for suppressing the revolt. Yet it is maintained, upon good authority, that the marshal's nomination was given under another pretext; and that the King was kept in complete ignorance of the troubles in the south of France. The ill judged measures Louis had been persuaded to adopt, were in train to falsify the assurances by which he had been deceived. Madame de Maintenon, as usual, endeavoured to spare him every additional anxiety; and the whole council joined in deceiving the monarch, who fondly imagined Court, vol. i, p. 349. The bull, dated 1 May, 1703, was addressed to the bishops of Monlpellier, Nismes, Usez, Viviers, Monde, and Alais, each of whom published it, with a *mandement* addressed to their clergy. It is not in the *Bullariura;* but its existence appears to be admitted, as M. Court has not been attacked for advancing it, although severely criticised for other statements. An anonymous author gives the *mandement* of Ambrose, bishop of Alais, dated 29 May, 1703, with a copy of the bull in question. *Hist, des Camisards,* vol. ii, p. 119.

his sway was absolute. Yet the new appointment demanded the allegation of some motive; and the duke du Maine facilitated the views of that influential lady. As governor of Languedoc, he requested that the forces should be commanded by a marshal; and Louis, far advanced in dotage, consented to please his illegitimate son. Montrevel was unquestionably tutored before he left Paris; and the minister at war, wrote to Basville: " Take care not to give this, the appearance of "a serious war." These instructions contributed greatly to prolong the resistance of the Camisards.

CHAPTER XIV. CONTINUATION OF THE CAMISARD WAR UNDER MARSHAL MONTREVEL.

Marshal Montrevel arrived at Nismes on the fifteenth of February, 1703. Basville, Julien, and another general, named Paratte, waited there to confer with him upon the state of the province. His presence inspired the catholics with great hopes, as the increased military force rendered the suppression of the revolt a comparatively easy matter. But the combat of Mas de Serieres showed that impending danger produced no intimidation on the Camisards: on that occasion, Ravanel had the honour of measuring his strength with the marshal. He had approached Nismes with between three and four hundred men, less with any hostile design, than to procure supplies from his friends in the city. He had even expressed the desire and hope of passing a day or two quietly; but some straggling soldiers having discovered his presence, the marshal immediately collected his forces, and sallied from Nismes at the head of a little army. Ravanel accustomed to engage with superior numbers, was undismayed at his approach. Although attacked on all sides, the Camisards fought with a desperation, which their opponents could not refrain from eulogizing. Night alone terminated the conflict; ibr the marshal's force enabled his soldiers to repose by turns, and Ravanel considered defeat as certain from the onset; yet surrender was out of the question, and in their determination to perish, rather than be captured, they displayed prodigies of valour. After all, their loss was very trifling; being only twenty-three men and two women. Their enemies however say it was considerable, *f* But one circumstance connected with this engagement, proves the victory was dearly bought: Montrevel immediately ordered the bodies of the slain to be stripped, in order that the soldiers might not be distinguished from the Camisards. Bulhiere, vol. ii, pp. 281—283.

20 Feb., 1703. f Flechier, *Letlre du 25 avril,* 1703, says, " *about A* hundred;" Brueys, vol. ii, p. 87, " *above* two hundred;" while the troops lost only one dragoon and a few wounded!!'.

Montrevel proceeded upon his task of pacifying the province, by acts of extreme severity; ordering several towns, inhabited by protestants, to be pillaged and burnt: Among others Marvejols on the Gard, for no other cause than the misfortune of some troops being defeated by the Camisards, in the neighbourhood. This " guilty place," as it has been called, was destroyed and burnt by the troops in consequence.-f-He likewise issued two ordonnances: $ the first declares accomplices, all who assisted the insurgents directly or indirectly; enjoins all absent from their houses, to return within eight days;.and forbids the presence of all who are not regular inhabitants of the province. Any such "being seized without a passport, to be reputed an insurgent, and executed as such. The second ordonnance confirms a previous disposition of the intendant, rendering every commune responsible for all violence committed within its limits.

Like Basville, he was impressed with the idea of a general conspiracy of the protestants; and as a further measure, proposed to seize a number of new converts from different parts, confine them in citadels, and declare that for every murder or conflagration, he would hang three or four persons as hostages of the place, where such outrages were committed. This scheme was too violent to obtain the sanction of the government; and Montrevel having summoned the protestant nobility of Languedoc, addressed them with an apparent wish to be tolerant. He urged their cooperation in suppressing the revolt; and concluded by declaring, that although he wished every one to be catholic, he would not constrain any: all he demanded was fidelity to the King.-J Court, vol. i, p. 246.

f 25 Feb., 1703. Brueys, vol. ii, p. 84.

£ Dated 23 and 24 Feb., 1703.

If the marshal's arguments had no weight with the assembled protestants, his *reign of terror* was sufficient to subdue them; for he not only gave up to pillage, places where the Camisards had been well received; he even inflicted his severity on villages where the inhabitants were unable to resist them. He condemned numbers to be burnt alive, or broken on the wheel, on the bare suspicion of having favoured the malcontents, or for being absent from their cottages: they were mostly executed without any form of trial. The heroism of these sufferers is noticed by a magistrate of Nismes, who bears ample testimony to the awful frequency of the executions. "There were "many shot by the troops, and a great number "perished by various tortures at Montpellier, Mende, "Alais and especially Nismes; but as we have already "stated, these dreadful spectacles made no impres"sion—the new converts regarded the condemned as "martyrs. The resolution they displayed in death confirmed them in their old religion; and if I may "be permitted to say it, the examples given to the "public, produced quite a contrary effect to what was "intended." The bishop of Nismes likewise bears witness to the terrible fact, in a pastoral letter addressed to his clergy; wherein he laments that many of them are present at the *frequent* executions; and adds, "The church, so circumspect and so cha"ritable, cannot approve of such sad and indecent "curiosity."-j Court, vol. i, p. S55. f Court, vol. i, p. 296.

A more summary mode of punishing the protestants was adopted on the occasion of an assembly for worship, held at a mill in the suburbs of Nismes. $ According to the statement of a hostile writer, "it "was not a body of armed men; it was merely one "of those religious meetings, convoked contrary to "the King's orders, where they preached in spite of "his prohibition." § About one hundred and fifty were collected; principally old men, women, and children. Montrevel, indignant at the circumstance, surrounded the mill, and on a signal being given, dragoons broke in and massacred the party. A lew attempted to escape by the windows, but a sentinel drove them back to the butchery; and as the work of horror was too long for Montrevel's impatience, he set fire to the edifice, which was soon envellopped in a body of flames. Some unfortunate creatures, wounded and burned, were still able to clear the flaming pile; HUl. de la Rivolte des Fanatiques, par de la Baume, conseiller au presidial de Nismes, quoted by Court,

vol. i, p. 305. f Flechier, *Lettre pastorale.* % Palm Sunday, l April, 1703. $ Braeys, vol. ii, p. J 28.
but the dragoons forced them back, to expire in the conflagration. A girl of seventeen was saved by the marshal's valet; his generous deed, the result of compassion, only served to display the diabolical feelings of his master, who ordered his valet and the girl to be put to death on the spot. The poor girl was executed; and the valet bound for a similar fate, when some religieuses pleaded in his behalf, and obtained his life. But Montrevel blamed himself for his weakness in yielding, and banished the valet from the town. Some catholics who were amusing themselves in a neighbouring garden, were killed by the marshal's orders: in vain they asserted their religion; he declared they had escaped from the mill, and they were executed. In his access of fury, he was even on the point of devdting Nismes to devastation.

De la Baume's account corroborates the foregoing; with a trifling difference as to the numbers killed: "It cost," he says, "the lives of eighty persons, all of the dregs of the people," and afterwards adds, "the court approved of the marshal's conduct." *f* To the disgrace of the bishop of Nismes, he also justifies the deed, while he distorts the truth, in order to diminish its odium. "They even dared, on Palm Sunday, to hold a meeting at a mill, without any precaution, at the gate of the town; and while we were chanting vespers, they sang psalms and preached. The marshal left his house, assembled some troops, and put to the sword, men and women composing the assembly, to the,number of more than fifty persons; and burned the house where it was held. This example was necessary, to stay the arrogance of these fellows." Court has minutely related this horrible scene: he was intimate with those who had witnessed it. Vol. i, p. 309. — Ménard seems unwilling to censure the marshal. *Hist, de Nismes,* vol. vi, p. 387.
f Quoted by Court, vol. i, pp. 313—315.

It is unnecessary further to portray the character of Montrevel's adminis-

tration; for a complete narrative of this epoch of blood-thirsty tyranny would be fatiguingly voluminous. Its duration is well attested by historians, inclined by their undisguised prejudices, to throw a veil over such occurrences. Brueys mentions the fact of six executions occurring in one day;-fand observes in another part of. his work: "I should 44 weary the reader if I were to give an exact detail of "all those who were arrested and punished; for "scarcely a day passed, without several of these "wretches being made examples." And de la Baume informs us, that the court of which he was a member, judged in the month of August alone," a great number of fanatics, who were condemned to various kinds of punishment. "$

As a natural result, the Camisards resolved upon selling their lives dearly, when attacked; and embraced every opportunity of wreaking vengeance on their pitiless enemies. The inhabitants of La Salle had been prominent in causing vexations to the protestants in general; those who remained quiet, suffering as much as the relations of those in arms. Cavalier in consequence determined on giving them a lesson of severity. Having dressed his followers in uniforms, taken from the soldiers killed in recent encounters, he advanced at their head, in the full dress of an officer; fully persuaded that on his approach to that town, the most violent of the inhabitants would come out to hail his arrival. The company of zealots advanced to express their joy, at the arrival of the troops, by whose aid their district would soon be freed from the Camisards. Their congratulations were mingled with boastings upon their individual deeds; and each took credit for something done against the protestants. A lame man surpassed all others in his accounts: he claimed the honor of contributing to the arrest of several preachers who were hanged, and declared his readiness to indicate the dwellings of Huguenots, where numbers might be seized. To his awful surprise, one of Cavalier's men addressed him fiercely: "Hast thou finished?" The boaster with trembling, asked why such question was put, and almost immediately the poor wretch and his companions, nearly forty in number, were put to the sword. Fl&hier, *Letlre du 25 avril* 1703,' f Brueys, vol. ii, p. 179. $ Court, vol, i, p. 426.

Similar deeds of violence followed on both sides; and more frequently towards the close of the year, when Basville deliberately prepared for destroying the resources of the insurgents by devastating thirty-one parishes, comprising one hundred and sixty-six villages. This scheme, which menaced ruin to all the catholic gentry of the district, was not adopted without hesitation; but as the alternative of indemnifying the loyal part of the inhabitants, was a trifle compared with the suppression of the revolt, the project was ultimately approved by the court. April, 1703. Court, vol. i, p. 33).

Montrevel then published an ordinance for collecting the catholics in the towns, where the authorities would provide for their subsistance. Another decree enjoined the new converts to return to their houses, within eight days; and forbade their stirring out, upon any pretext, without a passport, under pain of the galleys for life. Basville at the same time prepared lists of the new converts, in the different parishes, in which the names of absentees were to be carefully noted. The gentry among them were allowed to choose the town in which they would reside; and were promised a share of the property to be confiscated. The parishes and towns marked out for destruction, were four hundred and sixty-six in number; f and the inhabitants were ordered to bring their corn,cattle,etc, to certain places, with notice that the infraction of this order would be punished by the seizure of their goods; and for themselves, the treatment of rebels. To complete the list of barbarous preliminaries, the marshal gave orders that his officers, on arriving at a condemned village, were to read the proclamation forbidding the inhabitants to go home; but promising that no harm should befal them, as the King would not hear of any bloodshed!!! Brueys, vol. ii, p. 219.—Court, vol. i, p. 463. *f*

Court, vol. ii, p. 49. Brueys, vol. ii, p. 220.

Montrevel commenced his inhuman expedition on the twenty-sixth of September, 1703. The approach of so many troops coinciding with a summons for the whole population, convinced the unhappy villagers that they were all to be massacred: as many as could, immediately joined the Camisards. f

The marshal's first idea was to pull down the cottages, but the work proceeded too slowly for his impetuosity; and fire was substituted for manual demolition. The ravages of the devouring element speedily covered the land with desolation, and the horrors of reprisals and executions became more than ever frequent; for many ill-fated villagers avoided the towns through fear, and being seized were declared in contravention of the ordinance; while the aggravation of misery became an additional incitement to violence. % This scene of horror which was capable of calling forth the language of intercession, did not however move the bishop of Nismes, who wrote to the marshal in a style of warm approbation. "The project you are executing is severe, and will be doubtless useful. It cuts at the very root of the evil; it destroys the asylums of the seditious, and confines them in limits, where it will be more easy to subdue and discover them." In a subsequent letter is the following passage: "The court has been too long in deciding upon the remedies, which must be employed for staying such great ills. Those which might have sufficed some months since, are no longer adequate; and it will be necessary to adopt chastisements, more severe than those rejected as too cruel."- f Court, vol. ii, p. 52..

f Brueys, vol. ii, p. 225. % To this cause may be attributed the murder of Madame Miraman, a catholic lady,- killed by four Camisards. Cavalier, in his Memoirs, admits that the men had joined his troop; but, to mark his indignation at their crime, he had them tried by a council of war: three were shot— the fourth proved that he endeavoured to prevent the murder, and was acquit-

ted.

The proclamations issued at this period against the Cadets de la Croix, prove that the Camisards were not the only disturbers of the peace of the country; and when their ravages were found oppressive, the troops were as inadequate to suppress them, as the protestant insurgents. But when the Cadets were seized, the treatment they experienced was very different: they were acknowledged brigands, but the others were fanatics.

After a long series of encounters in which the results had been varied, Cavalier was surprised at Nages, by the count de Fimarcon. £ Two catholic historians claim the victory for their party, and greatly exaggerate Cavalier's loss; § but other accounts give a very different result; and a letter from the bishop of Nismes, written on the day of the battle, to the priest who sent intelligence of Cavalier's movements, is far from ascribing a triumphant result to the assailants "The information you gave of the march of the fana"tics was very good; and if the troops of the neigh"bourhood had been summoned in time, and M. de 4 Fimarcon had collected a greater number of dra"goons, or had been better supported,. the affair "would have been very important. They had then "joined the rebels, who would have been entirely de"feated: but they have escaped,. and have lost but a "few men."" Flechter, *Leltre du* l" *octobre* 1703.

t Ibid., 23 Oct.., J703. % 13 Nov., 4703. Nages is a village two leagues west of Nismes.

§ Brueys, vol. ii, p. 238.

The Camisards had time to quit the place and gain an eminence, before they were attacked; and their energetic resolution compelled their enemies to retire. About thirty women were with the Camisards when the alarm was given. They had carried provisions to their husbands and brothers, and found themselves compelled to fight for their lives. A girl of seventeen, named Lucrece Grignon, displayed great intrepidity, and stimulated her friends by her example. "Shouting, "The sword of the Lord and of Gideon!" she disarmed a wounded dragoon, and joined in the pursuit of the flying soldiers. A reinforcement was coming to the assailants; but their rout was too complete to allow a renewal of the combat,. in which Cavalier lost five of his comrades: on the side of the troops there fell a major, a lieutenant, and about thirty soldiers; besides a number of wounded. Cavalier himself was nearly taken at the outset: he had gone out to reconnoitre; and was intercepted by a cornet and two dragoons, concealed behind some olive trees. He was within pistol shot when he perceived his danger; and the cornet called to him by name, offering quarter. Cavalier replied by instantly shooting him through the head with his musket. He then awaited the attack of the dragoons with a pistol in each hand. To encounter such a foe was almost certain death: they advanced upon him; each pistol carried true; and Cavalier rejoined his comrades, drawn up ready for battle. After his victory he proceeded to Clarensac, where he dined and remained three hours; during which interval he destroyed the walls, and preached a sermon. Conduct highly characteristic of men, who aimed at imitating Joshua and the Israelite chieftains, on entering Canaan.

Flechier, *Letlre du* 13 *novembre* 1703.

Laborde, one of Fimarcon's officers, was defeated hy Cavalier at Roques d'Aubais.-f-He had four companies of dragoons, which he divided into two troops, in order to surround the Camisards. Cavalier likewise divided his force, to present a face to each opposing body. Confident of victory, the dragoons galloped down upon the insurgents; when to their astonishment, their progress was arrested by a band of sixty recruits who had recently joined Cavalier; and who for want of better weapons, were armed with slings. A shower of heavy stones threw the troops into confusion; and the main body of the Camisards, rushing forward, completed their defeat. Twenty-five dragoons remained on the field of battle; their horses and arms were a welcome prize to Cavalier, who celebrated his victory by divine service; at Gongenies.

Court, vol. ii, p. 121. f 17 Dec, 1703,

The sufferings of the Huguenots of Languedoc were not disregarded by the English and Dutch; but the supplies sent for their relief, were diverted from their destination. Pamphlets had been published, shewing the benefit which would accrue to the allies, from supporting the Camisards; and several individuals were actively engaged in promoting a movement of that nature — the abbe de Bourlie, better known as the marquis de Guiscard; the marquis de Miremont; and lord Galway, a nobleman of French origin. In addition there were a number of intriguing characters, who speculated alike upon the confidence of the Camisards, and the liberality of the allies. It is however certain that some measure to assist the insurgents was in contemplation: ships were perceived off the coast of Cette, in the autumn of 1703; and two refugees, bearing Dutch commissions, were arrested on their way to join the Camisards. Their names were Jonquet and Peytau: the former was induced by promises to make important revelations; he was kept in prison until the peace of Utrecht. Peytau was firmer: he yielded only to prolonged torture; and although his communication preserved France from invasion, it did not obtain any commutation of his sentence: he was broken on the wheel at Alais, and died with resolution, f Court, vol. ii, p. 175. t Ibid., vol. ii, pp. 80—86.

This incident occasioned some admonitory despatches to Montrevel; who in addition to his former horrors, ordered general arrests of the protestants, and the massacre of all who were/ound away from the places assigned them. He sent among other agents, the brigadier Planque, who scoured the Upper Cevennes; killing every one he found abroad, regardless of sex or age. He destroyed all the mills and ovens in the villages, with a view to compel the peasantry to retire into the towns. Some did so; but others unwilling to abandon their homes, were put to the sword, to the number of nearly six hundred.

Were it desirable to crowd these pages, with affecting or revolting scenes, this epoch would supply entire

volumes. The troops were excited to violence —unhappily we know that they were urged on by the clergy. The bishop of Nismes has penned the following lines. "I see in a part of the troops, so little zeal for the service of God and the King, that I do not expect great success from the contemplated expeditions, unless heaven give ardour to our warriors."-fHis appeal was so well answered, that the Cadets de la Croix outstripped all expectation; and he found himself soon afterwards, obliged to write to one of his clergy: "You must restrain the armed catholics. They should combat, and fight the wars of the Lord; and not plunder friends and foes."$ The wholesale murders recently committed were not alluded to; but the plunder of a catholic demanded repression—alas! for the blindness of bigotry!

20 Feb., 1704. Villars, vol. ii, p. 137. . f " Si le del n'echauffe nos guerriers. " Flechier, *Letlre du* 9 *fevrier* 1704. $ *Letlre* du io *avril* 1704.

There were scenes of barbarity on every side; if the cruelties of the troops, and their allies, the Cadets de la Croix, were described, justice would demand a list of the atrocities committed by the Camisards; and in contemplating the chronicles of the time, it is some relief to meet with a military engagement, as a less frightful scene. The victory obtained by Cavalier at the Devois de Martignargues was highly important, as it led to Montrevel's recall; it was besides a brilliant achievement in a military point of view.

The marshal being at Uzes, was informed that the Camisards were in that diocese; and sent La Jonquiere against them, with a detachment of marines, and some companies of dragoons. A reinforcement of a hundred horsemen followed to support him. This detachment La Jonquiere sent back, as he had full confidence in his men, who were impatient to wipe away the disgrace of a former defeat by Cavalier. Some heavy rains facilitated his tracking the insurgents, who finding themselves discovered, awaited the attack with their accustomed resolution. Cavalier made a suitable prayer, in the hearing of his men; and having exhorted them to fight manfully for their religion and liberty, he selected his ground, and made his arrangements for the expected conflict.

As soon as La Jonquiere had received the reports of his officers, he advanced upon the Camisards, ordering a general volley within musket shot: that discharge however produced no effect, as Cavalier had ordered his men to lay on the ground, when they perceived the enemy prepare to fire. The movement was so well executed, that La Jonquiere imagined they were nearly all killed or wounded; and commanded his soldiers to charge with the hayonet. To his astonishment, the Camisards suddenly started up, singing their accustomed psalm. They attacked their enemies with energy, and were supported by concealed bodies of men, who advanced on every side. The troops in dismay lost all power of defence. La Jonquiere escaped by swimming across the Gard; leaving twenty-five officers, and almost all his men, dead upon the field. The Camisards had twelve wounded, of whom two died. The spoils supplied the Camisards with arms of every kind, besides a number of good horses; with money and jewels to a considerable extent which afforded the means of procuring many necessaries. Cavalier had scarcely retired from the scene of action, when the marquis de Lalande arrived with eight hundred men: too late to attack the Camisards, he gave orders for removing the wounded, and burying the slain, f 15 March, 1704. It is about midway between Alais and Uzes.

The troops were often paralysed by the religious fervour of the Camisards. The anonymous historian mentions a conversation with an officer, who declared, as soon as his men heard *Que Dieu se monire,* they were no longer under his command. Vol. i, p. 244. f The *Mem. de Villars* (vol. ii, p. 138) state that La Jonquiere' division consisted of five hundred marines and fifty dragoons; yet, further on (p. 142) we find: " the troops lost five or six hundred meu the insurgents only two hundred." Louvreleuil estimates the troops killed at above 300; and de la Baume mentions that only

four officers and 180 men escaped. Court has summed up the conflicting accounts. t Villars, vol. ii, p. 143.

Montrevel had daily fresh proofs that the majority of the population favoured the insurgents; and to counteract their plans, he ordered a strict search in Nismes, which led to the arrest of above two hundred and fifty persons: they were confined in a fort. He also built a new wall around the city, to enclose the suburbs; and the discovery of two thousand loaves at a baker's in the faubourg, was a proof that the Camisards drew their supplies from such sources.

Montrevel's removal from the command of the troops in Languedoc, was ordered in compliance with the suggestions of Basville and the clergy. The marshal had at first opposed the cruel measures of the intendant: when the government ordered him, he obeyed with the unreserved ardour of a soldier; but he had raised secret enemies, and was deprived of the honour of tranquillising the province. Marshal Villars was already named as his successor; and Montrevel determined on gaining before his departure, some important advantages, for the sake of his reputation. The day was fixed; and knowing that Cavalier was well informed of all that passed in Nismes, he announced his intentention of passing into Guyenne; an escort was ordered to attend him to Montpellier: Cavalier relying on the the information he received, proceeded to Caveirac; where he reposed his troop, whom he lodged by billets in the town and surrounding villages. '

The marshal was well informed of Cavalier's movements; and sent a battalion, and some dragoons under colonel Grandval in pursuit of him. An action took place at Caveirac, in which the Camisards were defeated by their own impetuosity,-j-Cavalier endeavoured to rally his men, and effect a retreat, when he discovered fresh bodies of troops collecting on every side; and among them, a division under Montrevel in person. In vain did the intrepid Cavalier force his way through a difficult pass; he immediately perceived new obstacles to his escape: he retired

upon Nages, and hoped to reach the plain of Calvisson; but every road and outlet was occupied by soldiers. The marshal had five thousand men; while his troops consisted of only eight hundred infantry, and a hundred horsemen. After vainly contending with such a superior force, Cavalier addressed his comrades: "My children, "if our hearts fail us, we shall be captured and broken "on the wheel. We have only one resource: we"must cut our way through those men. Follow me! "and keep close together!"$

An impetuous charge was made after this allocution, and the conflict was most obstinate and fierce. The Camisards opened for themselves a way to a bridge, across which they forced a passage. Montrevel was indefatigable in the action; and the pursuit was maintained until night-fall, when the approach to a wood,.

Villars, vol. ii, p. 147. f 16 April, 1704. $ Hist, des Camisards, vol. ii, p. 21 i. and the broken nature of the country put an end to this disastrous affair, which lasted from three o'clock till nine. The battle was considered as decisive; and Montrevel is reported to have said, "It is thus I take leave of my friends."

There is some difference in the statements of the force of the Camisards, and the number they lost; both are exaggerated by the catholic writers. But all concur in describing their retreat, as displaying unparalleled courage; and Cavalier's conduct on this occasion has obtained from an enemy the following eulogy: "Every one was surprised to see a man of low.4 origin, and without experience in the art of war, "behave under the most difficult and delicate cir"cumstance, like a great general, "'ƒ

CHAPTER XV.

CONCLUSION OF THE CAMISARD WAR, UNDER MARSHAL VILLARS.

Cavalier's recent defeat was not so overwhelming a misfortune as to dishearten his party, had the disaster been confined to that battle. His friends had sufilcient forces scattered throughout the Cevennes to complete his battalions; and the course of the war had shewn that the King's troops were, in general, more harassed and fatigued than the insurgents; even when the results of an expedition were otherwise satisfactory. But a new dilemma befel the Camisards; a calamity of far more serious character, in the discovery of their principal magazine, near Hieuset. It was a vast cavern which served as hospital, arsenal, storehouse, and asylum for their wives and children.

Court, vol, ii, p. 313. f Villars, vol. ii, p. 152.

An aged female who was observed to proceed occasionally to the wood which concealed this retreat, was charged with carrying supplies to some of the insurgents: she was arrested and threatened with death, if she did not reveal the objects of her visits. Her answers were evasive, and Lalande, who commanded in that district, ordered her to be hanged. Her firmness withstood the effects of that threat until the moment of execution; when she purchased her pardon by revealing the fatal secret. A strong detachment proceeded with her to the cavern, where about thirty wounded Camisards gave evidence that her denunciation was true. Some of them were not expected to recover from the wounds received at Nages; but although their condition was sufficient to inspire pity, they were all put to death by the soldiers. As the troops advanced, they discovered large quantities of provisions of every kind, arms and ammunition, and a store of medicines and surgical instruments. This *Hist. des Camisards,* vol. ii, p. 244. was followed by the pillage of Hieusel and other towns, with the massacre of the inhabitants.

The discovery completely destroyed Cavalier's resources, as the province was too much empoverished to afford a renewal; but whether his genius could have rallied under such difficulties, so as to withstand the fresh troops who would accompany marshal Villars; or what plan he would have adopted for the personal safety of his followers, can only be conjectured. Hap- pily for the province, and no less so for the marshal himself, aprotestant noble had ventured upon a mission to appease the insurrection.

The baron d'Aygaliers of Usez, who lamented the dreadful state of affairs, was of opinion that the advice of a protestant might be effectual in persuading the Camisards to lay down their arms; and he further considered that such an important service would induce the King to appreciate the unchanging loyalty of the persecuted Huguenots. His plan was to commence with a journey to Paris; but without a passport he could not leave Usez: how to obtain one was difficult, as he could not expect it would be given by Montrevel or Basville. Circumstances favoured his projects: he dined one da yin company with the brigadier Paratte, an officer so blind in his bigotry, that in his view the religion followed and favoured by the King must be good, and he could not. refrain from invective against those, whose conscience did not permit such servility in their creed. On meeting d'Aygaliers, he animadverted with violence against all who had borne arms against their sovereign. This was intended for the baron, who immediately after the revocation, had joined the prince of Orange; he did not however notice the allusion, but on the following day took occasion to call on Paratte, when he declared that his observations had made such an impression on his mind, that he was most anxious to prove his zeal and fidelity to the King—he concluded by asking a passport, which was readily given.

Court, vol. ii, p. 323.

'J-De Rossel, baron d'Aygaliers, composed *Memoires sur lesderniers Troubles de la Province de Languedoc.* Court had the use of this account, which is of great value, as the author relates only what he positively saw.

On reaching the capital, d'Aygaliers drew up a memorial, in which he declared the protestants of Languedoc were anxious and able to terminate the insurrection, provided the government would allow them to act. The dukes de Chevreuse and Montfort seconded his views, and the minister Chamillard introduced him to marshal Villars, who was preparing to set out for his command. After some conversation respect-

ing the affairs of Languedoc, the marshal desired he would await his arrival at Lyons.

Villars left Paris on the thirtieth of April for that city; having received the King's commands to bring back the insurgents to their duty by mild measures, -f He was accompanied by d'Aygaliers on leaving Lyons; and during the journey down the Rhone, the baron spared no efforts in cautioning the marshal against the prejudiced opinions he would receive from the clergy of Languedoc, who openly maintained there was no other way of settling the insurrection, than by exterminating all the protestants. Villars heard him with attention, and promised impartiality; and it is due to the marshal's character to state, that beset as he was with advocates of severity, he encouraged d'Aygaliers in his laudable effort; and when the protestants of Nismes signed an act, requesting permission to march against the rebels, he thanked them, and authorized the promise of amnesty to all who would return to their homes within eight days. Still Basville exerted his influence to prevent Villars from granting the required permission; and d'Aygaliers at length overcame his repugnance, and demanded an interview with the sanguinary intendant; whom he told on entering, that although he would rather die than accept a glass of water at his hands, his desire to pacify the province induced him Jo intreat that the marshal might not be dissuaded from giving his project a trial. All difficulties were soon after removed, and d'Aygaliers received his commission to wage war against the Camisards. Such were the terms used, although d'Aygaliers had no design of using other weapons than exhortation and argument. He set out the next day, and in every town announced amnesty to all who would surrender.

Court, vol. ii, p. 271—281. f Villars, vol. ii, p. 156.

Basville and Lalande instantly became jealous of the importance which d'Aygaliers was likely to acquire; and without loss of time engaged La Combes, by whom Cavalier had been employed as shepherd's boy, to use his influence with the Camisard chief. Cavalier himself was inclined to despair of his cause, and the advice of his old master harmonized with his feelings; yet it is said that his answer was haughty, inasmuch as he declared he would never lay down his arms, until liberty of conscience was established. This was followed by an invitation to a conference from Lalande.-jCatinat was sent by Cavalier, to fix the place and time of meeting. The bridge of Avenes was selected; and within two hours Lalande and Cavalier were in presence. $ 4 May, 1704. Court, vol. ii, p. 339.

Lalande was attended by thirty dragoons, colonel Menon, about ten officers, and Cavalier's brother, a youth of fifteen, who was lately taken prisoner; and who was to be restored, with a view to promote conciliation. Cavalier was accompanied by sixty picked men of his infantry, and eight horsemen. § Each party left his men at some distance from the bridge, and advanced singly to the parley, which lasted nearly two hours. The result was kept secret, and subsequently deprived Cavalier of the confidence of his men; but Lalande was so pleased with the conclusion, that he expressed a wish to see the Camisards under arms; and having approached them, scattered a handful of louis d'or before them. The present was refused by the men, who said they did not want money, but liberty of conscience. "That is beyond my power to "grant," replied Lalande; " but you wiH do well to "submit to the King's wishes." "We are ready," rejoined Cavalier, "to obey his orders, provided he "will grant our just demands; otherwise we will die "with arms in our hands, rather than be exposed to "the cruel violence we have had to endure." Before they separated, Cavalier informed his men that they might accept the money, as peace was concluded,-f-There was in fact an amnesty; for Cavalier's troop went that evening to Vezenobre, where they were quartered by billets; and divine service was performed in the temple which had escaped demolition. Cavalier himself preached and prayed with such effect,

that he drew tears from his hearers; and marshal Villars sent his nephew to inform the court of Cavalier's proposals. $ Court, p. 343.

T la the *Mem. de Fillars* it is said that the overture came from Cavalier; but that chieftain, in his own Memoirs, says that Lalande wrote first to him.

£ U May, 1704.

§ This is Cavalier's account: Flechier says there was a troop of three or four hundred, of whom eighty were mounted, and that M. de Lalande had only twenty dragoons. In the *Memoires de Fillars,* we find Cavalier was attended by about thirty badly mounted horsemen and two hundred infantry, in which account Brueys coincides. If so much discrepancy is discovered in a detail of no moment, need we be surprised to find variance on questions of real importance?

Flechier, in a letter written the day following, after expressing himself in the coarsest invective against the *fanatics,* remarks that Cavalier entered into the negociation because he was afraid of being surrendered. "The reasonings of this peasant," observes the prelate, "are very coarse and savage, although he be "preacher, prophet, and general: still he is not with"out a fund of good sense, for effecting his object." *Mem. de Cavalier,* quoted by Court.

f Villars, vol. ii, p. 173.—Brueys, vol. ii, p. 315.

£ Court, vol. ii, p. 350.

On the very day of the conference, Rolland completely defeated a strong detachment at Fondmorte. It was commanded by Courbeville, who was killed with four captains, six lieutenants, and above two hundred soldiers. Yiala, an advocate, who had been active in troubling the protestants, was taken with his son and nephew; all three were massacred. Rolland obtained great booty in money, arms, and clothing.-f-This event doubtless contributed to render the government more willing to accede to Cavalier's proposals.

Cavalier's troop was meanwhile quartered like the divisions of the royal army. He exchanged visits with the King's officers; and in every place had

public worship, with all the freedom of the best times of protestant liberty. He wrote to marshal Villars expressing his regret at the engagement of Fondmorte; and having met d'Aygaliers, was urged by that gentleman to request a conference with the marshal. D'Aygaliers, whose mission was to make war against the Camisards, was no sooner in their presence than the divisions mingled, embraced, and joined in singing psalms; while the leaders conversed on the line of conduct to be adopted. D'Aygaliers convinced Cavalier that the happiness of all his brethren in religion demanded his submission, and the Camisard chieftain signed an offer to submit with his troops to the King's clemency. After this preliminary, Villars hastened to bring the insurgent leader to positive terms; speculating probably on the effect which this increase of importance might have on the mind of an uneducated youth. The arrangements for the meeting were speedily concluded; hostages were left under the custody of Ravanel; and sentinels and piquets were posted to maintain a communication with the main body of the Gamisards, before Cavalier ventured on entering Nismes.-J Fllchier, *lettre du* 13 *mat.* f Villars, vol. ii, p. 177.—Brueys, vol. ii, p. 319.

Sandricourt, governor of that city, conversing with the marshal, endeavoured to prevent the conference, by representing the' astonishment which would be caused by a low bred man,. known only by his crimes and rebellion, succeeding in concluding a treaty of peace with his sovereign. Villars replied by an allusion to the general advantage of the state; and Cavalier was soon after announced. He presented his sword to the marshal, who desired him to retain it; after which they conversed at length upon the projected pacification. $

After the conference Villars wrote again to court, and Cavalier sent a dispatch to Holland urging him to follow his example. The Camisards were left in possession of Calvisson, awaiting the reply of the government; and during the interval were treated with more consideration than is usually shown for the regular troops. This did not however deter Cavalier From detaining hostages, and placing sentinels, as if hostilities had continued. The clergy were horrified at the consequences to be apprehended; the whole population was in such rapturous joy at free opportunities for worship according to their conscience, that the town resounded with accents of praise; and psalms and thanksgivings were openly heard in the streets and public places. The bishop of Nismes thus alludes to the spectacle: "We have seen Cavalier at our gates: "his interview with the marshal and M. de Basville; "his submission and his pride; the boldness of the "*scelerals* who accompany him: the assembly of so "many unpunished murderers; the concourse of new "converts who go to see-them; the psalms they "chant, and with which the Vaunage resounds; *4* their sermons in which they utter a thousand ex travagancies, applauded by all our people; the pro"phets and prophetesses who spring up among them, "and encourage the hope of the speedy re-establish"mentof their religion.—All this greatly scandalizes "and afflicts the catholics; and seems sad to endure." But he adds: that the hope of restoring the Romish religion makes them overlook many things. Court, vol. ii, p. 360. t 16 May, 1704.

: Villars, vol. ii, p. 180.—Brueys, vol. ii, p. 327.

Basville represented to the marshal, that such a scandal ought not to be tolerated: that the assemblies should be forbidden, and the troops ordered to fall

"Flechier, *lettre du* 23 mat 1704.—The language of Brueys is similar. Vol. ii, p. 331..

upon them. Villars would not listen to a project calculated to revive the insurrection; and desired the intendant to be patient for some time. He sent word however to the chiefs to restrain their preachers from extravagance. The marshal's biographer makes no attempt to disguise his dislike to the Camisards, whom he styles miserable fanatics; but d'Aygaliers, who was present when Basville urged a renewal of persecution, has recorded an observation, highly to

the marshal's credit. "There is something very ridiculous in the 4' impatience of the priests on this subject: I have re"ceived I know not how many letters, filled with 44 complaints, as if the prayers of the Camisards blister "not only the ears, but the skins of all the clergy. I "wish from my heart, I knew all those who have "written to me, that they might be bastinadoed. For "I think it a very great impropriety that those "who have caused these disasters, should complain "and disapprove of the means used to make them "cease."-j

On the twenty-second of May, the chevalier de St.Pierre returned with the answer of the government to Cavalier's proposals. What were the terms demanded, is not known. Cavalier being accused of betraying his party, for the advancement of his own interests, has given a prolix statement in his Memoirs, which on a close scrutiny will appear full of improbabilities; such for instance, as the asserted fact of Villars and Basville signing a complete approval of his demands, on the day following the conference. Common sense would require the submission of such terms to the King's approbation; and narrators of every party agree that Villars did so send them for the opinion of the court, before he ventured to sign the treaty. Basville was averse to the very last; and only signed as a matter of necessity, such was his hatred of the *scelerats.* Villars, vol. ii, p. 187.

f D'Aygaliers, quoted by Court, vol. ii, p. 401.

In consequence of the marshal's instructions from court, he delivered to Cavalier a commission of colonel, with the right of appointing the officers of his regiment, which was to serve in Spain: and a pension of twelve hundred livres. f

Rolland had not yet submitted; but hopes were entertained that Cavalier would persuade him to accept terms, such as had been granted him; and for thai purpose the Camisard chieftains met at Anduze. Cavalier repeated to Rolland all the arguments which d'Aygaliers had used in persuading him; but Rolland was not so easily

drawn from what he deemed the path of duty. He accused Cavalier of having betrayed the cause; and vowed that he would not submit to any thing, short of recognized liberty of conscience. The interview was very stormy, and might have had fatal consequences, without the interposition of Salomon Couderc, who offered to proceed to Nismes and learn the conditions offered. Villars and Basville met and discussed the terms as before; and Salomon Couderc was authorized by the marshal, to offer Rolland a colonel's commission, with privileges equal to Cavalier. It was soon evident that Rolland would refuse such terms; for Couderc before he quitted Nismes, delivered to Lalande a letter from the inflexible chief to the marshal, observing as he gave it, that peace could not be expected, without granting liberty of conscience. Holland's letter was to the same effect: his conscience he declared, would not permit him to depose his arms, until the edict of Nantes was completely re-established, and the imprisoned protestantswere freed.

Brueys, vol. ii, p. 341. ƒ Villars, vol. ii, p. 187.

There were unfortunately at this period, some intriguing individuals who if commissioned by any party, must have obtained their authority by misrepresentation; such were Sallier,Guiscard, Belcastel, and others, induced by the desperate condition of their fortune, to obtain the means of improving it, by serving the allies, in preventing the restoration of tranquillity in France. Two of these agents were arrested at Avignon; their object was to encourage the Camisards by the promise of assistance. They were punished, but other emissaries were more successful;-f-and to this cause it is reasonable to attribute the extraordinary scene which occurred at Calvisson, when Cavalier returned there, after meeting Rolland.

In composing the regiment to be formed by virtue of Cavalier's commission, Ravanel was named Lieutenant-Colonel; a post to which his bravery and successful expeditions fully entitled him. His mind was under that violent excitement, which when based upon religious feeling, excludes all idea of lear,i disregards every earthly consequence, and almost renders martyrdom an object of glory. The life he had led, the dangers to which he had been exposed, the plaudits of his brethren, which were obvious even in the thanksgivings offered to the Almighty, and the constant habit of mingling warfare and worship; altogether, it was no more than a natural result, that he, one of the most active of the Camisards, should have taken fire the moment a suggestion was made to him, that their cause was betrayed.

Court, vol. ii, p. 110 *el seq.* f Villars, vol. ii, p. 194.

Cavalier on his return to Calvisson, was questioned by Ravanel in the presence of the principal officers, on the conditions of his treaty with the marshal. A refusal to impart particulars increased the eagerness of the demand; threats were uttered; and when at length Cavalier informed them that they were to serve in Portugal, he was assailed with the epithets *coward* and *traitor.* Ravanel vowed that for his part, he would not lay down his arms till religious liberty was granted, and their temples were restored. His violence caused Cavalier to draw his pistol; but Moyse, a preacher, appeased the rising quarrel. With the exception of forty men, the troop of Camisards followed Ravanel; and when Cavalier endeavoured to change their resolution, above twenty muskets were levelled at him. Moyse again addressed the Camisards, and saved their late. leader's life; but fearing a sentiment of attachment might win them over to the man, who had formed them to victory, Ravanel and Moyse hastened the departure of the troop, which took the direction of Pierredon; shouting 44 The sword of the Lord!" 28 May, 1704.

This unexpected scene, at a moment when the complete pacification of the province was hoped for, caused some display of severe intentions, deemed requisite as a warning.

Almost immediately after Ravanel's mutiny, an ordinance was issued, forbidding religious assemblies;-fand another fixed the termination of the period of submission for the fifth of June; after which day the devastations of the preceding year would be renewed. £ At the same time Villars expressed his complete approval of Cavalier's conduct; the remains of his troop were quartered at Valabregues, an island on the Rhone, and his offices were accepted by Villars, who postponed his measures of rigour, until after the result of another effort in concert with d'Aygaliers, to persuade the insurgents to submit: with a further view of conciliation, he ordered the gibbets and scaffolds to be generally removed. §

D'Aygaliers induced Rolland, and Ravanel who had joined him to meet on a mountain near Anduze. Cavalier's appearance gave rise to some animated reproaches between him and Rolland; but they afterwards embraced each other. Not so Ravanel: he repeatedly called Cavalier a traitor, and a slave of marshal Villars. Rolland was persuaded to accept the proffered terms; which considering all the circumstances were very reasonable. Cavalier and Rolland were each to have a regiment, to serve out of the kingdom; each might be attended by a minister; the prisoners were to be freed, the exiles recalled, and free permission to be generally granted for the emigration of the new converts. The Camisards who remained were to lay down their arms; and none were to be molested for their religion, if they remained peaceable. There was moreover full and complete amnesty. But Ravanel could not suppose good faith, on the part of a King who had violated the most solemn engagements with the protestants; he suddenly quitted them to harangue the troop, and impress his comrades with distrust. In consequence, when the negocialors of both parties proceeded to announce the result, an advanced guard seized on Rolland, and upbraiding him, carried him off to the main body. Cavalier was obliged to spur his horse, or he would have been sacrificed; and d'Aygaliers, who was too far advanced for retreat, found himself assailed with reproaches, and his life in great danger, having six muskets close pointed at his breast, and a pistol at each ear. His good intentions were however so well appreciated by the preachers, that the Camisards were pacified, and he was permitted to depart without injury. Meanwhile small parties of the Camisards occasionally rejoined their late commander: they were well treated by the marshal, and received great attention from the protestants and new converts. They prayed and sang psalms so much, that the catholics became indignant; and would have thrown them into the Rhone, but for the soldiers. Court, vol. ii, pp. 424—431,—Villars, vol. ii, p. 189.—Brueys, vol. ii, p. 343. f Dated Nismes, 29 May, 1704.:£ Dated Saint-Genies, 1 June, 1701. § Court, vol. ii, p. 455.

Court, vol, ii, p. 459.

Gavalier quitted Valabregues on the twenty-second of June, accompanied by one hundred and fifty men. It was considered that if the Camisard leaders had acted in concert, they might have obtained favourable terms for the protestants in general: the efforts of d'Aygaliers, however well intentioned, created jealousy, and destroyed combination. The little band was well received on their route. At Macon they found orders to halt; and Cavalier came on alone to Versailles, to confer with Chamillard. The King wished to see the far-famed mountaineer. Cavalier was placed on the grand staircase, and was pointed out to the haughty Monarch, as he passed: surprised and perhaps indignant, that one so young and homely should have braved his authority, he shrugged his shoulders and passed on.

Cavalier being suspicious of some treacherous design on the part of the government, communicated to his followers a project of evasion. It was generally approved: they traversed Montbelliard, entered Porentruy, and proceeded to Lausanne.

Villars recommended a system of severity the day after Cavalier's departure, by arresting every one supposed to be connected with the Camisards. AH the prisons were crowded; and above five thousand agricultural labourers were imprisoned on that suspicion, until they could give evidence of their catholicity. At the same time a band of Cadets de la Croix who had been imprisoned for their atrocities, were let loose upon the province, asauxiliaries to the King's forces.-fThe Camisards on their side resumed a hostile position; but although they continued their former system of warfare, they were less inclined to violence, than before the armistice, of which de la Baume has recorded two examples, $ De la Baume, quoted by Court, vol. iii, p. 4.

Rolland meanwhile sent letters and messages to the marshal, declaring his willingness to surrender, but explaining that he was restrained by his own followers. Villars then informed the King, that he had to deal with madmen, who after consenting to submit and receive the royal pardon, suddenly broke off, and stood upon the defensive. In one of his dispatches the marshal observes: "If they continue this state "of indecision, I shall constrain them by force." §

The appearance of a hostile fleet off the coast of Provence, gave Villars some apprehensions. A storm dispersed the squadron, and drove some of the vessels ashore; by which means two French refugee officers were captured. The aspect of affairs became serious, and Villars devastated and massacred, in imitation of his predecessor; at the same time the judicial vengeance was n« less active.
Court, vol. iii, p. 54.

'J-Plusieurs villages furent piltes et brulds par les troupes; on fit de nouveaux enlevemens parmi les protestans suspects, et on autorisa de nouveau les courses des Cadets de la Croix.... les troupes régulieres fusillaient tous les Camisards dont elles s'emparaient. Saragnon, *Ab. de I'Hist. de Nismes,* vol. iii, p. 203.
$ Court, vol. iii, p.' 25. § Villars, vol. ii, p. 260.

D'Aygaliers continued his efforts to persuade Rolland into submission, and a meeting was held at Durfort for discussing the subject; but Ravanel's obstinacy prevented the success of the negociation. That enthusiastic man, accustomed to regard martyrdom as the highest honour, was insensible to all idea of consideration for others, desirous of leading a peaceable life; although they would prefer death to the disgrace of abandoning their party in its decadence. In reply to an observation made by d'Aygaliers, he declared with energy: "I adore God! Cavalier is a traitor— "but for my part, 1 will serve the Lord; even though "thirty thousand devils would prevent it." f

The promise of a hundred louis d'or induced a young man named Malarte, to betray Rolland's retreat, $ Paratte sent a battalion of infantry and some dragoons to Castelnau, where the formidable Camisard was to lodge. The approach of the troops was not discovered until escape was no longer possible. Rolland half dressed, with five of his officers, contrived to reach some trees behind the house; where they were discovered and surrounded. The resolute air of these desperate men caused the officers present to hesitate: the marshal would have preferred taking them alive; but a dragoon speedily settled their doubts, by levelling his piece at Rolland, who fell dead. His companions made no further resistance, and died upon the wheel with great firmness. Five bishops who were present at their execution, were so lost to the requirements of propriety, as to manifest an indecent joy at the spectacle. Rolland's body was brought to judgment, and condemned to be drawn on a hurdle and burnt,-f Pierre Martin, a captain in the English service; he was hanged. His companion was Charles de Goulaine, holding a Dutch commission; he was beheaded.
t D'Aygaliers, quoted by Court, vol. iii, p. 36.

£ Brueys, Louvreleuil, and the *M6m. de Fillars* exult upon a bit of scandal, respecting the demoiselles Comely, said to be the mistresses of Rolland and his companion Mallie". If true, the fact is not very important; because the Camisards, from their station and circumstances, couid not be selected as specimens of protestanl conduct: but, if false, how disgraceful for a party to advance such a calumnious argument!

From this time the Camisards sustained repeated losses and discouragements. Ravanel remained undaunted, until all the other leaders had made terms with the government; and by the end of September the insurrection was terminated. The Camisards were conducted under escort to Geneva; they received the assurance that their captive brethren should be liberated, and that no protestant should be molested on account of his religion. $

Cavalier served with distinction in the allied forces: and at his death was a general in the British army. The arrangements he had concluded for his companions, would have opened for them an equally honourable career; but after the pacification of Languedoc, their position as discontented exiles, made them an easy prey to political adventurers and agents; and particularly to such intriguers as Miremont, Guiscard, and Flotard. At the instigation of one or another of these men, most of the Camisard leaders returned to Languedoc. The duke of Berwick had replaced Villars in the command; and his vigilance detected a conspiracy for rekindling a civil war in the Cevennes, as a diversion to favour the alliance against France. The death of Basville and the arrest of Berwick were to be the signals of insurrection: at least it is so asserted, and with some probability. The plot being discovered, the result was fatal to all the conspirators. Castanet was arrested in the Vivarais, and died upon the wheel at Montpellier. Ravanel and two others were taken in Nismes; and Catinat was seized while passing the gates of the city in disguise. Ravanel and Catinat were burned alive; their two comrades were broken: all four suffered with almost incredible resolution; and as it was feared they would address the spectators, drums were beaten during their execution. They had been previously tortured; but although three of them confessed projects and accomplices, no pain could extort a single confession from Ravanel.-j 14 Aug., 1704. Court, vol. iii, p. 56.
t Brueys, vol. ii, p. 377. $ Court, vol. iii, p. 92. Menard attributes the most atrocious projects to these misguided men; but his accusation is too violent to merit

refutation. *Hist, de Nismes,* vol. vi, p. 415. f 22 April, 1705. Brueys, vol. ii. p. 484.—Court, vol. Hi, p. 194.

A frightful list of executions followed; and notwithstanding these severe examples, fresh projects were set on foot in 1707 and 1709. The principles of the insurgents were still founded on the claim of religious liherty; but they were the mere instruments of political purposes.

Ere we quit this period of cruelty and vengeance, the unfortunate destiny of the baron d'Aygaliers claims a passing remark. This nobleman's well-meant exertions procured him the King's approbation, and a pension of twelve hundred livres. But his residence in France was not permitted. On the payment of his pension being withheld, he considered himself entitled to return to his estates, as the natural resource for his supply. The authorities of Lyons were informed of his project; he was arrested as he passed through that city; and conducted to the castle of Loches in Anjou, where he perished in an effort to recover his liberty. He had escaped from his chamber, by removing one of the window bars, with which he despatched the first sentinel, when another soldier fired upon and killed him. Court, vol. iii, p. 69.

CHAPTER XVI. REIGNS OF LOUIS XV AND XVI.

The remainder of the reign was occupied with military disasters, and controversies between the contending sections of the Romanists. The amiable Fenelon and the dignified Noailles became involved in serious disputes, through the vehemence of the Jesuit or Molinist party: and even Madame de Maintenon was in some measure embroiled. The Jesuits were victorious, and the destruction of Port-Royal displays the measure of their resentment.

The death of father La Chaise, an event seemingly to be desired by the Jansenists, and their off-set party the Quietists, became a misfortune to the sects thus designated, on account of the morose and vindictive character of the new confessor, Tellier; of whom the following sketch is given by a writer of some note: "Animated with the pride of a wicked angel, endowed with a robust body, a mind strong and capable of great efforts; without the least social virtue, he had all the vices of a vigorous understanding. Imbued with the desire of power, of subjugating all to his society, and his society to himself; incessantly devoted to his purpose, he was feared by those whom he obliged, whom he enslaved; and abhorred by all others, even his society, which he rendered powerful and odious."

His first appearance at court sufficiently announced his disposition. Aware that his penitent would be more struck by an apparent contempt of courtly honour, than by the obsequious flattery with which he was usually surfeited, he manifested from the outset that sternness of disposition which alone could impress the King with awe. When his name was first mentioned, Louis asked if he was not related to the late chancellor Tellier deLouvois. "Very far from it," replied the Jesuit, bending reverentially: "I am a "poor peasant of Lower Normandy, where my father "was a farmer."-j

The confessor, steady to the tactics of his society, immediately commenced his measures for injuring the Cardinal de Noailles, archbishop of Paris, whom he accused of Jansenism, to be avenged of that Cardinal's assertion, that he sold church preferment. Circulars were addressed to the bishops, with directions for their conduct, and orders to denounce Noailles and Quesnel to the King: this scheme was however defeated, by a copy of the circular falling into the Cardinal's hands. It was made public, and Tellier was on the point of being dismissed. $ Having failed in that plan, the Jesuit resolved on persecuting Quesnel, whose works had been patronized by Noailles; and in searching for propositions to be condemned, he took care to select those opposed to the Molinist views. Yet as they were conformable to the doctrines of St.Paul, St.-Augustin, and St.-Thomas-Aquinas, one of his assistants represented the danger to which he would be exposed, if he thus assaulted those pillars of Christianity. "Saint-Paul!" exclaimed Tellier with earnestness: "St.-Paul, and St.-Augustin were "hotheaded fellows, who would in these days be "sent to the Bastille; with regard to St.-Thomas, "you may judge how little I care for a Jacobin, when 4 I scarcely trouble myself about an apostle." Duclos, *Memoires secrets sur le regne de Louis XIV,* v©l. i, p. J 35. f *Mem. dnduc de Saint-Simon,* vol. iii, p. 201. Paris, 1818. % La Beaumelle, vol. v, p. 134.

Under the influence of such a confessor, it is quite natural that sanguinary edicts should be issued until the close of the reign; and a declaration published not long before the death of Louis, is at once a monument of cruelty, injustice, and incapacity,-j It declared that a residence in the kingdom of those who had heretofore professed the pretended reformed religion, was more than sufficient proof that they had embraced the catholic religion, without which they would not have been tolerated. Further on, and in direct opposition to the concluding article of the edict of revocation, the whole body of Protestants were exposed to the rigours decreed against relapsed heretics; all who 'persisted in the pretended reformed religion being deemed in a state of relapse.

Within six months Louis ceased to live-; and the heavy yoke which hypocrisy and bigotry had laid upon the nation during the period he filled the throne, was exchanged for the sway of a prince, completely the reverse of the *Grand Monarque.* Duclos, vol. ij p. 142-T Dated 8 March, *nib.*

In this work it would hardly be fair to attempt a delineation of his character: the subject of these pages being almost exclusively connected with his blemishes; while the more brilliant scenes of his protracted reign have had no claim upon our notice. The numerous panegyrists, whose pens were enlisted to throw an aureole of glory around this "great era" of the French monarchy, have contributed to mislead the judgment of subsequent times; but his policy, his published sentiments, and his personal conduct must suffer seriously, when subjected to the analysis of impartial men. While his courtiers were lavish in abject adulations, he was detested by the people at large; and the indecent joy displayed on the day of his interment, must have been grounded on some very obnoxious sentiments.

It may not be misplaced to insert here the opinion of a modern writer, comprising an idea which certainly should enter largely into the estimate of this monarch's character. "I demand of all sound minds, "of all upright hearts, free from passion. The Con"vention, whose chiefs are justly stigmatized for "having substituted the legislation of murder and "vengeance for the code of. liberty, does it present "in its decrees, a single barbarous or immoral com"bination, the example of which has not been given "by the council of Louis XIV?" The question contains an overwhelming accusation, the answer to which is beyond doubt.
Lacretellf, *Hist, deFrance pendant le i s Steele.* Vol. i, p. 132.
As his successor was a mere child, the duke of Orleans was appointed Regent; and during the period of his government, a different policy was followed. His reputation for impiety was an earnest that persecution on account of heterodox opinions would cease; and he commenced his reparatory measures immediately after the late King's burial, when the doors of the Bastille were thrown open to the victims of father Tellier, who at first relied upon the authority of the deceased monarch's will, by which he was appointed confessor to Louis XV. He presented himself with confidence; and inquired of the Regent, what were to be his functions, until the King was of an age to need his ministry? "That is no concern of mine," the regent coolly answered; "apply to your superiors." This rebuff tormented the imperious ecclesiastic, whose brethren took revenge, by preaching most fanatical sermons against the government,-f

Under other circumstances the Huguenots might have complained of the Regent's administration, for he maintained all the edicts against Protestant worship; and whatever may have been his real opinion in their favour, as has been pretended, he did nothing to improve their condition. Yet by com-

parison they were

"*De VEtat des Protestans en France,* par M. Aignan, de 1'Académie franca ise. p. 23. f Lacretelle, *ut antea,* p. 134. $ An ordinance dated 20 July, 1720, permitted the establishment in a happy state: emigration in consequence ceased, and although no positive favour could be expected, they were free from apprehensions of fresh persecution.

The duke of Orleans was succeeded in the direction of affairs, by the duke of Bourbon, who had the weakness to imagine he could immortalize his administration, by renewing the severities of Louis XIV; a new persecution was in consequence commenced, by an absurd and odious edict, more cruel than that of revocation. Children were torn from their parents, to be educated in the Romish religion; death was again decreed against pastors, confiscation against relapsed converts, and every kind of oppression endured in the late reign was renewed: and this disgraceful measure has been styled a masterpiece of Christian policy, f

There was some abatement of the horrors of persecution while cardinal Fleury was prime minister; yet the system did not terminate for many years: and to judge from the writings of more than one prelate, an unabated desire existed to be freed from the presence of heretics. A memorial from the clergy in April, 1745, declared there was no hope of their conversion, and that there was rising up a generation of Protestants, more obstinate and headstrong than their fathers. "They may protest fidelity, and publish that the spirit which pervades their assemblies is free from revolt and insurrection; but they will be goofl subjects no farther than fear constrains them." of a burial place in Paris, for Protestant *foreigners;* but every precaution was taken that no French body should be interred there; and the Cth clause especially declares that the public profession of the protestant religion was not permitted, even to foreigners, whowere forbidden all ceremonial in the sepultures; nor could any French man be present.
Dated May, 1724. This declaration, ob-

serves M. Boissy d'Anglas, forms the summary of all the penal provisions scattered throughout the laws of Louis XIV, some of which it renders even more severe. *Essai sur la vie de Malesherbes, yol.* i, p. 18. f Caveyrac, *Jpologie de Louis XIV,* p. 449.
Monclus, bishop of Alais, in reply to an intendant who Was a friend to tolerance, thus writes. "The "magistrates have relaxed the severity of the ordi"nances, and thus caused all the evils of which the "state has to complain."f Chabannes, bishop of Agen, about the same time published a letter, in which he laments the incurable obstinacy of the heretics, and recommends that the state should be freed from them by permitting their departure.

The bishop had heard indirectly that the edict of Nantes was to be re-enacted: this horrified his intolerant soul, and he composed a tract which is no credit to the Romish party. He commences by praising the piety of Louis XIV, who made the greatest sacrifices at the peace of Ryswick, rather than listen to any proposal in favour of the protestants. "He renounced "the fruit of his victories, purchased with so much "blood and toil; he even acknowledged the usurper "of England, notwithstanding the ties which bound "him to the dispossessed King—he granted all, he "yielded all; he surrendered every thing except the "return of the heretics." The bishop then argues, that what Louis XIV refused, being in the greatest difficulty, his successor cannot yield in the midst of prosperity. *Proces Ferbaux de I'AssemblUe generate du Clerge,* quoted by Menard, vol. vi, p. 609., f *Beponse de M. I'eveque d'Alais,* dated 6 *octobre* 1751.

This correspondence arose out of the inconvenience perpetually springing up, respecting marriage and baptism among the protestants; a subject which renders it necessary to revert to an earlier period. Ever since the edict of revocation, the jurisprudence had assumed that there were no protestants in France; while edict rapidly followed edict, inflicting penalties upon protestants and new converts leaving the kingdom. The church of Rome declaring marriage a sacrament, could not administer that rite to any who denied its ecclesiastical authority; and in consequence, the new converts were called upon to give proof of Roman Catholicism, before their marriages could be celebrated. The Huguenots sought their proscribed pastors in the deserts and forests. When the benediction of a minister could not be obtained, the blessing was pronounced by aged heads of families, awaiting the occasion of a pastor's arrival; and whenever it was known that a minister was in the country, multitudes hastened to meet him, to have a religious sanction conferred on their unions, to present their children for baptism, and to receive the sacrament of commu. nion. *Lettre deM. ttvique dAgen A M. le conlrdleur-genSralcontre la tolerance des Huguenot dans le royawne, i" mai* 1751. This pamphlet was so eagerly sought for that it could not be procured without difficulty; but it was reprinted, in 1756, by Court, along with the *Patriote francais* and *Impartial,* which is a severe commentary on the letter.

As the assemblies in the *Desert* consisted of many thousand persons, a fresh persecution occurred for the purpose of effecting their suppression,-f-In a report addressed to the secretary of state, the severities are not concealed. In Languedoc twenty-eight persons, and in Guyenne forty-five, were condemned to the galleys, and attached to the chain of *forgats,* for nothing else than attending these meetings for worship. In Normandy, the goods of those who had not allowed their children to be baptized by the cure, were sold without any form of procedure. These iniquities occurred in 1746; $ and in 1752 an attempt torebaptize by force, the children of protestants, caused such resistance at Ledignan, in the diocese of Nismes, that the measure was relinquished. §

The punishment of death was inflicted upon all ministers who fell into the power of the government. M. Desubas, a young preacher, was arrested in December, 1745, and conducted by a body of soldiers to Vernoux in the Yivarais. Some of his flock learning his capture,

assembled on the road, unarmed, to implore his liberation: a discharge of musketry was the reply to their appeal, when six persons-were killed, and four were made prisoners. Crowds arrived at Vernoux to intercede for their pastor's life. The assemblage was fired upon — thirty-six were killed, and two hundred wounded; the greater part mortally. The feelings excited by this wanton cruelty might have led to serious consequences, as the majority of the population was protestant, and the escort not very powerful; the pastors however exerted themselves in persuading the people to abstain from violence. Desubas was conveyed to Montpellier, where he was condemned to death, and suffered on the first of February, 1746, in presence of an immense concourse of people: his conversation with those who visited him in prison, and his calm behaviour at the time of execution, kindled much commiseration, even among the Catholics. Rulhiere, vol. ii, p. 174. Menard also testifies their steadfastness in describing their assemblies in 1743. *Hist, de Nismes,* vol. vi, p. 590. f Comme les protestans ne discontinuaient pas leurs assemblies, il *fallait* punir les nouveaux convertis des lieux de l'arrondissement dans lesquels elles se tenaient. Menard, vol. vi, p. 626. $ Rulhiere, vol. ii, p, 340. § Menard, vol. vi, p. 632.

The minister Benezet, arrested at Vigan, was executed at Montpellier in January, 1752. Francis Rochette, another minister,-suffered at Toulouse in 1762 with three brothers, named Grenier. The eldest was not twenty-two years of age. They had endeavoured to release their pastor from captivity, and were beheaded close to the gibbet, on which Rochette was hanged,-f-They were offered their lives if they would abjure; but their firmness did not relieve them from the obtruding solicitations of four priests, who beset them until the fatal moment. As the crucifix was occasionally presented to the brothers, the eldest observed: "Speak to us of him who died for our sins "and rose again for our justification, and we are ready "to listen; but do not introduce your superstitions."

Rochette was forced to descend in front of the Cathedral, where he was ordered to make the *amende honorable;* but he boldly declared his principles, refused to ask pardon of the King, and forgave his judges: to the last he displayed a martyr's constancy. The brothers Grenier were equally firm. After two had suffered, the executioner entreated the youngest to escape their fate by abjuring. "Do thy duty," was the answer he received, as the youth submitted to the *Hist, of the Persecutions endured by the Protestants of the South, of France,* by Mark Wilks, vol. i, p, 7. f Rulhicrc, vol. ii, p. 351.—Boissy d'Anglas, vol. i, p. 379.

The celebrated Calas, broken on the wheel upon a false charge of having killed one of his children, who was disposed to become a catholic—an injustice discovered too late; and the filial tenderness of Fabre, who suffered condemnation to the galleys in the place of his father, are so well known, that allusion to them is sufficient. The effect produced upon the public mind when the circumstances were made known, contributed essentially to the removal of a great reproach upon French legislation.

An effort was however made by the clergy, in 1765, to resist the tendency to toleration, by a remonstrance to the King: "It is in vain," that body declares, "that all public worship, other than the catholic, is forbidden in your dominions. In contempt of the.wisest laws, the protestants have seditious meetings on every side. Their ministers preach heresy and administer the supper; and we have the pain of beholding altar raised against altar, and the pulpit of pestilence opposing that of truth. If the law which revoked the edict of Nantes—if your declaration of 1724, had been strictly observed, we venture to say there would be no more Calvinists in France. Consider the effects of a tolerance, which may become cruel by its results. Restore, Sire! restore to the laws all their vigour—to religion its splendour. Let the solemn renewal of your declaration of 1724, the fruit of your wisdom and piety, be the happy result of our remonstrance." Similar representations were made by the clergy in 1770 and 1772, against the prolestant assemblies. The hostility shewn to this meagre, half toleration, has inflicted a permanent evil on France. Protestantism was suppressed to the extent of administrative power; but as no enactments could enforce sincere respect for the victorious church of Rome, a spread of irreligion has been the consequence. Ardent Huguenots defied authority and braved martyrdom; while the indifferent, although they declared themselves converted, were unable to submit their conscience to papal tyranny, and became the leaders and teachers of the Encyclopcedist school.

From the *Toulousainez,* a series of letters published in 1763.

"Boissy d'Anglas, *ut antea,* vol. i, p. 18.

The philosophic party in its hatred of the clergy, co-operated with the enlightened members of the educated classes, in producing a mitigation of the code, under which the Huguenots groaned; and the writings of Caveyrac and the abbe L'Enfant,--in favour of bigotry, were received with general contempt. Louis XVI gave an edict in 1787, which improved the condition of protestants in a small degree. This ill-fated King, although remarkable for humane feelings, was still influenced by education, as well as by respect for the opinions and policy of his immediate predecessors; and without the exertions of the admirable Lamoignon-Malesherbes, it is doubtful whether this edict would have been obtained, $ That eminent man was indefatigable in the council, and by his writings. "It is the least," he observed on one occasion, "that I can do, to repair in the eyes of the "protestants, all the harm which M. de Basville, "my uncle, did to them in Languedoc."§ The astonishing popularity of Voltaire's writings effected much; and he exerted his influence with eminent persons in behalf of toleration—particularly marshal Richelieu,to whom he addressed an admirable letter on the subject, in 1772. f This writer, after grossly disfiguring history, observes:—" Telle "est, Sire, la filiation de l'irreligion, dont le calvin-

ismc est la souche." *Discours a lire au Conseil,* etc, p. 223.

£ Gilbert des Voisins, conseiller d'etat, composed a *Memoire sur lei moyens de donner aux Protestans un etat civil en France.* It was written by order of Louis XV, and read to him in private; but remained unpublished until 1787. The consistorial library of the Oratoire has a number of pamphlets on this subject, which drew forth much controversy.

§ lioissy d'Anglas, vol. i, p. 31.

The concessions were no more than what could not lie with safety withheld; and the terms of the edict expressly statc, " that the non-catholics cannot claim "under its provisions, more than the law of nature "forbids being refused. " In short it only conferred the means of recording the civil existence of the Huguenots: nothing like a privilege was granted; and an express stipulation was made to prevent any protestant minister from signing certificates, establishing the birth, marriage, or decease of one of his flock. The religious assemblies were no longer the object of such vigilant pursuit; but the protestant worship existed by sufferance, rather than by permission.

The boon was trivial, yet the edict was opposed in its progress, and the cause of fanaticism found a zealous defender in M. d'Epresmenil, who resisted to the last; and called upon the magistrates to avoid "crucifying the Lord anew," by the sanction of such a sacrilegious measure. It may indeed be doubted whether any concession would have been made, if the different parliaments had not, on several occasions, given decrees in favour of the protestants. One or two instances will display the civil degradation of the Huguenots, until the sanctuary of justice afforded some relief.

Andre Greffeuille, a protestant, left by will certain The bishop of Rochelle issued a *mandement* dated 26 Feb., 1788, enjoining his clergy to refuse their ministry to all non-Catholics, referring them to the secular authorities. The King was displeased, and by *arret du conseil,* 3 April, 1788, declared the *mandement* very reprehensible, and or-

dered it to be considered as *non avenu.* property to his daughter; and his widow, to whom he had been married in the *desert,* proceeded to act as guardian of her child. But Jean Roche, the residuary legatee, iniquitously endeavoured to take the whole property; and obtained a favourable decree from the seneschal of Nismes, on the grounds of the absence of legal forms in the marriage: the child was in fact, baptised at the church as the natural daughter of Andre Greffeuille and Susanna Metge, *living in concubinage;* for such was the invariable mode of describing the children of protestants. However a declaration from the paternal relatives, that the parents had been married in the protestant form; and that the child was always regarded as legitimate, sufficed to obtain a decree in her favour.

The same parliament gave other decisions in favour of widows, to whose prejudice collateral relatives had raised claims, grounded on their pretended concubinage; or restoring the heritage to children, whose legitimacy was disputed.-j-These conclusions were based upon equity: there had existed impediments, arising out of contradictory enactments; and the principles of justice were defended, in opposition to conflicting technicalities. Yet on one occasion, the parliament of Toulouse gave a judgment which involved a still greater principle. Antoine Benech, a protestant, being on his death-bed in 1747, was summoned by a cure, in the presence of three witnesses, to receive the sacraments of the church. He refused, and the court of Montauban confiscated his property, as a relapsed heretic, under the enactments of 1715 and 1724, by. which all persons persisting in the pretended reformed religion, are declared *relaps.* An appeal-was presented against this decision in 1769; and after a delay of eight months, the parliament decreed, that as no one could be declared a relapsed heretic who had not abjured, the memory of the deceased was free from calumny, and his property must in consequence pass to the next of kin. *Arret duparlement de Toulouse,* 9 mars, 1759. f *Arrets* dated 19 Aug., 1769; 9 July,

1770; and 17 July, 1776: the parliament of Grenoble gave a similar decree, 16 Feb., 177S.

The decrees of the National assembly opened a new era for the Huguenots. In the sittings of August and September, 1789, the non-catholics were declared eligible to all public functions. They were no longer an inferior caste, and became candidates for civil and military employments. It was therefore natural that the revolution should be hailed with joy, by those who from their cradles had endured severe persecutions: they received a benefit, far beyond the range of their expectations; their forlorn-condition forbidding the contemplation of a change so favourable. Yet the adversaries of religious freedom accuse them of disturbing the good feeling which prevailed at the commencement of the revolution: and represent them as aggressors, where evidence abounds to substantiate their intended doom as victims.

The news of the destruction of the Bastille gave rise to the most joyous enthusiasm at Nismes. The nobility and clergy of that province had been foremost in promoting the establishment of a limited monarchy; and until the church property fell under discussion, and was devoted to public purposes, the greatest harmony prevailed; for at that time, the new constitution was generally, in favour. But a proposal in the National assembly *f* to sequestrate the ecclesiastical revenues kindled a sympathy between the secular clergy of all ranks," the regular clergy of all denominations, and the noblesse, who could duly appreciate the retreat of a rich benefice, as a good provision for younger sons. The nobility and clergy had already begun to quit the country; and their adherents prepared, for the organisation of parties in the municipal councils of Nismes and for raising separate companies in the national guard. These intrigues began in December, 1789, when meetings were held at the house of a cure, and in the church of the Penitens Blancs. Other cures co-operated, and their efforts were directed to inflame the people. $ In all subse-

quent elections, the catholic and protestant interests were placed in hostile array; and at the municipal elections in February, 1790, out of eighteen members, only one protestant was elected. The catholic clergy had previously circulated some inflammatory, on more properly speaking, incendiary pamphlets, to excite a feeling against the protestants; and urging the necessity of their destruction. *Arret du parlement de Toulouse,* 10 *juillet* 1770.

The election of twelve commissioners for organising the *milice Nismoise,* in July, 1789, passed off with perfect harmony. M. Vidal, subsequently a violent *ultra,* was among the successful candidates. f 10 Oct., 1789. *f* Lauze de Peret, 2' livraison, pp. 174—210. This author will be frequently referred to. His work consists of two parts: *Eclaircissemens historiques,* in three livraisons. Paris, 1818; and *Causes el precis des Troubles,* etc., in one vol., Paris, 1819.

One of the chief instigators in this unhappily business, named Froment, being disappointed of the full recompense for his services, at the restoration of the royal family, published a statement of his exertions in behalf of the clergy in 1790; and it is not assuming too much to declare, that the intrigues of such persons were the sole causes of the trouble and confusion which followed; and of the animosity displayed between the protestants and catholics of Nismes.-j

"Faithful to my religion and my King," says M. Froment, "I endeavoured to diffuse the spirit by which I was animated. I published in 1789 several writings, in which I exhibited the dangers that threatened the altar and the throne. My fellow countrymen being struck. with the justness of my observations, displayed the most ardent zeal; and with a desire to avail-myself of the favourable feeling, I went secretly to Turin in January, 1790, to solicit the approbation and. assistance of the French princes. At a special meeting held on my arrival, I shewed that if they would arm the partizans of the altar and the throne, making the interests of religion march with those of loyalty, it would be easy to save both..,,' „ After a gener-

al plan was decided upon, and a secret correspondence arranged, I returned to Nismes; where while I awaited the promised assistence from Turin, and which I never received, I employed myself in exciting the zeal of the inhabitants. It was at my suggestion they adopted the declaration of the twentieth ef April, which demanded that the catholic worship *alone* should be permitted, and which was signed by three thousand citizens."

' I hare fortunately procured two of these violent tracts, the character of which may be gathered from an extract from each:—

"Je ne crains pas d'assurer qu'accorder aux protestans la liberté "du culte, l'admission aux charges et aux honneurs civils et mili"taires, c'est un mal qui ne renferme aucun avantage réel pour vous "ni pour l'Etat, mais qui bien plus expose l'un et l'autre aux pins "grands désastres." *PierreRomain aux catholiques de Nismes,* p. 4.

"Les catholiques de la Sène-Chaussée n'ont jamais entendu don"ner à leurs députés le droit de les soumettre au despotisme de leurs 4 4 plus cruels ennemis, et ils deviendraient réellement les esclaves des "protestans si on accordait à ces fanatiques républicains la liberté du"culte." *Charles Sincère à Pierre Romain,* p. 16.

f This was so evident that Froment's pamphlets were soon suppressed: he published one in 1815, another in 1817. The latter I have been able to procure; but I only know the other through the extracts given by Lauze de Peret and Mark Wilks.

Unhappily this band of conspirators was encouraged by the municipal authorities; f and with such support, they were enabled to create some confusion at the elections for departmental officers. Yet not to the extent expected by Froment and his friends, who prepared for a vigorous effort. The thirteenth of June was the day fixed upon; when about two hundred leaguers attacked some dragoons, who drove them hack after long resistance. At the same time Froment dispatched messengers into the country parishes, to claim help; asserting as a motive to enforce the appeal, that unarmed catholics were massacred in Nismes. The messengers were arrested, and their letters thus falling into the hands of the electoral assembly, created as may be well supposed, much indignation at such a perfidious attempt to cast upon their intended victims, the odium and initiative of the project framed by the conspirators, *f* In the fermentation which ensued, all the protestants who fell into the hands of the rustics, were murdered. $ Lauze de Peret, 2 livraisen, p. 196.—Prudhomme; *Rivoluliffns de Paris,* n 44, p. 309.

ʄ *Viritis historiques sur les ivenemens arrivis a Nismes-lie 13 de juin et les jours suivans.* Pubises par le club des Amis de la Constitution, en juillet 1790, p. 2.

On the following morning at seven o'clock, the procureur du roi proceeded to verify the number of slain; when he was informed that there was fighting in the adjoining streets. The national guards were drawn up on the esplanade facing the convent of the capucins; a place notorious as the focus of the conspiracy, and whence the most inflammatory libels had been issued. The convent being suspected was searched, but nothing was discovered; however to the surprise of all, a firing was heard: it was supposed to proceed from the convent, and M. Massip, municipal officer of St.-Come, was killed. The national guards rushed forward to attack the convent; and the superior, from a window, insulted the assailants; while the convent bell was rung to summon aid. The expected support did not arrive in time; the gate was forced open; and five capucins with three laymen, were killed on the spot. The edifice was then attacked; and while it is slated by one party that even in their rage, the people respected the chapel and *objets du cuke,* their opponents charge them with rapacious pillage.-f-.

These were the cavalry of the national guard; they were composed of the wealthiest among the inhabitants of Nismes, and comprised many protestants. The companies raised under party influence, and consisting of violent

catholics, had frequent quarrels with them. They prepared on the 8th June to express their contempt by proceeding through the town mounted on asses; but the authorities prevented them. *Resumi des Procis verbaux,* p. 21. .j-On searching the houses of the abbe Cabanel and Brajouze, curate of St.-Paul, arms were discovered. *Veritis hutoriquei,* p. 13. % Lauze dePeret, 3" livraison,pp. 21—34. —Thisauthor has drawn largely for information from the official report made to the national assembly by M. Alquier. Meanwhile Froment and his partisans kept up a fire from the ramparts, whither they had retreated. He was not aware of his letters being intercepted; % and maintained the conflict, fully expecting the arrival of multitudes from the country to support him. He placed thirty men in the Dominican convent, decidedly against the wishes of the monks; while another party took a position in Froment's house. With a view to prevent the threatened loss of life, the electoral assembly sent a flag of truce, accompanied by the town trumpeter: a parley ensued, and the leaguers consented to surrender to the assembly. The white flag was displayed, and preparations were commenced for executing the terms, when the firing was renewed from the ramparts, and reconciliation became impossible. A vigorous attack followed immediately, and the leaguers experienced the effects of popular fury. Most of them were killed on the spot; and among the number was Pierre Froment, brother of the chief conspirator. Vide Appendix. N 4.

f Lauze de Peret, 3" livraison, pp. 39 et 44.—*V iritis hisloriques,* etc., p. 12. The letter states that four men were with the monks, and refers to a proces verbal, drawn up by the cure of St.-Castor, to show that no profanation occurred. The *liisumi ties Prods verbaux* (p. 32) pretends, on the other hand, that plunder and devastation took place. :£ The letters of Froment and Descombies to the marquis de Bouzzols, commandant of Languedoc, are given at length in the *Veriles historiques,* etc., p. 26.

The disturbance created a great sensation in the National Assembly, as it was

represented in the light of an attack upon the catholics by the protestants; a charge which has been frequently repeated since the restoration. In consequence Rabaut-St.-Etienne, deputy of Nismes, addressed the assembly: "A number of facts demonstrate that the affair of Nismes, far from being a war of religion excited by the animosity of protestants against catholics, had religion only for pretext; but for its principal object, the restoration of the old government; and that the two parties of Nismes, far from being protestants against catholics, were on one side, the friends of liberty and the constitution, both protestant, and catholic; and on the other, all those of both religions who were discontented with the revolution; ci-devant nobles, canons, etc." This assertion has been denounced as a calumny; but Froment's publication, has established its correctness,-f

This conflict has obtained the name of the *bagarre de Nismes.* One hundred and thirty-eight persons were killed: four were severely wounded; and twentyfour houses were pillaged or destroyed. The loss was most severe on the side of the Leaguers, two-thirds being of that party: but it was a combat, and not a massacre, as the catholics maintain; and-which they have exaggerated with shameless effrontery, declaring that in 1790, fifteen hundred victims were massacred, and that priests were slain at the foot of their altars. $

During the reign of terror the protestants suffered in the same proportion as the catholics; this being incontestably established by the list of condemnations, is a proof that religion was not in question. § To condemn the protestants in general, as Jacobins and revolutionists, is therefore a monstruous injustice as well as an absurdity; yet such was the prevalent opinion among the ultraroyalists after the restoration; and the sentiment was strengthened by an expression attributed to Malesherbes, who after expatiating on the benefits which Louis XVI had conferred on the protestants, exclaimed: "Some gratitude was due "from them; but it is known that the King had no "enemies more cruel.

" This was repeated and enlarged upon, although there is not the least proof that Malesherbes ever uttered such a phrase; and the illiberal feeling gave rise to a series of events, which prevent the conclusion of our task at this period; for the rights of conscience and liberty of worship were legally admitted when the anarchy of 1792 was replaced by a regular government. The spirit of party then vanished; during a period of nearly twenty years, none ever dreamed of inquiring into his neighbour's religious opinions; and if any fanatical feeling existed, it was silenced by the irresistible authority of the laws.

Stance du 24 fevrier 1791. .J-Acette epoque (Janvier I790),jefuscharg6par S. A. R.Monsieur le comic d'Artois, alors a Turin, de former un parti royaliste dans le midi, de l'organiser et de le commander: je remplis ma mission avec succes; maisle 13 juin 1790, ayant 6t6 attaque a Nismes par des forces tres-supeneuresavant d'avoir recu les armes et les secours *qu'on m'avait promis,* je perdis dans cette lutte un de mes freres et sept a huit cents royalistes. Froment, *Leltre a M. le marquis de Foucault,* etc., 1817, p. 24. % *Memoires, Rapport,* etc. , presented to the King, 23 Aug., 1815, Another account, hostile to the protestants, was published in Sept., 1790, entitled *Details circonstancies,* etc., but the event was then too recent to permit such gross exaggeration—at least in the numbers; although a distortion of the facts is very glaring, even there. 5 JLauze de Feret gives the name and residence of each victim: there were ninety-one catholics, forty-six protestants, and one Jew. Boissy d'Anglas expresses great doubt on the subject. Vol. i. p. 3T.

CHAPTER XVII. RESTORATION OF LOUIS XVIII.—TROURLES AT NISMES AND ENVIRONS.

The return of the Bourbon princes was sincerely hailed by the French protestants. In most towns their numbers were too small to attract observation; but at Nismes, and in the surrounding districts they constituted a large proportion of the inhabitants. There were instances of protestants being appointed mayors; but none were ever named prefect, pro-

cureur-general nor chief president of the *Cour Royale,* in the department of the Gard.

As the majority of the protestants were engaged in commerce or manufactures, the fall of Napoleon was to them the dawn of prosperity: a wide field was opened for their operations, and they had no motive for any concealed affection towards the deposed dynasty. In the religious services with which they celebrated the restoration, their loyalty was manifested in an unequivocal manner; the return of the Israelites from the Babylonish captivity, being selected as the closest parallel in sacred history. The catholics on Wilks, p. 97. the other hand did not conceal their regret at the change; and when the royal government was established, the more zealous among them renewed their demonstrations of animosity, and persisted in representing the protectants as Jacobins. In their view, none but catholics could possibly entertain correct political sentiments; and the members of the rival religions were on a sudden enrolled in opposing interests — such a division was at least assumed by the ultraroyalists, who styled themselves /es *honnetes gens.* The marquis d'Arbaud Jouques, in attempting to justify his party, indirectly admits an agression. "The popular joy among the catholics was unbounded, hut not without a mixture of bitter recollections, and imprudent threats against the calvinists. The sentiments manifested by the latter, on this occasion, were on the contrary free from reproach.-j

The mayor of Nismes M. Castelnau, member of an ancient noble family, wasaprotestant; and he quickly experienced the insults of a bigoted faction. Being in public with the other authorities, on occasion of a *fete* to celebrate the restoration, while shouts of applause greeted the prefect, numerous voices exclaimed, *a bas le maire!* some even ordered him to resign his office. M. Vincent Saint-Laurent, whose influence had, in 1790, preserved the property of a violent partisan named Vidal, was in the prefect's box at the theatre: immediately the public insisted on his being

sent away, calling out to the prefect, to purify his box.-fWhen catholics met protestants in the streets, they cried out *Vive le roil* with menacing gests; and insulting songs were constantly heard. One in particular had a refrain worthy of the sixteenth century— "they would wash their hands in protestant blood/'$ The lower orders were speedily trained to ferocity, and the cabarets and market places resounded with pihrases such as these: *"Marianne* will soon come 4 down—The black throats must go back to the *fri goulettes—The* charter will last but a month—The 4 St.-Bartholomew is not far off."§ Protestans ou revolutionnaires, disait-on, c'est synonyme. « *Journal du Card* l'imprimait. Lauze de Peret, liv. i, p. 55.

f *Troubles et agitations du de'partement du Gard,* etc., par marquis d'Arbaud Jouques, p. 3.

To these portentous warnings must be added the proceedings of some influential individuals. It was currently reported, that according to the declarations of persons of rank, the country would never be quiet without a second St.-Bartholomew. In May, 1814, an address to the King was drawn up, at Nismes, in direct opposition to the declaration of St.-Ouen, on which the charter was founded: it boasted of the principles of 1790, and called for the establishment of absolute power. Addresses were also voted in other towns, declaring that there ought to be *only one* religion in Finance — One God, one King, one faith: that was the motto of the party, and it was inscribed over the gates of Lyons, when the count d'Artois entered that city. The celebrated Carnot has also denounced the manifestation of a similar feeling; for he mentions that some individuals connected with the old parliament, were advancing the most senseless pretentions of vengeance, the necessity of absolute intolerance, and of one exclusive religion,-j Vidal was a zealous supporter of Froment's conspiracy; he was very conspicuous in the troubles of 1815, as commissary general of police for the southern departments.

f *Purger sa loge.* Lauze de Peret, 3 livraison, p.94. The first volume is in three distinct parts; the second has a continued 'pagination. $ Lavaren nostri mans

Din lou sang di proutestans.

§ *Marianne* is the bill of the protestant temple; *gorges noires,* a name given to the protestants; *les frigouleltes* means the worship in the desert. Lauze de Peret, 3" livraison, p. 95. Wilks, p. 100.

BibliothSque historiqwe, vol. i, p. 251.
Another symptom of reaction was the organised demand for restoring the bishopries, suppressed by the revolution; this was coupled with uniform recommendations given by the clergy to their penitents, to say a certain number of *paler* and *ave* for the prosperity of the throne, and the re-establishment of the Jesuits. $

Yet, notwithstanding this state of irritation, the King's authority was sufficiently maintained to prevent any outbreak. Castelnau resigned his mayoralty, on account of the hostile feelings publicly manifested: Louis XVIII immediately named as his successor another protestant, M. Daunant, to whose energy the people of Nismes were indebted for the preservation of order: but the zealous discharge of bis duties drew upon him the sneers and malevolent insinuations of the violent royalists.

Lauze de Peret, vol. ii, p. 11. f *Memoire adresse au Roi,juiUet* 1814. $ Wilts, p. 108.

The "men of 1790"continued indefatigable in the prosecution of their designs; and fresh insults were daily offered to the protestants, whose conduct was cruelly misrepresented to the government. A writer who has carefully investigated the proceedings of this period, observes, in alluding to the service in January, 1815, to commemorate the death of Louis XVI: " The sermons and prayers delivered on the occasion at Nismes, were printed and distributed by the consistory; but this, like all other acts of respect and loyalty, was despised and perverted: they were told it was in vain for them to dissemble; that in spite of their pretended loyalty, their security had terminated with the reign of Napoleon; that their temples would

soon be rased, and their ministers proscribed."

It has been surmised, and with great probability, that the ultra-royalists wished to goad the protestants into some act of rebellion, by which they might obtain an occasion for acquiring importance; because unfortunately for those ambitious notabilities, the King did not dismiss all the functionaries whom he found in the public service. The inferior classes discerned the impending storm much earlier than the wealthy protestants; the merchants and manufacturers indulged in the hope of better times, when the King would be more amply. informed; but the labourers and husbandmen soon abandoned their confidence in the promises of Louis XVIII; and when Napoleon returned from Elba, they hailed his appearance, as a preservation from the Jesuits. The *Cafe de I'ile d'Elbe* was thenceforth therendez-vous of all who disliked the perspective of sacerdotal influence; among whom were many catholics, and almost all the disbanded officers: it is therefore with injustice that the cafe has been designated as the seat of a protestant conspiracy for restoring Napoleon.

Wilfcs, p. 122.'

There is now no doubt of the essentially military origin of the revolution of 1815; and it is equally well known, that Nismes was one of the very last places in France to submit to the Emperor. However the purposes of faction required an accusation against the protestants of the Gard, the only department where they form an important body; and for a time the party wreaked its vengeance on the unhappy inhabitants, while the tribunals were either enlisted as assistants in the relentless work, or had become powerless to afford protection or redress.

The duke d'Angouleme arrived at Nismes on the twelfth of March, 1815. In reply to his proclamation, the protestants of the higher classes volunteered their services for the royal cause; but the faction prevented their offer from being accepted. Accused of dissimulation, they were obliged to withdraw from the

ranks, as they heard repeated on all sides: 44 We will not al44' low these rascally protestants to join us."

The prince it is notorious, was unable to keep the field, and having capitulated at La Palud, his army of *miquelets* was disbanded. These men being hastily levied, deficient in discipline, and excited by political animosity, frequently conducted themselves in an unruly manner; but only in one instance did any thing serious occur, although they had to pass in detachments, through a district inhabited by those who are designated as their bloodthirsty and savage enemies. The unfortunate exception has however been so much exaggerated, that it demands a circumstantial mention. Not far from Uzes is the village of Arpaillargues, inhabited almost entirely by protestants. Through this place fifty royalist volunteers had to pass; and they would undoubtedly have traversed it, as quietly as their comrades had passed other towns, if a mischievous individual, named Bertrand, a catholic, had not hastened on horseback to Arpaillargues, to announce that the miquelets were advancing, and that on their route they had plundered houses, violated females, and murdered forty protestant ministers, *f* Lanze de Peret, *Causes et precis,* p. 37. *Miquelets* are volunteers enrolled for local service, without uniform, and armed according to the means at their command. The term was used in the Camisard wars, and appears peculiar to the south, where it is applied only by opponents. f This man's culpability, as to the original cause of the affray, was amply proved at the trial, and was declared in the speech of the procureur-genéral Bernard:—-" Si tous les accuses etaient devant vous, "je signalerais d'abord, comme les plus coupables, Bertrand.... Bou"carut—qui ont mis eux-memes les armes a la main aux habitans "d'Arpaillargues: Bertrand, qui a dit que les volontaires royaux pil"laient, violaient les femmes, les jetaient ensuite par les fenetres, et "qu'ilsavaient assassine quarante ministres protestans." Page 3? of the speech, printed separately at Avignon, in 1816.

Such a report being spread, Boucarut,

mayor of the village, summoned the inhabitants who prepared for defence. On the other hand, the miquelets who had no hostile intentions, on hearing the tocsin, reversed their arms as they approached, to manifest their friendly disposition. Having stated their desire to pass through the village, the mayor offered them safety and accommodation, if they would lay aside their arms; but refused them even the permission to enter, unless they complied with that stipulation of the treaty of La Palud; and to infringe which, they had been advised by their commander, general Vogue, *as they might soon require them again.* At the same time their ungenerous leaders had abandoned them, to reach their homes as they best could.

At first there appeared a willingness to yield to the mayor's demand, but some of the party attempted to enter the village, without complying with the terms. The suspicion of the inhabitants were aroused, confusion ensued, and in apprehension of the horrors reported by Bertrand, the miquelets were attacked and severely treated. Four were wounded, of whom two died; one in the village, the other in the hospital of Uzes.-j-The affray was truly lamentable in itself; but its consequences were rendered still more so. At the second restoration, the villagers of Arpaillargues were selected as objects of judicial vengeance; when three men and two women were guillotined, for the alleged assassination of Royalist volunteers. In addition, the melancholy event has been repeatedly put forward to justify the barbarities committed by the ultra-royalists, who endeavour to shelter the excesses of religious fanaticism under the pretext of political reaction. Even the King's proclamation f is not free from party colouring: it contains the following unjust assertion— "Atrocious persecutions have been committed, "against those of our faithful subjects, who under "the banners of our beloved nephew, courageously "attempted to save France."

"Lauze de Pcret gives the depositions of three of the volunteers, to this effect. Vol. ii, p. 79.

f In no other country would the public accuser be allowed to use such language as this: "Fourrier et Calvet ne furent pas lesseuls qui "perdirent la vie dans cette funeste soiree; raais il n'a pas *616* possible "de faire le denombrement exact des volontaires royaux qui *n'ont "plus reparu;* et qui, par consequent, *sont presumes avoir piri."* Requisitoire de M. Bernard, p. 16. Fifteen months had elapsed, and there had not been lime to see who was missing in a company of fifty!!

But to return to the affray at Arpaillargues—the proces-verbal of the juge de paix of Uzes, corroborates the preceding account. 44 We learned from a royalist volunteer, who Avas confined in the prison of Arpaillargues, that the stranger was killed for endeavouring at the head of armed men, to enter by violence the said commune of Arpaillargues, at the moment when the inhabitants offered to furnish them with every thing they could want, on condition that they should not enter without surrendering their arms: a condition which they would not accept, wishing to enter armed. This occasioned the insurrection of the inhabitants and the death of the stranger. The same statement has been made to us, by several inhabitants of the commune." Boucarut, the mayor, was included in the accusation; but being absent was condemned only by *contumace.* He subsequently returned to Arpaillargues, where he remained unmolested: the return of tranquillity insured him a fair trial, if called to account; but the true circumstances of the case being well known, he remained unmolested. On the other hand, Berlrand, the malicious and mischievous cause of the disaster, being placed on his trial, was acquitted. The abbe Raffin his employer, ex-vicar general of Alais, testified in his favour, "that being born and "educated in the catholic religion, he scrupulously "practised all its duties, and professed all its holy "principles."f The testimonial further mentioned that Bertrand had exposed himself in the royal cause at Aries, in 1790. At the period under consideration, such a man could defy justice before the tribunals of the Gard.

The court of assizes, by decree dated it July 1816, condemns eight persons to death, and one to the galleys for life. The sentence was commuted in favour of three. The others suffered at the close of September following: three at Nismes, and two at Arpaillargues. The details of their behaviour at the awful moment, as related by Rev. Mark Wilks, have been confirmed to me by a most respectable inhabitant of Nismes. In 1819 the King granted a free pardon to the survivors. .J-Dated 1 Sep. 1815, countersigned ". Pasquier." This *procis-verbal,* dated the 12 th April, the day after the occurrence,was commented upon by the procureur-géneral, Bernard, who maintained the right of the soldiers to force an entrance, as it was a public road. He had the prudence to say nothing of the trealy concluded three days previous. f Wilks, p. 155. Lauze de Peret, vol. ii, p. 91.

The affair of Arpaillargues is not the only charge of cruelty exercised by the protestants, during the "hundred days." One zealous partisan has had the hardihood to aecuse them of assassinating three hundred royalist volunteers. This calumny drew forth a reply from a magistrate of Nismes, who declared that inquiries made with scrupulous care, had established the proof that only two volunteers perished in the department of the Gard; and they were traversing the village of Arpaillargues with a numerous troop, of which they formed part.-f

The news of Napoleon's defeat at Waterloo revived the spirits of the catholics; and the remains of the army collected by the duke d'Angouleme, reassembled at Beaucaire, where they were rapidly joined by numbers, ever ready to enlist in the ranks of the stronger party. No opposition was made to the proclamation of Louis XVIII, at Nismes, after it was known that the government was changed at Paris. The urban guard, a corps raised under the imperial government, was disbanded; and the readiness of the protestants to surrender their arms, deprived the partisans of civil war of all pretext for an attack upon Nismes. $

But the precautions which common

responsibility demanded of the superior military officers, were converted into a ground of accusation, and perverted to justify a scene of horror. The *braves de Beaucaire* gave early proof of a predatory-disposition; and the measures adopted for preserving Nismes from plunder, were construed into a defiance of the King's authority, The religious prejudices of the rabble had been artfully excited, and in an official harangue delivered soon after, D'Arbaud-Jouques declared that the department was agitated by resentments, recollections, and rivalries, more religious than political.-j Alphonse Beauchamp, *Hist, de la Campagne* de 1815.

.J-Letter of M. Achille Daunant, in *Journal de Paris,* 11 Sep. 1817. 4: Lauzede Perel, vol. ii, p. 182.

Count Rene de Bernis, one of the royal commissioners for directing the government, allowed the army of Beaucaire, an undisciplined horde, to enter Nismes, without attending to maintain order by his presence. The chiefs of a ferocious band already collected in the town, were Jacques Dupont, surnamed Trestaillons; Graffan, alias Quatre-Taillons; Truphemy, a butcher; and about six others—names devoted to execration. Their first exploit at Nismes, was equal to the worst episodes of 1793.

The garrison of that city consisted of two battalions of infantry; there were also in the barracks five pieces of artillery. The accounts of Waterloo caused great desertion; and at this time, their numbers were reduced to about two hundred, officers included. The soldiers had assumed the white cockade, and only waited orders from the competent authorities, to regulate their future movements. After the departure of general Gilly, who resigned his command on the fall of Napoleon, his authority had devolved on general Maulmont, who no sooner heard that the royalists were advancing from Beaucaire, than he took a position on an eminence, as a measure of precaution: however as no hostile movement followed, the troops returned to their barracks. At length the populace was fully ex- cited, and being backed by the royalist forces,

a mob assembled, and demanded the surrender of the cannons. In vain did Maulmont endeavour to convince the people of the impropriety of their demand; they replied to his harangue by a discharge of fire-arms: he retired with his officers into the barracks, and closed the gates. The mob meanwhile was rapidly increasing, as the alarm bell was rung; and the country population thronged into Nismes, deluded by a report, that the catholics were being murdered by protestant insurgents.

This has been confirmed to the author by one who joined the levy. f Speech on occasion of his installation as prefect at Nismes, 30 July, 1815.

As the mob continued to attack the barracks, and threatened the utmost violence, the soldiers resolved to sell their lives dearly, and a few shots were fired from the windows, which killed some of the assailants, and induced their main body to retire to a distance. In the evening a commissioner approached the barracks, to converse with general Maulmont upon the terms of surrender. That commander claimed as a just right, that his soldiers should leave with their arms and baggage; and proposed that they should wait at a certain distance from Nismes, for-orders respecting their march. It was near two in the morning when the commissioner returned, to announce that the troops

"17 July, 1815.

must depose their arms; and the decision was accompanied with an intimation, that if the offer were not forthwith accepted, it would soon be too late to capitulate, as the popular fury might be beyond restraint.

Maulmont had loyally waited the arrival of the King's representative at Nisraes; and although the proposed sacrifice was painful, he consented from honourable motives, that the soldiers should depose their arms before they quitted the barracks; and when a murmur from the ranks announced the disappointment caused by his arrangement, he convinced them that among fellow-countrymen, the surrender could not be viewed as a disgrace.

It was agreed that the disarmed col-

umn should be protected by gendarmerie; and in full confidence, the soldiers piled their muskets and quitted the barracks, at four o'clock in the morning. Scarcely however had fifty made their appearance, when the royalists began firing upon them, killing or wounding the greater part. General Maulmont was one of the victims. Those inside immediately closed the barrack gates; but the royalists forced an entrance, and the greater part of the soldiers were massacred. Some in attempting to escape by the roofs, or over garden walls, fell and broke their limbs; and in that condition were mangled by their relentless enemies. The gendarmes, drawn up to protect the unhappy men, remained inactive. To use the expression of an eyewitness, "they doubtless thought it was a judicial "execution, which it was their duty to preserve free "from interruption." However when the populace had terminated their butchery of the soldiers, the gendarmes were, in their turn, attacked; and many of them were killed, wounded, or plundered.

In defiance of notoriety, M. de Bernis thus describes this tragic scene: "The barracks had capitulated; "the troops quitted to proceed to Uzes. Peasants "arriving from the country, attacked them on the '4 road; *some* soldiers were killed: it was a misfortune "which could neither be prevented nor foreseen, "-jSuch a misrepresentation is not surprising, since the writer so far degraded himself, as to wear a cockade *of white and green,* the distinctive mark of Trestaillon's band. $ That sanguinary troop, assured of impunity, and excited by the effects of their own crimes, proceeded to fresh atrocities at Nismes; while QuatreTaillons wreaked his fury upon the protestants of Uzes. During several months the department of the Gard presented a frightful scene of massacre and devastation; and it is melancholy to reflect that the arm of the law was paralysed, and the tribunals became powerless before a secret influence, which emboldened many of the individuals implicated, to brave the authorities no less than public opinion. § The press was at the same time employed to misrepresent the facts; and unblushing falsehoods have been sent forth to the world, by a party, incessantly charging its opponents with exaggerations and calumny.

Lettre d'un offlcier de la garnison de Nismes, inserted in Durand, *Marseilles, Nismes,* etc., part 2, p. 65.—Lame de Peret, vol. ii, pp. 185—191.— Wilks, pp. 191—197. — *Bib. Historique,* vol. i, p. S53. f *Precisdece qui s'est passe en 1815 dans les de"partemenls du Gard et de la Lozire,* par le comte Rene de Bernis, p. 63. $ Wilks, p. 211.
S *Fide passim,* Madier Montjau, *Du gouvemement occulte.*

It is therefore indispensable to detail some of the terrible occurrences of this period; for otherwise the old assertion of political reprisals may be again brought forward to colour the misconduct of the royalists. Not only were the houses of protestants and JeWs selected for destruction; but in cases where the lawless bands had any doubt of a man's opinions, they would call upon him to declare his religion. Several courageously acknowledged they were protestants, and were almost instantly murdered. The aged housekeeper of the farm of Chambaud was thus addressed by some ruffians. She was a catholic; but as the wretches entertained doubts, they compelled her to recite her *Paler* and *Ave,* as proof. Alarm made the poor woman hesitate, and she was at once knocked down with a musket. A serving man named Daniel Ladet, entering soon after, the same question was addressed to him. "lama protestant," he firmly replied. A musket was immediately discharged at him, and he fell wounded. The monsters perceiving he was not killed, made a fire with straw and planks, threw the dying man into the flames, and left him to expire in protracted agony. After they had regaled themselves and plundered the premises they rejoined their savage comrades in Nismes.

Lauzc de Peret, vol. ii, p. 217.—Wilks, p. 109. This diabolical deed was committed 17th July, 1815.

D'Arbaud-Jouques in extenuation of

this cruelty, which was too notorious for denial, represents it in the following light. One Ladet a *valet de ferme,* aged about fifty years, was suffocated in the smoke. On the approach of a band of armed men, all the servants who were protestants fled; but Ladet, *a Catholic,* remained. Alarmed at such a visit, he concealed himself in some straw, where he was neither sought for nor discovered. The brigands having set fire to the straw, little supposing that Ladet was there, this unfortunate man, unable to extricate himself before the flames encircled him, was suffocated by the smoke and reduced to ashes.

The victim's fate was clearly substantiated by the depositions of witnesses; his protestantism was attested by the ministers Juillerat and Vincent; and his age proved to be sixty-three.-f-All these shew the ex-prefect's disregard to accuracy; while his anxiety to prove Ladet a Catholic, is an indirect evidence of the persecution.

M. Negre had a chateau near Nismes, called Vaqueirolles, which was pillaged and burnt. His daughter, recently deceased, had been interred in the garden: the wretches untombed the body, and treated it with gross indignity. *$*

The condemnation of Bois, of Milhaud, has established that he had several conferences with his friend Trestaillons, previous to uttering cries of *vive l'empereur!* in the country towns: which cries they were to charge upon the protestants. D'Arbaud Jouques, pp. 97—98.

f Lauze de Peret, vol. ii, p. 219. Wilks, p. 200. $ Conculcaverunt corpus exanimum, et super illud minxerunt.
Madier de Monijau, *Petition d la chambre des deputes.* Madier de M., *ut antea.*

The following is the declaration of a catholic magistrate, when compelled to justify himself for courageously denouncing the iniquities of this time. "The people excited to pursue the protestants, dragged them to prison. In open day I saw a protestant woman, stripped of all her clothes, led round the boulevarts of the town. Two forked sticks, held under her arms by men, sustained the victim as she proceeded. She

was struck at intervals; and her cries were stifled by shouts of *vive le rot!* I beheld this barbarous procession pass between a company of newly raised troops of the line, and one of the national guard, "-f

From the moment the army of Beaucaire was directed upon Nismes, a great emigration had taken place. M. de Bernis issued an arrete or decree, commanding all absentees to return home within eight days, under pain of sequestration of their property. The injunction was absolutely barbarous, while the protestants were exposed to assassination. It surpasses in fact every thing in the annals of tyranny; for,.as it has been justly remarked: "The despots of "Asia send the fatal cord to their slaves, but never "order them to seek it."§ f Madier de M., *Plaidoyer devant la cour de cassation,* 30 Nov. 1820, p. 32. 4-" Dated 20 July, 1815. % Madier de M., *Petition d (a chambre des deputes.*

At the close of July, the King revoked all the extraordinary powers, conferred during the crisis of a revolution; and the regular authorities were again summoned to activity. D'Arbaud-Jouques, the new prefect, entered on his functions; but his arrival had disconcerted the violent faction, and Jules de Galviere, the provisional prefect, refused to quit his post. D'Arbaud-Jouques addressed the inhabitants in a proclamation recommending unity; he concluded by inviting all to join in one sentiment—the King, the Charter andFranee."-j

This was most unpalateable to the "white and green" faction, who clamoured loudly against the new prefect. "Down with him!—Calviere for ever! "—Down with the protestants! — *Vive le roi!"* D'Arbaud-Jouques quitted Nismes in consequence, and joined the duke d'Angouleme at Toulouse: nor did he return to his prefecture, until the eighteenth of August. $

On his second arrival he was very differently received; and the leaders of the faction, perceiving the necessity of obeying the King's indisputable command, allowed his nomination to take effect. § At the same Unhappily the King's wishes were disregarded at

Nismes. Alexander Deferal, a Piedmontese captain, was condemned to death by a court martial, for having joined Napoleon on the third of April; although the royal ordinance amnestied all who remained loyal until the twenty-third of March. Deferal was shot 5th August, and his body was treated with indignity. —Political vengeance alone operated in this case, for the victim was a catholic. + 30 July, 1815. D'Arbaud Jouques, p. 131. :£ Wilks, p. 231.

§ The interval had witnessed some curious negociations. D'Ar time, the new functionary speedily convinced them of their mistake, respecting his character; and his address on this occasion made no mention of the charter. It was now—44 The King—order— peace."j Trestaillons and his band were as free in their murderous career as under Calviere; and protestants who had returned to Nismes, on the faith of proclamations, were assassinated in the bosom of their families, f

Among other methods of inflicting vengeance, one was disgustingly barbarous. The ruffians would raise the garments of protestant females, and beat them with a bat, (such as is used by French washerwomen), on which was traced a fleur-de-lis in sharp points. This was repeatedly done; and in several cases, caused the death of the sufferers. £ The minister Juillerat appealed to D'Arbaud-Jouques; and endeavoured to move him, by a pathetic description of such horrors; but the prefect received his address with a smile, and gave an evasive answer, replete with cruel insult. § baud-Jouques had previous to the first restoration, published a proclamation in which the duke d'Angouleme was described un quidam. The ultras threatened to reprint it, and the price of its suppression, was to be the unrestrained exercise of party vengeance.

20 Aug. Lauze de Peret, vol. ii,p. 312. An inhabitant of Nismes, whose house was destroyed by incendiaries, assures me that when he called upon D'Arbaud Jouques in consequence, he found him quite indifferent to the terrible state of the town, and employing his leisure in translating Juvenal!! M. Juillerat re-

ceived for answer to an appeal in consequence of the death of M. Affourtet: "Il n'y a pas grand mal; on n'a encore tug" qu'un chapeau noir.".,,
£ Bib. Historique, vol. i, p. 265. Lauze de Peret, vol. ii, p. 39.

§ "Allez, Monsieur! les magistratsde Paris auraient trop a fairc, s'ils avaient a s'occuper des querelles de la place Maubert."

At Uzes the terror was equal to, if it did not surpass that of Nismes. There the sub-prefect, Vallabrix, after humbly soliciting employment during the "hundred days," proclaimed that the protestants were violent Bonapartists; and on that account, permitted the,most violent excesses against them. Graffan surnamed Quatre-Taillons was his worthy co-adjutor, and proved that the menace of a second SaintBartholomew was not entirely unfounded. On the third of August every quarter of Uzes presented a spectacle of organised plunder, conflagration and murder, amid shouts of vive la croix! vivent les Bourbons! At midnight, Thedenat, commissary of police proceeded to the prison; and after liberating a catholic, informed the gaoler, that the other prisoners were to be shot the next morning. Six protestants were accordingly led out, two by two, and shot upon the es-' planade, while the air resounded with shouts of vive te Roi! a bas les Protestants! Among the victims was Ribot, who had just before returned to Uzes, relying upon a proclamation, f which promised protection to persons and property. Two other victims were doomed; but the gaoler's firmness saved them, $ D'Arbaud Jouques did the same; and notwithstanding his fulsome phrases respecting the " wisest, most august, and best or Kings," he had applied to Fouche for a prefecture, soon after Napoleon's return to Paris. He even accepted the patronage of Manuel, who introduced him; and with the most loyal assiduity,waited among a herd of applicants in the police minister's antichamber.
'. Issued by the commissary-general of police, Vidal, whose life was saved in 1790, by the interference and aid of a protestant, named RiBot. Lauze de

Peret, 3 livraison, p. 51.
$ Lauze de Peret, vol. ii, p. 260. Wilks, p. 33C
As St.-Bartholomew's day approached, a general massacre was apprehended as well as threatened.

This produced an extensive emigration, which fully answered the purposes of the chief leaguers; for the absence of protestants at the approaching election, enabled them to secure the return of partisans, who would do their utmost to efface the detested liberty of worship from the charter, by legislative means. To effect that object, nothing appeared too violent or too cruel; and it has been subsequently declared in the chamber of deputies, that sixteen protestants were murdered on the eve of the election. The result was such as might be expected: four violent ultra-royalists were chosen deputies for the Gard. But if the chiefs were contented with this success, the wretches by whose co-operation they had succeeded, were not yet satisfied; and Trestaillons, Truphemy and Quatre

Taillons marched with armed bands, under pretence of maintaining order; but really with the design of murdering and plundering the protestants.

A corps designated as the royal chasseurs of Vezenobre quitted Nismes, on account of the arrival of some Austrians. They were proceeding to Alais, and unexpectedly made their appearance in the protestant commune of Ners, on the twenty-fourth of August; the day so fatal in the annals of protestantism, and publicly announced for a repetition of the awful drama. The presence of such a force, and at such a time, seriously alarmed the inhabitants of Ners, who assem Discoursde M. Devaux, 25 April, 1820; Moniteur of 26th.
bled in arms to protect their families and sell their lives dearly; a most tragical event was the result.

It may not be superfluous to notice here, that as many of the fugitives from Nismes had taken refuge in the Cevennes, whither their enemies did not dare to follow them, it became essential for the persecuting faction to exhibit that district in a state of insurrection,in order to procure the assistance of the

Austrians in suppressing the revolt: this may in some measure explain the catastrophe at Ners The opinions of the Austrian commanders were poisoned against the inhabitants, who were represented as barbarians and savages; and at the same time, the advance of the chasseurs was preceded by emissaries, who announced that the miquelets were coming to pillage their town: there was a violent desire to create a collision with the protestants. *f*

On the evening of the memorable day in question, M. Perrier a protestant, who had filled the office of mayor until the second restoration, when he was superseded, accompanied by M. Bruguier a minister, had exhorted his fellow-townsmen to disperse quietly, and return to their homes; and the consideration he enjoyed gave him such influence, that the object of his mission appeared effected. He was retiring, when an officer of the chasseurs induced him to return to the assemblage. On reaching the extremity of the village, M. Perrier was fired at, and killed on the spot. Cambon the deputy-mayor, and two other inhabitants were instantly arrested and conveyed to Nismes, where they arrived the following day, in the midst of the festival of St.-Louis. D'Arbaud-Jouques gave on that occasion, a splendid dinner to the principal Austrian officers; and without the least inquiry placed the captives, as rebels taken in arms, at the disposal of count Stahremberg. Deceived by the misrepresentatioris'of the local authorities, that general at once ordered them to be shot; and without the least investigation — not even the semblance of a military trial, three unoffending persons were inhumanly sacrificed. *Bib. Historique,* vol. i, p. 255.

t This has been assured to me by several inhabitants of the Gard. Lauze de Peret, v. ii, p. 379. Wilks, pp. 269 et 400.

Independently of all other evidence, the apologetic account published by d'Arbaud-Jouques, is sufficient to condemn his conduct; for in raising a quibble upon a trivial point, he establishes the important part of the accusation.-f-This is the statement drawn up for his

OAvn justification: "In the combat which took place "between Ners and Boucoiran, on the banks of the "Gard, the *twenty-fifth* of August, 1815, between the '" royal troops and the imperial forces of Austria "united, against the insurgents of the Gardonnenque "and the Cevennes, three men were made prisoners by the Austrians, at the very moment they were tiring upon the Austrian troops. Conducted by an "Austrian detachment before the general count Stah"remberg, the French authorities were informed by 44 that general, that those prisoners belonged to the 44 Austrian army and its military justice; and accord44 ing to the laws of that justice, inhabitants in revolt "against the lawful authority, and taken in arms "against the regular troops, could not be considered "as prisoners of war, and should have been shot on "the field of battle. There was therefore no com"mission formed to judge them, neither French nor 44 Austrian. The order of general count Stahremberg "was their only judgment. " To estimate the value of this writer's veracity, the preceding justification may be compared with the preamble of a decree issued by himself at the time. "The *royal* troops were *yes"terday* attacked at Ners; an officer was wounded, "and a *magistrate* killed by the rebels."--It has been already observed that Perrier's functions had ceased.

Durand *(Marseille, Nismes, etc., en* ISIS) had deplored Ihe fatal rapidity with which they *were judged* and condemned; and d'Arbaud Jouques in reply, declares they had not even the form of trial!!

The proces-verbal drawn up on the inspection of Perrier's body, establishes that the piece fired was placed close to his breast; the wound being about three inches in diameter. $ This renders it impossible that it proceeded from the inhabitants of Ners, who were drawn up at a distance. Indeed the esteem enjoyed by the deceased, was alone sufficient to refute the charge. On the other hand, the indecent haste with which Cambon and his companions were murdered, is best explained by supposing a desire to remove those, who could have borne testimony against the assassin. After Perrier's death, the people of Ners were not likely to depose their arms; and several skirmishes took place on the following day; but nothing of consequence occurred, as the presence of the Austrians restored order.

D'Arbaud Jouques, p. id. + Dated 25 August, 1815. So far from alluding to the presence of the Austrians on this occasion, the decree states, that in consequence of the insurrection, the French and Austrian troops *are to be sent there.* 4: See the *proces-verbal* ai length in Lauze de Perei, vol. ii, p. 334.

The sub-prefect Vallabrix did more than follow the example of his superior—he surpassed him. On the very same day, the twenty-fifth of August, Quatre-Taillons was sent on an expedition to Hieuset a commune not under his authority, being situated in the arrondissement of Alais. That ruffian arrived in the night with thirty men at St.-Maurice, a protestant commune, where a post of the national guard was stationed by the authorities. Being challenged by the sentinel, the band fired on the post; and instantly rushing in, seized six of the national guards, who were carried off to Montaren, before the inhabitants could make any effort for their rescue: one of their comrades was killed by the fire. At Montaren, Quatre-Taillons prepared to shoot his prisoners; but the inhabitants interfered and prevented him: in the discussion which arose, the wretch exhibited a written order to justify his proceedings. He then hastened to Uzes and marched his captives to the esplanade, where they remained while he consulted M. Vallabrix. That unworthy functionary with characteristic brutality said: "Do as you please: they were taken in arms." Qua

"As St.-Maurice was not in the direct road to Hieuset, that place must have been the real object of the expedition. tre-Taillons immediately caused them to be shot. Twenty-two children were rendered fatherless, by this butchery.

An account of the sad affair was published in the official journal, denying much and distorting the whole. It is false that the sub-prefect ordered Graffan to re"connoitre an assembly at St. -Michel-d'Yeuzet; the "sub-prefectcorresponds with the commandant alone, "respecting the service of the national guard; the ex"pedition of Graffan with his band was only tolerated 44 by the civil and military authorities, to spare Uzes the horrors with which it was threatened that very night; and this measure would have been a real be nefit to the town if his return had not bathed it away 4 in blood. Finally it is false that the persons brought "in by Graffan, were convicted of rebellion: they were purely and simply shot on their arrival, and without the knowledge of the authorities; and unknown even to the majority of the inhabitants, who have shuddered with horror on hearing of this barbarousexpedition." -f

This explanation, as may be well supposed, was far from appeasing the public indignation. Graffan was protected by powerful individuals; he knew it, and relied upon impunity. He was however arrested and conveyed to Montpellier, where a formal trial was got up, in which he was honourably acquitted. But a dispatch addressed by d'Arbaud-Jouques to the Minister of the Interior, fully establishes that Graffan was ordered by the authorities of Uzes to make a military reconnaissance at St.-Maurice; and in addition convicts the prefect of entertaining extraordinary sympathy for the infamous assassin; for he advances an absurdity to palliate the atrocity, and declares that the prisoners were killed by the population of Uzes, not only without his participation, but to his great regret, f Lauze de Peret, vol. ii, p. 360.

+ From the *Journal officiel du Gard*, 2 Sept., 1815. Quoted by Lauze de Peret, vol. ii, p. 365.

The melancholy death of the abbe d'Egrigny which likewise happened on the twenty-fifth of August, was notoriously regretted by the protestants in general; for he was on the most friendly terms with many among them. It was the act of an unprincipled miscreant named Laporte, whose opinion of the parly in power induced him to abjure protestantism, in the confident hope of obtaining a pardon: he was however, executed, as he justly deserved; and the incident would hardly have been noticed here, if its omission were not calculated to give occasion for an unfair inference. $

The events of Nismes, Uzes and their immediate vicinity have hitherto engaged attention, almost exclusively; but similar scenes occurred throughout Languedoc and the Vaucluse. Some years later, when the authority of the laws was restored, a few cases were selected for prosecution; and the evidence then adduced amply confirms the violence of these troubles. The long impunity allowed the villains who infested the department of the Gard, proves that they were merely the instruments of influential persons, on whom they relied for protection. Every functionary was encouraged in promoting the work of persecution. When the widow Landoz applied for an *acte de deces* of her husband, murdered in July, 1815, she was informed that his death was not registered; and when a similar demand was made by a widow of the unfortunate family of Civas, (five of whom were assassinated), she received for answer: "We do not certify "the death of such wretches, "f The prisons were filled with protestants, confined without any warrant; the good pleasure of the lawless bands was sufficient; and no magistrate ventured to interpose his authority. It has been observed in reference: 44 Every thing proves that an unknown but formidable power, exercised its unhappy influence upon this country." $ Dated 27 Sept., 1816.

f D'Arbaud Jouques, p. 77. In the same letter he states that when Graffan arrived at St.-Maurice, and answered the sentinel's challenge by *Five le Rpi!* the post replied by *Five I'Empereur!* M. Vallabrix would have been too happy to advance such a justification, had it occurred to him in time. $ Lauze de Peret, vol. ii, p. 386.

What else could have induced the prefect of the Gard to issue a proclamation § in which we read: 44 Inhabitants of the Gard! Justice is the basis of all "order and public prosperity. In the first moments "which followed the tyrant's fall, and in your noble "efforts for the restoration of the King's authority, an "indignation *too natural, too general, and too thought"less not to be excusable,* burst forth among you "against those whom general opinion designated as "the most violent enemies of the best of Kings. "Some public places where they held their fatal "councils, some private dwellings were by you at"tacked and destroyed: but illegal as was this ven"geance at least it was not stained with the disgrace "of pillage, and popular indignation was not de"graded by the spirit of robbery. Yet, inhabitants "of the Gard! see notwithstanding, what have been "the consequences of a *simple error!!!"*. Servant was convicted of robbery and murder in Nov. 1819. Ha was tried a t Ri om; and after his execution, a magistrate did notscruple to assert: " Innocent blood has been shed at Riom." Madier de M. *Petition d la chambre. .'* Lauze de Peret, vol. ii, p. 227. *Bib. Hist.,* vol. i, p. 269.

$ *Bib. Historique,* vol. i, p. 2—59.

§ Dated 7 Sept., 181S.

Encouraged by such a palliation, the ruffians plundered with increased activity; and when money could not be obtained, signatures to bills were extorted under threats of murder, j-Impunity rendered them more violent, and in October, a plan was formed for a general massacre of the protestants. The sixteenth was the day fixed upon: Trestaillons reviewed his satellites, and encouraged them to their dreadful task. The arrangements were complete: eight hundred men, divided into bands, were to scour the faubourgs; a concerted signal was to summon their partisans from the country; and in order to insure complete success, it was decided that in the massacre, any catholic who sheltered a protestant, should himself be treated as one. To the eternal disgrace of the magistrates, no measures had been adopted for learning the movements of the faction; and Nismes would have rivalled the St.-Bartholomew, if general Lagarde had not providentially discovered the plot, at ten o'clock of the night it was to be put in execution.

Overwhelming proofs could be adduced to substantiate the contrary, were such evidence necessary. The falsehood of the prefect's assertion is not only notorious; it is indirectly admitted in the apologies of the faction. f This occurred to M. Cremieux, now a distinguished advocate. One Casteras was sentenced to imprisonment for the extortion; but the endeavour to avert the compulsion of an illegal obligation, exposed M. Cremieux to great danger. D'Arbaud-Jouques was well aware of the circumstance; for M. C. applied for redress, as soon as the brigands had quitted him. The prefect treated the matter lightly; but finding the complainant was resolved to publish the affair in Paris, he observed: "If you are assassinated on leaving me, I cannot help it!"

It was then too late to prevent the commencement of crime, for the murderers had already entered upon the realisation of their scheme. Lagarde, almost in despair at the alarming state of affairs, summoned the garrison to arms, and endeavoured to arrest the progress of the mischief.

The horrors of this night alone would fill a volume; these pages therefore will scarcely admit an outline of the enormities committed: the bandits did not hesitate to assault the troops on meeting them in small parties; which frequently occurred as detachments were sent to protect the houses attacked. The general in consequence resolved upon arresting the chief insurgents. Trestaillons was on the Cours Neuf, with an immense crowd; his agents were at his side; and he was armed with sword, pistols and a carbine. To seize him in the midst of his accomplices was a hazardous attempt; yet general Lagarde was so resolutely bent upon securing the chief miscreant, that he undertook the perilous commission, and proceeded thither with a few officers. As they advanced to arrest the ferocious wretch, they shouted *vive leRoi!* then rushing in upon him, he was quickly secured. Trestaillons expressed great indignation that *he* should be thus ignominiously treated; and threatened signal vengeance on those who had arrested him. His safe detention at Nismes

being hardly possible, he was immediately sent off to Montpellier, under strong escort: the completion of the intended mischief was thus prevented.

Some incidents, connected with this dreadful effort of faction, will in a great measure account for the hardihood of the wretches, who were most active on the occasion. One Maurin was arrested in the act of robbing a dwelling, where the military force present was only twelve men and an officer; the robbers not only rescued their comrade, but were proceeding to murder the officer, when a reinforcement arrived. Maurin was retaken and committed to prison, under the double charge of robbery and assaulting an officer; yet the prefect, attended by a judge and the commissary of police, set him at liberty; while hundreds of protestants remained in prison, where they had been placed by Trestaillons, without any order or warrant.

Lebeiber, chef-d'escadron, in attacking a horde of miscreants, was almost miraculously saved: two muskets pointed at his breast, missing fire at once. As a recompense for his endeavours to maintain order, he was placed on the retired list a few days after.

The duke d'Angouleme was expected at Nismes; and in order to foment animosity against the protestants, a measure, under the specious appearance of a charitable design, was proposed to celebrate the expected honour. An address was published, stating that many royalists had been ruined by oppression, during the three months of the usurpation; and a subscription was announced for their relief. A religious ceremony was to grace the occasion; and the protestants were grossly insulted in the official journal, as violators of treaties and blasphemous jacobins.

It is a singular coincidence, that on the very day-fthat d'Arbaud-Jouques announced his project, M. Voyer d'Argenson was called to order in the chamber of deputies, for merely alluding to the massacres in the south of France. As soon as he mentioned that such reports had reached him, his voice was overpowered by the exclamation: "It is false." A scene of confusion fol-

lowed, in which the calls "to order" were incessant: the deputy was not even permitted to explain his observation. $ If the correspondence between the agitators of Nismes and the ultra-royalists be not thus established, a mutual sympathy is incontestably proved. Indeed, nothing short of a consciousness of guilt could have induced the majority of a legislative body to act with such indecency. There appeared a determination in the chamber to stifle discussion on the subject, and the enemies of the protestants derived additional assurance from the impunity thus promised.

Not by the government, but by the local authorities. Durand, *Marseilles, Nismes,* etc., p. 68. f 23 Oct., 1815. $ *Moiuteur,* 24 Oct., 1815.

The duke d'Angouleme entered Nismes on the fifth of November, when he gave an audience to the consistory; after hearing the statement of their grievances he expressed a desire that the temples should be reopened on the following Thursday: at the same time, he ordered general Lagarde to take measures for securing the public tranquillity.

Such attentions from the prince disconcerted the catholics, whose disappointment was augmented when they learned the failure of a scheme, closely interwoven with their policy. The grand-vicar, Rochemaure, the cure Bonhomme, and some ladies of respectability, unblushingly solicited the liberation of Trestaillons and his infamous comrades. The duke in a tone of displeasure recommended them to leave the prosecution of assassins and incendiaries to the tribunals. This reproof inflamed their desire for vengeance, and their partisans declared that the protestant temples should not be reopened.

In the disturbed state of the town it was not deemed prudent to renew divine service until the Sunday following (12 November) when it was arranged that only the smaller temple should be opened, that the ringing of the bell should be omitted, and that the organ should not be played. General Lagarde approved of r Lauze de Pcret, vol. ii, p. 428.—Wilks, p. 477.— D'ArbaudJouques, p. 46.

the precautions, and declared he would answer with his head for the safety of the congregation. The protestants privately informed each other of the time and place of meeting, and they assembled with silence and caution, as if committing an offence instead of exercising a right. The minister Juillerat was to preach: he soon had reason to anticipate danger; for in proceeding to the temple, groups of ferocious men scowled upon him; and he heard on his way, threats of most ominous import.

A crowd had early assembled at the door of the temple, and the measure of the popular rage may be inferred from the violent cries of the assembled populace. *"A bas les protestants! sarre les grilleurs!"* "The brigands come to their temple, but we will so "serve them, that they shall have no wish to return! "They shall not use our churches; let them restore "our churches, and go to the desert, *dehors! dehors!"* The service was scarcely commenced, when a band entered the church shouting " *Vive le Roi!* Death to the "protestants! kill! kill!" The gendarmes succeeded in expelling the disturbers; but the continuance of worship was impossible.

After a most painful interval, a detachment of troops passed: they were returning from mass, and the protestants were encouraged to escape in their ranks. This deliverance baffled the plans of the fanatical party, who purposed murdering the protestants as they quitted the temple: at the same time, to create greater excitement, emissaries had announced in the cathedral, that the catholics were being killed. M. Olivier Desmond, a venerable minister, above seventy years of age, escaped with difficulty: the Grmness of some officers alone preserved him from the ruffians, who surrounded him, vociferating, "Kill the chief of bri"gands!" Yet M. Desmond was a decided royalist; and his son had joined the forces under the duke d'Angouleme. M. Juillerat was pursued and pelted with stones, and his mother received a severe blow which placed her life in danger for some time. Other protestants were treated with great violence, and two females died in conse-

quence of wounds received.

A patois expression, meaning *Kill the protestants!*

General Lagarde advanced to suppress the tumult, when a villain named Louis Boissin seized his bridle, a'nd discharged a pistol close to his body. The assassin was well known; yet no one attempted to arrest him; and when Lagarde had given orders to the commander of the gendarmerie, to protect the protestants, he hastened to his hotel, where his first care was to inform the government from what quarter the blow had proceeded. He would not even allow his wound to bc examined until he had discharged that duty; so important did it appear to him, to secure the protestants from being charged with his death, which was then deemed most probable.

Meanwhile the disturbance continued. The national guards from the environs joined the populace of Nismes; and the authorities were so terrified with apprehensions lest the mercenaries might make disclosures, that the energy of the magistrates was directed to sheltering, rather than punishing the assassins. This is clear from the tone of the prefect's proclamation, when he was shortly after compelled to order a reorganisation of the national guard. Wilks,pp. 478 *and-seq.*—LauzedePeret, vol. ii, pp. 430—436. Dated isNov., isii.

The protestants decided on deferring their public worship for a time; they thus removed a pretext, which their enemies looked for with impatience. It was the King's desire that they should enjoy complete liberty in the exercise of their religion; and the duke who knew his uncle's sentiments, sent for a president and an elder of the consistory, to declare the sovereign's wishes on that head. The truth respecting the events at Nismes had been so concealed by affiliated functionaries in the interest of faction;-f-and publicity was so stifled by the censorship, that the excellent monarch who sincerely anticipated beneficial results from his charter, was not aware of the iniquities perpetrated for the destruction of its most precious provisions.

A royal ordinance $ admits the religious character of these troubles, and the arrival of a reinforcement of troops afforded some respite to the afflicted population of Nismes. The deputies of the Gard published a palliative statement, in which they declared that the assassin would have neither protection nor support from the inhabitants; yet Boissin was not brought to trial till after the lapse of a year, when he was acquitted on the ground of having acted in self defence. f To such extent were the abominable machinations carried, that agents were placed to shout *Five I'Empereur!* in the hearing of the duke d'AngouIeme. A most respectable witness has assured the author, that the cry was uttered, even in the courts of the prefecture.

£ Dated 21 Nov., 1815: countersigned Marbois.

In January, 1816, the law of amnesty was discussed in the chambers. The successful candidates at the elections carried under the influence of terror, could not withhold their support fronrthe ruffians who had prevented the protestants from voting; it is not surprising, therefore, that the deputies of the Gard made an effort to include the murders and pillage of Nismes. in the abolition for political offences.--Their effort to comprise them in the amnesty failed; but they succeeded in obtaining an ordinance; $ exculpating Nismes from the stigma recently cast upon its population. The reason assigned is "that the assassin of general Lagardehas neither asylum nor protection in Nismes, that the protestant temple is open, and every security guaranteed by law is enjoyed." It is true that the protestants were allowed to celebrate divine service at the end of December; but it is at the same time a matter of notoriety, that no effort was made to arrest Boissin, although his retreat was well known.

The indecorous proceedings at this trial (in Jan., 1817) were related by M. Madier, in his address to the court of-cassation; 30 Nov., 1820, p. 39. The disclosures in the evidence were apparently the cause of M. d'Arbaud's dismissal from the prefecture. That functionary had composed a jury before which an acquittal was almost certain: the majority were either chevaliers de St.-Louis, or Vendean chiefs. f *Moniteur,* 7 Jan., 1816. £ Dated 10 Jan., 1816.

The notice issued by the mayor of Nismes on the subject of the protestant service, is a fair sample of the misrepresentation resorted to by the ultra-royalist party. "The protestant temples will be opened on "Thursday next, the twenty-first instant; and that "day will prove to the King, to France, and to Eu"rope which accuses us, that the blind infatuation "of *a few women and children,* is not the crime of the "city of Nismes."

From this time until the celebrated ordinance of September 1816, which delivered France from a violent faction, by dissolving the chamber, the condition of the protestants was very afflictive.-f- The fanatical party had powerful abettors: Trestaillons and Truphemy were brought to trial, but the proceedings were a mere mockery of justice. None dared to depose against them, and for want of evidence they were acquitted. On the other hand, Trupheniy and his accomplices immediately afterwards came forward as witnesses against some protestants; five of whom were condemned after midnight. Nismes was on the eve of another convulsion; and an acquittal might have cost much loss of life and property, as the populace of the surrounding districts had filled the hall of justice, and thronged about the entrance. This notice was published 19 Dec, 1815. Wilks, p. sio.

f The change of system which followed is termed by M. Clausel de Coussergues, "Une persecution atroce et constante contre les hommes "les plus devours a la monarchic." *Projet de la proposition d'accusation conlre M'. le due de Cazes,p.* 63. M. Lanjuinais however observes, " L'ordnnance a fonde le credit public et a sauvela France.'' *li'ssai tur-la Charte.*

The cause of religious liberty was too dear to the British public to allow indifference towards the sufferings of their French brethren, for the rights of conscience. A warm sympathy was manifested; and interference in behalf of the protestants was loudly called for. This feeling was at first chilled by the misrepresentations addressed to the duke of Wellington, in which political reprisals were stated as the cause of the troubles. But when the subject was discussed in parliament, f lord Castlereagh in opposing the motion, could allege nothing beyond an anonymous letter from the south of France. The truth has been long since established, though the persecuting party has spared neither pains nor expence to throw discredit on the public statements. $

It is admitted that in the first details given by Clement Perrot, there were inaccuracies, arising from slight confusions in the names of persons and places. The general facts were however decidedly true; and several inhabitants of Nismes, presentat the disastrous scenes, have corroborated the details which precede. At the same time, the admissions and contradictions to be found in the apology for d'Arbaud-Jouques are sufficient to prove his administration very faulty; they moreover show that his statements are very far from commanding or deserving implicit belief: and if any assertion required positive proof, it was unquestionably requisite to substantiate the authenticity of a letter, said to be found among the papers of sir Robert Wilson, inviting a general charge of religious persecution, real or imaginary, as the most effectual method of injuring the Bourbons. M. d'Arbaud-Jouques makes this discovery a complete stalking horse, and presents it repeatedly, as a sufficient reply to those who censure his administration of the Gard.

9 Mar., 1816. *Bib. Hist.,* vol. i, p. 264. f Debate of S7 Feb., 1816, on the motion of Sir S. Romilly. $ M. Marron, president of the Paris consistory, being informed that his correspondence with England on behalf of the protestants, exposed him lo a prosecution for high treason, under the 76th'article of the Penal Code, he was induced to publish a letter, declaring that no persecution had taken place, and that the reports in circulation were false. The *acte d'accusation* mentions it; but although

sir Robert Wilson was questioned several times on the subject of his papers, this letter from his brother Edward was not brought forward. And M. Dupin in his defence of sir Robert, stated: " Ce passage ne,se trouve pas dans la Iettre du frere de Wilson, du moins avec le sens qu'on lui pnSte. Lc frere, enumcrant dans cette Iettre les causes qui ont indispose quelques individus contrc le gouvernement francais, place au nombre de ces causes, la persecution reelle ou imaginaire contrc Ics protestans. C'est' le vrai sens de la phrase." *Proces des trots Anglais,* p. 138. CHAPTER XVIII. ADMINISTRATION OF M. DE CAZES. —INTRIGUES OF THE ULTRAS. — REVOLUTION OF 1830.—PRESENT CONDITION OF THE PROTESTANTS.

A new era dawned upon the protestants of Nismes, when count d'Argout was named prefect of the Gard, in 1817. His energy repressed the factions, and restored the authority of justice. Vexations and heartburnings continued; for a commotion so violent could not speedily subside. In the hospitals, repeated attempts were made to obtain abjuration, from sick and dying protestants; and in several places, disputes arose, concerning the obligation for protestants to ornament their houses with hangings, on occasion of Romish processions. In 1817, the mayor of Puylaurens enjoined the inhabitants to place hangings for the *fete-Dieu.* Three individuals being cited for contravention, pleaded in justification that they were protestants: they were each sentenced to a fine. The case was ably argued on appeal in cassation; but that court decreed that the mayor's order contained nothing contrary to the charter, and confirmed the sentence. In 1818, a precisely similar case occurred in the canton of Cadenet (Vaucluse): on this occasion the appeal was successful; the court of cassation annulled the proceedings, and sent the affair to the tribunal of Aix, for a new trial. The decision of that court being unfavourable, there was a second appeal in cassation, when the proceedings were definitively quashed, f The organic law respecting public worship is unequivocal on this head: " No religious ceremony shall "take place, outside the edifices devoted to catholic "worship, in towns where there are temples destined "for different religions, "$ To what extent the provisions of this statute were disregarded, is a matter of notoriety; positive persecution was however at an end. Yet in 1819, the discussion of a proposed change in the election law revived party animosity; and Nismes was again threatened with a renewal of discord. By a strange fatality which never occurred in other towns, on changing the garrison of Nismes, the new troops did not arrive for some days after the departure of the old force: an unpardonable negligence at a period of excitement. The violent men of 1815 immediately resumed their audacity; and the protestants were openly insulted and assaulted, amid shouts of *Les Bourbons ou la mort!%* Wearied with so much harrassing persecution, the protestants determined on assuming a defensive attitude; and their enemies were in turn seized with alarm, when they heard that the inhabitants of the Cevennes were preparing to aid their brethren. A collision was happily prevented by the more eminent citizens; but assemblages on both sides continued for several days.

t 29 Aug., 1817. *Joumaldu Palais,* vol. li. 20 Nov., 1818. f 26 Not., 1819. *Journal du Palais,* vol. lvi. 4: Loi du 18 germinal an X, *art.* 45.

§ 6 March, 1819. The cry of *Five Charles X* was heard oil this occasion, which coincides with the hopes of the party, founded upon that prince's hatred of the charier. Masse, *les Protestants de Nismes et lewsperseeuteurs,* p. 14.— Paris, 1819.

At length the procureur-general requested M. Madier de Montjau to attend a meeting, at which the protestants were to concert their measures of defence. The authorities knew that M. Madier enjoyed the confidence of the protestants, more than any magistrate in the department; but that gentleman was unwilling to accept the mission, for two principal reasons: if he failed, the fanatical party would certainly accuse him, as instigator of the animosity which must ensue, should a conflict arise—

while a successful mediation would cause him to be denounced as a dangerous person, on account of his influence over a detested party. Nor did he consent, until the procureur-general repeated his request, and declared that " he believed "the firm and calm attitude of the protestants had "saved the department," M. Madier attended the meeting; and in consequence of his persuasions, the armied bodies dispersed.

The military governor of the department summoned the garrison of Montpellier; and within two days, those troops were employed in dispersing the catholic bands, who had again become boisterous, immediately after the protestants had separated. Happily the troubles were suppressed without any serious consequence.

12 Mar. Madier deM., *Plaidoyer devant la cour de cassation* p. 48.

In the year following, the death of the duke of Berry became the signal for another attempt by the faction. That event, so afflictive to all sincere royalists, was hailed with satisfaction by the Leaguers, as an incident calculated to promote their object. Two circulars rapidly followed the first intelligence of the catastrophe: they were numbered 34 and 35. The previous circulars were more carefully preserved; but the contents of these explain in a great measure, the mysterious influence which had directed the troubles of 1815. No. 34 gave intimation to the party, that although the minister (M. de Cazes) was not yet overthrown, they might act as if he were: it recommended organisation, with a promise of instructions and supplies. No. 35 speedily arrived, to announce the dismissal of M. de Cazes, and explained that tranquillity was, in consequence, essential to their interests. This order stayed the violent designs, for which preparation was making on the reception of No. 34. The old emblems and signs of recognition had reappeared; and the mercenaries were heard to say openly: "Why did we "not make an end of this race, in 1815!"-f

The author of these circulars was denounced to the chamber of deputies, by M. Madier de Montjau, as the func-

tionary, who in 1815, thus reproached a magistrate for having saved the life of marshal Soult, when he was arrested. *"Insensé! apprenez de moi que* 4 4 *dans les conjonctures où nous sommes, on n'arrête pas "un maréchal de France: on le tue!"* The allusion although obscure to the uninitiated, was so clear to the politicians of the day, that the leading ultra-royalist paper of that period, contained thereon some very sensitive passages, proving it was well understood. Madier de ML, *ut antea,* p. 50.

'J-Discours deM. de Vanx a la chambrcdesdeputes, 25 April, 1820.

In the debate which followed the reading of M.Madier's petition, M. de St.-Aulaire described the sufferings endured by the protestants of Nismes; bore testimony to their good conduct; and appealing to the other deputies of the Gard, declared that nota drop of blood had been shed in Nismes during the " hundred days."-f M. de la Bourdonnaye, the Achilles of the ultra faction, made no reply; yet his tacit admission of the fact, did not prevent his partisans from repeating their hackneyed assertions, that catholic blood had flown in torrents.

The possession of power by the ultras enabled them to gratify their adherents, without the necessity of signal services; the protestants in consequence ceased to be denounced as revolutionists, and were allowed the rights of conscience, as stipulated by the charter. Yet there was still manifested a great reluctance on the part of the government, to permit the establishment of protestant temples and schools.

Le Journal des Débats, 21 Nov., 1820, contains a long article on a publication by M. Madier, entitled *Pieces et documents relatifs à son procès:* " Il s'agira dans ce procès de justifier le silence qu'il s'obstine à garder sur les membres d'un gouvernement occulte, dont au mois de mars dernier il a dénoncé l'existence à la chambre des députés; et sur les auteurs de deux circulaires de ce prétendu gouvernement qu'il a déclaré bien connaître, et que, sans les nommer, il a désignés par *des indications assez précises* pour se ménager tous les avantages de la calomnie, sans encourir les peines dues au calomniateur." f *Moniteur,* 26 April, 1820. Séance du 25.

The encouragement afforded to the ultra-montane section of the Romanists, during the reign of Charles X, requires no more than a passing allusion: the Jesuits were paramount; and the affiliated members of the *congregation* were found in every department of state. The catholic church, arrogantly enjoying the distinction of state religion, its clergy were impatient to regain all lost prerogatives. In the long struggle between the *parti prdtre* and the advocates of liberty, the royal influence was frequently committed. By a fatal system of policy, the interests of the royal family appeared identified with hostility to the charter: one impolitic measure led to another; and the revolution of 1850 produced an additional phase in the history of religious freedom.

In the newly modelled charter, all religions are placed upon an equal footing; and an invidious distinction was soon after remedied by a legal provision from the public treasury, for the expences of the Jewish worship. This tolerance has galled the partisans of Rome; and brought down upon the existing government, the reproach of being atheistical. It is notwithstanding an indisputable fact, that public worship is better attended now, than when presence at mass was the price of court favour; and every thing indicates the probability of some great change in the prevalent opinions, on religious subjects. Materialists have astounded the world by their audacious attacks upon the elementary principles of all religion, while Romanists have persisted in unmeaning formalities: the necessity of a medial course, avoiding both extremes, naturally leads to revealed religion. The ancients tacitly admitted that consequence, by the importance attached to oracular decrees; and in our day, the extensive circulation of the Scriptures necessarily invites examination, and cannot fail of producing important consequences.

The subject was brought under discussion when the articles of lite eharter were under revision, and the debate, as reported in the *Moniteur,* 8 Aug., 1830, is highly interesting.

It will be readily imagined that the election of LouisPhilip to the French throne, was generally regarded as the harbinger of a full development of the liberties, theoretically commented upon under the restoration; and in the department of the Gard, the public joy surpassed all precedent. The new Ring was proclaimed at Nismes on the fifteenth of August, amidst the most heartfelt expressions of enthusiasm; but it was remarked, that among the shouts which resounded from the assembled crowds, the cry of *Vive le Roi* was not heard. Those words had been the signal of massacre and devastation; and the present generation must enlirely pass away, before the people of Nismes can heartily join in that exclamation.

A victim of 1815 assures the author, that although he would joyfully shout *Vive Louis-Philippe,* he could not bring himself to cry *Vive le Roi!*

The change of dynasty did not however pass off without an attempt to excite troubles in the Gard, and an attack was made on some protestants in the night of the second of August. The principal inhabitants of Nismes, enlightened by experience, concerted for preventing fresh disorders. Anaddress, recommending peace and union, and signed by persons of all parties, had been distributed as speedily as possible, after the news of the revolution in Paris. It was hoped and expected, that the exhortations would be attended to; but scenes of confusion arose, which did not terminate until September, after the strong measure of declaring Nismes under martial law.

A conflict was feared on the fifth of August: both parties seemed ready for blows, and an irritating allocution would have renewed the horrors of former days, when the leading royalists accompanied by the protestant pastors, proceeded to the place de la Maison-Carree, where M. Monier des Taillades addressed the multitude in a short discourse explaining the necessity of union and peace. The speech produced a happy result, but its effect ceased in a few days; for the re-appearance of the tricoloured flag excited painful feelings among the adherents of the dethroned monarch. Nothing however occurred until the new king was proclaimed. Strangers, whose appearance was suspicious, then appeared in Nismes, and on the following night the most unprovoked attacks were made on the liberals; among whom were included all protestants, whose attachment to the new dynasty was assumedas beyond doubt. The national guards of the Vaunage hastened into the city, to support the authorities and protect their friends; the prefect, mayor, and other magistrates adopted energetic measures; and the protestant ministers exerted themselves to conciliate and pacify the public. By these means the senseless attempt of a few misled men, was quickly suppressed; yet not without bloodshed, for the catholics had two killed and six wounded—the loss of the protestants was six killed, and twenty-eight wounded. Brilliant indeed were the hopes which arose in perspective, as the consequences of the "Three days" of 1830. Little was it then supposed that police regulations, intended to counteract political combinations, would be brought into array against freedom of worship. It had been so under Charles X, but the Bomish church was then supreme; and those oldlaws were considered as annulled by the revolution. Even in 1834, when a law for preventing associations was under discussion, an amendment was proposed, to prevent its application to meetings for worship. M. Persil, keeper of the seals, declared on that occasion, that the law would not be applicable;f and in the report upon the same measure to the chamber of peers, the adoption was recommended, in express reliance upon that most formal declaration. It was signed 3d August.

Evenemens de Nismes, depuis le 27 juillet jusqu'au 2 sept, i S30, par E.'.;B. 1). Frossard, pasteur. t *Monitmr,W* Mar. , 1834.

But the rights of protestants require to be fully defined by law, before they can be assured of their enjoyment; and a new enactment for the regulation of public worship is greatly wanted. The law of the year X, which is the present authority and rule, was conceived in a spirit of despotism. It is therein clearly shewn, that the government wished to retain the direction of spiritual affairs; and when circumstances induced the legislators of 1802 and 1830 to render the state independent of the church, they were unwilling to abandon their influence over ecclesiastical matters. So long-as the protestants were satisfied with the listless enjoyment of their liberty, they encountered no opposition; but when a desire of extension followed, as the natural result of the political change; when the spread of the Scriptures manifested the existence of proselytism, the characteristic of earnestness in religion, obstacles were raised, and hostile feelings displayed, in quarters hitherto most friendly. Two recent trials will impart some idea of the present state of religious liberty.

M. Oster, a lutheran minister, opened a chapel at Metz. He had conformed to all the preliminaries required by law; and for several weeks, was permitted to celebrate divine service, without hindrance. But after a time, the mayor intimated that he should not have the permission of the municipal authorities, on account of the alarm which his publications had created among the Jewish population of Metz. M. Oster, relying on the justice of his cause, persisted in the service; and was in consequence, sentenced by the police court, for an infraction of the municipal laws. *Moniteur,* 6 April, 1834.

When the cause came before the court of cassation, M. Dupin after severely commenting upon the intolerant and unjustifiable conduct of the mayor of Melz, regretted the necessity of opposing the appeal, on technical grounds. The mayor's refusal was within his attributions; and an administrative act could not be reversed by judicial authority; 'the appeal was accordingly rejected.--Immediately after the conclusion of his speech as procureur-general of the court, M. Dupin proceeded to the legislative tribune, and called the attention of the government to the injustice. "The

motive for refusing the permission," he observed., "is most opposed to religious liberty, as we understand it; and to toleration, as we ought to comprehend it. It is alleged, that one religion displeases another; while the object of religious liberty, is to enforce mutual forbearance. The reason assigned by the municipal authority is made the text of a refusal, consigned in an administrative act. That refusal cannot therefore be remedied by judicial power. The supreme authority alone can restore right, in place of an unjust denial; and on these grounds, I recommend the case to the minister of public worship." $

The other trial is known as the *.proces.de Montargis,* and arose out of the following circumstances. JohnBaptist Doine, a preacher of the *Societe evangelique,* though not an ordained minister; and Joseph Lemaire, a schoolmaster, were charged before the police court of Montargis, with illegally meeting for worship in two neighbouring communes. Their sentence was a trifling fine; but the animosity which marked the proceedings, have given the trial a lasting importance. The royal court of Orleans, by an important decree, annulled the judgment.-f-The cause occupied three days; and the court was thronged with protestants who came from a great distance, as the entire question of religious liberty appeared involved. The joy manifested at the decision was very great; and a day was set apart for a religious service, to celebrate the triumph of justice. The procureur-general of"Orleans appealed against the favourable decree, and the affair was elaborately discussed before the court of cassation, $ A decision, technically favourable to the protestants was awarded by that court; yet the motives assigned were adverse, and M. Dupin's official declarations were far from friendly to religious liberty. Arguing from the restraints imposed upon the Romish clergy by the Concordat of 1802, he contended that protestants could not claim greater freedom; however as the sanction of government was implied in the present instance, his conclusions were for confirming the decree

of Orleans.

10 Oct., 1837. t 9 Jan., 1838. 4= The proceedings in both causes have been published in a compendious form, by Kisler.: they merit attention, and evidence great talent and zeal in the pleadings. M. Natchet advocated the cause of M. Oster. Messrs. Lutteroth and Lafontaine defended the Montargis cause at Orleans; M. Jules Delaborde pleaded at the court of cassation. The *arret* is dated 12 April, 1838.

The protestants must now be convinced that, if their religious feelings are such as will induce them to desire an extension of their numbers, they must expect opposition from the authorities. Yet there is no cause for discouragement. The mere exercise of independent reflexion upon religion, is a step towards protestantism; and public attention has been so much excited within the last few years, that the opinions of the multitude must of necessity be affected. The church of Rome admits the authority of the Scriptures; and the recent spread of that sacred volume cannot fail of ultimately creating a distaste for tenets, at variance with its precepts—for improbable legends; and miracles, such as that of Migne, near Poictiers, revolting to common sense.

The increased means of instruction in the present day, will eventually lead to a great change in the Romish religion. That part of it which is founded in truth must remain unchangeable, in common with the abstract principles of morality, taught even by the heathen philosophers; but the Papal superstructure, and the thousand devices engrafted on the ecclesiastical edifice, with the design of strengthening human influence, and gratifying ambition and avarice—all these must and will be swept away. And when the progress of intelligence shall have effected this great change, there will remain no cause for dispute; because that is not genuine protestantism, which desires any thing more than the truth. The difference between the rival creeds may be thus defined: one faith is induced by reasoning, the other is imposed by authority. In the catholic church, man seems made for the splendour of religion, while the protestant religion appears contrived for the happiness and advancement of man.

The numbers of French protestants at the present time cannot be correctly estimated. That they areincreasing, is beyond doubt; and that they will continue to increase, may be reasonably expected. Their organised ministry may be classed as follows: 1. The *Lutheran* church, or Confession of Augsbourg, has 6 inspections, 37 consistories, and 260 pastors or ministers.

2. The *Calvinist,* or Reformed church, has 89 consistories, and about 400 ministers. 3. The *Societe evangelique* employs three distinct classes of agents— viz: 16 ministers; eleven itinerant preachers, not ordained; and nine colporteurs, or distributors of Bibles and religious books. The latter by their conversations with the rural population, prepare the way for itinerant preachers; and their efforts have been sufficiently successful, to give rise to some virulent attacks in the episcopal *mandements.* This society has also ten schools. The expenses are entirely defrayed by voluntary contributions; and it frequently occurs, that when a congregation becomes sufficiently numerous, it is engrafted on the nearest consistory, and thenceforth receives a grant from the public treasury. The chapels opened for the use of the English and Americans, of various denominations, are distinct from our subject: still they have all in succession contributed to the formation of societies for advancing religious interests in France. 4. The *Wesleyan Methodists* have, for some years, been labouring as valuable auxiliaries. That body made an attempt to establish public worship in 1791; when Dr. Coke and two other ministers, visited Paris for that purpose; but the endeavour completely failed. M. Mahy, ordained by Dr. Coke, persevered for some time in the neighbourhood of Caen, where he had to contend with much jealous opposition from the Consistory: he withdrew to Guernsey, and afterwards to Manchester, where he died in 1812.

Pierre du Pontavice, a noble of Brittany, after self banishment to escape the ter-

rors of the revolution, returned to France in 1802, and entered upon the pastoral office. He translated many theological works into French; and was usefully engaged as a preacher, in various parts of Normandy, until his death in 1810. f

The successful results of preaching on board the prison ships in the Medway, encouraged the society to renew their efforts at the peace of 1814. Their congregations are now considerable; and the number of their French preachers is fourteen.

The Wesleyan Mission in France, by W. Toase, pp. 14—5'. + Toase.p. 22 5. The Church of England also contributes to the important work of extending the light of the reformation. The *Society for promoting Christian Knowledge,* has in Paris a foreign district committee, under the direction of Bishop Luscombe. None but members of the established church can take any part jn the direction of its proceedings; the object of which is "to collect and transmit information, respecting the best means of promoting Christian Knowledge in its district—to establish, enlarge or superintend schools— to supply settlers and natives with the books circulated by the Society—to promote translations, when necessary, into the language of the country—and lastly to make collections in aid of the Society's funds." In pursuance of these designs the Bishop has, for some time, been engaged in superintending a new translation of the Bible and Liturgy; in which he has had the assistance of several learned persons, whose knowledge of the ancient languages ensures a faithful version of the original idea, in the purest style of modern French. This important undertaking has, for some cause, been recently laid aside; yet a large portion being completed, the friends of revealed truth may still hope to see it resumed. 6. The *Eglise catholique francaise* must be mentioned as a co-operating means for promoting the Reformation. The abbe Chatel founded this church in 1831; and although his tenets do not at all resemble protestantism, they are calculated to induce investigation—a tendency nec-

essarily obnoxious to a body, which denies the right of private judgment. From the Society's annual report. The depot of its books is at No. 9, rue d'Aguesseau, faubourg St.-Honore".

With respect to collegiate education there is a faculty of protestant theology at Montauban; another at Strasbourg; and a college established in Paris, b the *Societe evangelique.* Application has been made to the chambers, during the present session (1838), for a protestant faculty in the capital: the result was not favourable; but its necessity is generally admitted, as well as that of a change in the legislation for public worship, which is found to be as galling to the catholics as to the protesfants.

The subject of these volumes has led the reader through many scenes of violence. Even wheh controversy has assumed its mildest forms, it has been rarely exempt from acrimony. The vanity and pride of resistance, have been frequently found in companv with the martyr's firmness; and reprisals, recriminations, and angry feeling, have in turn tarnished the character of both parties. Yet the Conflict of three centuries has produced much benefit to society, by teaching the necessity of mutual forbearance. At the outset, it was a struggle of numerical strength; in the following age, controversy had become systematised, and the writers and orators who withstood the encroachments of Louis XIV, have left abundant stores for enlightening their successors. The eighteenth century found an unexpected auxiliary for religious freedom, in the antipathy to Romanism, manifested by the philosophical school. Religious persecution was then reduced to its most pitiful character; and an ungenerous warfare was waged against widows and orphans, labouring under the stigma of concubinage and illegitimacy. To this cause principally may be attributed the vivid jealousy of the French, against ecclesiastical interference in the *etat civil;* it perpetuates an exclusion severely felt by the clergy; and which, excepting the general confiscation of church property, is perhaps the most severe blow inflicted on that body by the Revolution.

THE END. APPENDIX,

No. I. — *On the Origin of the term* Huguenot.

This epithet has been the subject of much 'discussion: it is considered by many a term of reproach; and several persons of erudition have, in consequence, objected to its introduction in the title of this work. However it is to be observed, that the terms Puritan, Methodist, and Quaker, were originally given in a reproachful sense; but custom has sanctioned their currency, and they are used unhesitatingly by those, who would scrupulously avoid the slightest tendency to abuse.

The French protestants are mentioned under a variety of names. — Heretics, Pr&endus reformed, Calvinists, Huguenots; and sometimes, though rarely, Protestants; for the fact of protesting against the infallible church is unpleasant to orthodox Romanists. Each of these designations carries with it an explanation of its meaning, with the exception of *Huguenot;* which is enveloped in obscurity, with respect to its etymology, no less than the period when it was first generally applied.

Marshal Montluc's commentaries shew that he possessed extensive information upon the events of his time. He took an active part in the religious wars; and was in a favourable position to know the origin of the word, because his brother the bishop of Valence was for a time suspected of favouring the reformation; but in his fifth book, the marshal says, "they were so called, I know not why. " Nor do we learn any thing more positive from Tavannes or Pasquier, who were extremely minute in their inquiries on all the prominent events of that age. They relate notions, at once prevalent and contradictory; and in examining subsequent writers, we find that the hypotheses on the etymology of the word have increased, in proportion as the period of its adoption has become remote.

Menage, in his *Dictionnaire Etymologique,* has collected a variety of opinions; some derived from original sources, while others are the result of previous inquiries. The following are the principal versions, supported by various critics; some of which are not alluded to by Menage.

1. *Hugon's Tower* at Tours, where the early protestants assembled secretly to worship. This is mentioned by d'Aubigne and Pasquier; and is in some measure confirmed by the latter, who states that they were also called *Tourangeaux;* from which it may be inferred they were numerous in that city.
2. The commencement of their petition to the Cardinal of Lorraine. —" *Hue nos* venimus, serenissime princeps." 3. *Heus quenaus,* which in the Swiss patois signifies seditious people. 4. *Heghenen* or *huguenen,* a Flemish word equivalent to puritans or *xxOotpot.* Caseneuve supports this opinion. It will also be remembered that the Albigenses were called Cathares for the same reason. Further, it may be possible that the term *Gueux,* applied to the protestants of the Netherlands, is a kindred derivation; for as the recorded conversations of the period are mostly Spanish, it is less probable that a French word would have been so generally used. 5. Verdier, in his *Prosopographie* says: " Les Huguenots ont 6t6 ainsi appels de Jean Hus, duquel ils ont suivi la doctrine; comme qui dirait les *Guenons de Hus.* "— Guenon signifies a female ape. 6. Another etymology, of a similar kind, is given in a curious book, entitled,44 *Genealogie el la fin des Hvguenavx, et descouverte du Caluinisme,* par M. Gabriel de Saconay, archidiacre et comte de l'eglise de Lyon. A Lyon, par Benoist Rigaud, 1573." No translation could do justice to the following extracts.

Que si onques personnes meriteren t de prendre le nom de la beste, a laquelle ils sont presque en tout conformes, ie lairray au iugement d'un chascun cognoissant le naturel des parties, si onques il y eust transmutation plus certaine, ni entiered'hommesen singes et guenons (reservee la semblance humaine et l'ame qui demeure eternelle) que de ceux qui pour cest effect sont nommez huguenaux, par voix corrompue du langage francois, qui nommc un guenau ce qu'on appelle une guenon, espece de singe. (P. 8.) le Francois heretique a pris ce nom pour s'estre plus tost transformed en singe et guenon qu'en autre beste, suyVant un certain naturel d'aucuns Francois, qui se rendent assez souvent imitateurs des nations estrangeres es meurs, gestes et habillemens, qui est le propre du singe, comme nous dirons. (P. 9 J 7. Coquille, *Dialogue sur les causes des miser es de la France,* derives it from Hugues Capet; whose posterity the protestants supported, in the persons of the Bourbon princes; against the Guises, who boasted their descent from the Carlovingian Kings. It is however by no means clear that the Guises contemplated their ambitious project, prior to the death of Charles IX; while there is proof that the word Huguenot was in use long before.

8. One *Hugues,* a sacramentarian, is also said to have given rise to the epithet. Respecting the two preceding derivations, it is to be noted, that Huguenot is a diminutive of Hugh or Hugues; as Jeannot of John, or Pierrot of Peter. Menage also mentions that it was a family name; for Jean Huguenot was substitut du procureur du roi in 1559, at Chaumont in Bassigny, a district of Champagne.

9. The etymology most generally received is that which ascribes it to the word *Eignot,* derived from the German, *Eide-genossen* — q. e. federati. A party thus designated existed at Geneva; and it is deemed highly probable, that the French protestants would adopt a term so applicable to themselves. This opinion is favoured by Mezeray, Maimbourg, Diodati, and Voltaire. 10. *Huguenote* is the name given to a common earthenware or iron stove: and as so many early Huguenots perished in the flames, that derivation is not impossible. Especially when it is considered that *sentir le fagot* was an expression used to denote an inclination for the reform; and is often found in writings of the sixteenth century. At the same time, it is stated in the dictionary of La Furetiere, that this utensil was so called, because the Huguenots used it for dressing meat secretly on fast days. 11. Benoit *(Hist, de I'edit de Nantes)* ob-

serves, that some persons supposed the term had originated with an incorrect pronunciation of the word *Gnostic*.

No. II. — *The MSS. de fa Reynie.*

Gabriel-Nicolas de La Reynie, lieutenant-general of police at the period of the revocation, has left a mass of papers, sufficiently interesting to deserve a separate notice.

This collection, at present in the Royal library, is invaluable to the historian, as it corroborates in a great measure, the contemporary statements published by the refugees; which it has been the fashion in France to condemn as libels. The documents are bound up in six volumes. They are chiefly originals; but such as are copies accompany original pieces, to which they refer. Among them are letters addressed to the lieutenant-general of police; but the most interesting portions, are the reports of police agents, employed to watch the Huguenots and suspected converts. The mere outline which can be given here will impart but an imperfect idea of the collection, as it is by no means well classed. It would seem, that the bundles of papers were placed in the binder's hands, just as they were tied together for preservation, when M. de la Reynie's functions ceased.

Vols. I to IV contain: 1 *Procis-verbaux* of books seized at the houses of booksellers and binders.
2. Reports concerning protestants who had taken refuge in Paris. 3. *Lettres de cachet* for protestants. 4. Reports on the condition and movements of the elders of Charenton. 5. Divers informations sent to the King. 6. Lists of fugitives, and of persons known to contemplate emigration. 7. Informations on the means used for escaping. 8. Lists of conversions, and of converts relieved by the King. 9. Names of persons usually relieved by the elders of Charenton. 10. Lists of *marchands de viit,* protestants. 11. Persons imprisoned on account of religion, in the Bastille, the Chatelet, and the For-l'Eveque.

The reports of the police agents are very numerous in vol. Ill; the following selections are copied, literally:

Dimanche 1 avril 1685. Les P. R. ont dit aujourd'huy en revenant de Charenton, que l'ambassadeur d'Angleterre estoit aujourd'huy au bresche, et que l'on ne fait plus d'exercice chez luy, parce que le Roy son maistre est catolique. 26 avril 1685. Les ambassadeurs des états protestants ou calvinists nalloient autrefois à Charenton que très rarement, pareequil y a exercisse dans leurs hostels; et depuis peu ils y vont tous, du moins tous les dimanches et l'on voit que c'est pour se faire veoir au peuple et le fortiffier. 12 juin 1685. Deux personnes furent exprès le jour de la Peritecoste à Charenton pour observer la femme et les enfans de Lejay, pretendus relaps, mais l'assemblée de ce jour fut si nombreuse qu'ils ne purent demêler ces personnes d'avec les autres et naiant pu les joindre ils s'attachèrent à observer les communians, mais il y avoit trois tables, deux dans le temple et une sous les tentes dans la cour, et comme ils ne purent observer qu'une seule table ou cette femme ny ses enfans ne parurent point il ny a nulle certitude s'ils ont communié pareequ'ils l'ont pu faire à l'une des deux autres tables; mais pour agir a lavenir avec plus de certitude Hervé sattachera cette semaine à la bien connoistre et dimanche prochain il se trouvera proche sa porte pour la veoir sortir et la suivra jusques a Charenton: Ion asseur quelle va par batteau. Il se mettra dans le mesme batteau et ne la quittera point de vue qu'elle ne sorte du temple, ce moien paroist infaillible pour scavoir au vray ce quelle fera pendant ce jour. 25 Juin 1685. Il y a une femme de consideration chez madame l'ambassadrice d'Angleterre quy attend le depart de madame l'ambassadrice pour passer avec elle en Angleterre je nen scait pas encore le nom. 30 Juin 1685. L'on a enfin decouvert que Rurnet est a Paris: il se fait nommer M. de Hornet, et il est connu par les P. R» pour un docteur en theologie, et ils l'estiment beaucoup plus habil que M. Claude. Il loge chez le ministre Alix rue neufve St-Eustache. 11 va presque tousles jours chez Rozemond rue des Marresls. Les P. R. ont dit aujourd'huy en confidence que ces deux hommes travaillent ensemble a des ouvrages ad-mirables,) et que la veufve de Varenne en doibt faire le debit. Rurnet va souvent chez cette veufve.

Vol. I contains this specimen of tyranny: *De par le Roy.*

Il est ordonné à Laguerre valet de pied de sa Majesté, de se transporter incessamment dans la maison du sieur Claude, ci-devant ministre de la R. P. R. à Charenton, et de lui faire commandement de la part de S. M. de sortir de la ville de Paris dans vingt quatre heures au plus tard, pour se retirer incessamment hors du royaume. A l'effet de quoi le dit Laguerre l'accompagnera jusque sur la frontière par laquelle il desirera sortir. Fontainebleau xxi Octobre 1685.

Louis.

Colbert.

The following is relative to the demolition of the temple at Charenton, commenced on the very day the edict of revocation was registered by the parliament:

Je viens d'ariver Monsieur, jay lessè une partie de mes officiers dans le temple pour y coucher. Les autres sont dans les plus prochins cabarets du temple pour se reposer pendant la nuict, et demain auront soin des auenues du temple et principalement des portes pour empescher l'incommodité des curieux. Jay fait aretter la fille et lay fait remettre entre les mains du commissaire Lamare qui la menée aux nouvelles catholiques. Je ferai encore un tour demain et receuray les ordres que vous aurez la bonté de me donner. Je croy que les menuisiers auront achevé leurs ouvrage sur les neuf heures du matin. Je suis monsieur avec beaucoup de respec vostre très humble et très obeissant serviteur DE Francini Grandhaison. Ce lundi au soir, 22 Oct. 1685.

Some idea of the extensive ramifications of the police may be formed from these extracts: 16 Jan. 1686. En mon quartier il ne reste que le sieur Destreville qui est un garçon demeurant rue des Mauvais-Garçons chez Corneille, vinaigrier à la 2 chambre lequel ne veut-ny signer ny faire abjuration. Jean-Louis Alexandre rue du Mouton n'a signé ny ne veut faire abjuration, n'a point de domestique.

Les deux garçons du sieur Ausvere et leur servante nont voulu signer ni faire abjuration, se sont absentez, jay scellé dans leur maison, Rue de la Poterye.

Rue de la Verrerie à l'hostel de Bourbon, maison, garnyc sont logez Monsieur le Marquis d'Inoncourt, madame sa femme, leur fils. et quatre filles et leur fille de chambre tous de la R. P. R. avec un laquais de même religion et 3 laquais Almands Lutheriens. Madame d'Inoncourt scayt que la declaration du roy porte 15 jours pour congédier les domestiques. Elle refuse de congédier les trois Lutheriens.

Le sieur Desguilly cydevant capitaine de cavalerie au regiment de Comminge loge a la teste d'or Rue de la tixeranderie. Il est de la R. P. Rson lacquais est catholique. Monseigneur de Louvois l'a fait mander pour lui venir parler. (Vol ii.) 21 Jan 1686. L'on m'a donné advis aujourdhuy, que dans le cabaret du Riche laboureur qui est à l'entrée de la rue des fossés M. le Prince. Il s'y assemble presque tous les soirs des marchands et artisans de la religion et de nouveaux catholiques ou ils se trouve quelquefois jusques à dixhuit ou vingtet qu'ils y tiennent des discours scandaleux. (Vol ii).

28 Oct 1686 Le ministre Gibert de la Rochelle ne s'est point logé en auberge dans la crainte d'etre decouvert. L'on m'a asseuré qu'il se retire chez la nommée Bot, revenderesse, qui est une nouvelle catholique de ses amis qui demeure Rue de la Corne au Faubg St. Germain. Il fut hier au presche chez M. l'ambassadeur de Danemarc, et l'on dit qu'ilydoibt entrer pour y demeurer et prescher en François. Cette nommée Bot est une femme qui a desja parut suspecte en d'autres occasions, (voliii)

Extract Of A Deposition Made 3 Dec. 1686.

Que le nommé Desbaux, potier d'estain rue des Fossés St. Germain est l'agent de tous les mecroians de Paris, et que sa femme va de maison en maison porter des livres et des lettres. Que chez le nommé Lebeuf à la PlaceMaubert on s'assemble quelquefois. Que la femme de Bezard cy devant ancien de Charenton est une seditieuse

qu'il faudrait mettre en lieu de sûreté. (Vol i.) . Report Of Olivier Cellier.

Ce 26 Jan. 1687. Jai esté ce matin chez l'envoie de Brandebourg dans le lieu ou ils font leur assemblée; je m'i suis trouvé le premier, et ai exactement observé tous les usages qui i ont paru. J'ai vei 5 personnes qui ont chanté en François. J'en ai suivi un lequel a fort observé ma contenance. Je l'ai suivi jusques dans la rue de Lavandières. Je l'ai veu entrer dans une porte entre deux portes carrées-vis-à-vis M. Boulo, cirrurgien.

L'homme que j'ay observé a bien quarante ans il a le visage un peu carré les hieux et la fasse un peu enflammez. Il a une assez grande espée a garde d'assié très luisant. Le juste corps gris un peu brun. (Vol.iv).

The fifth volume contains memoirs, correspondence, and accounts of books furnished to new converts, amounting to the enormous sum of 536,640 livres. There were evidently suspicions of peculation, as the inquiries appear directed towards detection; and the report made upon the accounts of one Clement, states, that he produces no proof, nor entries in books or journals either to justify his expenditure, or to shew what the booksellers have delivered to him. It is also stated, that the documents furnished by him had been altered. The reporter's opinion may be inferred from this observation: 4 4 Par ce moyen la despense effective de 4-à "500 mille livres, peut estre enflée et portée à 6, 7, 8, 9 "et un milion, ainsi qu'il aura plu au sieur Clement."

It is stated by Rulhière, that Pellisson did not leave his accounts in perfect order; and as he was concerned in the distribution of these books, it is probable that this transaction gave rise to the imputation.

Vol. VI contains the papers seized on the persons of fugitives, and in the houses of suspected *relaps;* with a number of abjurations, many of which are signed in blank, having neither the date, the name of the ecclesiastic receiving, or of the requisite witnesses attesting the declaration.

No. III. — *Recent act of intolerance.*

The following disgraceful circumstance has been related in the Paris journals, extracted from the *Phare de la Rochelle.* It will be found at length in the *Propagateur* of 30th June 1838..

A protestant lady, named Fleury, died at the village of Pont-1'Abbé (Charente-Inférieure) and was interred on the 2d of June by the protestant pastor of Marennes. As cemeteries are communal property, and under the control of the mayor, independent of the clergy, the deceased was buried in the only burial ground; which however the priests, according to their custom, consider a domain of thc church. Thc vicar had protested against the sepulture; and in the night of the 7th he had the corpse disinterred. He then wrote the following record of his own disgrace.

A Mons. Cambon, *Pasteur à Marennes.*

Monsieur, le bel œuvre que celui dont vous êtes venu vous illustrer à Pont-1'Abbé, la veille du saint jour de la Pentecôte. Vous avez grand sujet de vous en glorifier, la memoire en restera longtemps dans les coeurs. Le corps de MTM" Fleury vient enfin d'etre exhumé du lieu, ou contre mon droit et mon opposition, vous l'aviez fait déposer. Cette opération s'est terminée cette nuit entre minuit et une heure.

Courage, Monsieur, encore quelques actes de cette nature, et vous rendrez de plus en plus recommandable votre ministère, dejà si accredité par la solidité de vos doctrines. Le repos dont vous assurez le corps de vos fidèles après leur mort est une garantie du repos dont vous pouvez assurer leur ame.

Recevez, Monsieur, l'assurance de toute la consideration que vous avez su m'inspirer.

Labbo,

Pont l'Abbé, le 8 Juin 18 38. *Desservant de Pont-VAilé.*

This strange letter obtained a reply from the protestant pastor, the mildness of which presented a striking contrast to the unchristian boastings of the priest. He congratulated himself that he was not minister of a religion, which pursues men, even in their grave, and would deprive their mortal remains, of the rest they deny to their souls; and concluded by exhorting the vicar to inquire seriously, and as in the presence of his maker, whether his conduct and sentiments were Christian, or if he had not rather stifled the voice of charity and the feelings of humanity.

No. IV. — *Abrege de I'Histoire de Nismes, de Menard, continue jusau a nos jours,* par P. L. Baragnon pere, avocat a la cour royale de Nismes, vols. I to III.

The author was unable to procure a copy of the above work, until after his own task was finished. The third volume concludes with an account of the *Bagarre* in 1790. However with all possible deference for the advantages enjoyed by M. Baragnon, as an inhabitant of Nismes, his arguments have not induced any alteration in the volume now offered to the public.

From the sixteenth century, M. Baragnon's history is, almost without intermission, a» *Acte d'Accusation* against the protestants; yet his account of the Camisards has not necessitatedjnorethan a marginal note, wherein *his* testimony to the severe measures adopted has been adduced.

At a later period, where there is an allusion to the audacity of the protestants, in holding assemblies (1743 to 1745), it would certainly have tended to establish his character for impartiality, had he not withheld Menard's testimony to their loyalty. During a consistory held at Ledignan, news was received of the Ring's illness; on which the ministers instantly suspended their discussion, to offer a prayer for his recovery. (Menard, vol. 6, p. 603).

It will not therefore excite surprise, that M. Baragnon blames the protestants for the troubles of 1790. He admits that in the publications of the Catholic party there are exaggerations, as well as in those written by protestants; but his avowed preference for the statement made by M. de Mar guerittes, mayor of Nismes, has caused him to overlook the circumstance of its being a justification of the municipal body, then accused of counter-revolutionary principles; and for that reason, *ex parte.* How-

ever the mayor's statement contains an important admission.
Ce n'etait point une querelle de religion; les dogmes, le culte n'y entraient pour rien; mais c'etait l'inquictudc des calholiques d'avoir vu d'abord la force armee entre les mains d'un petit nombre des citoyens, dont plus de la moitie etaient protestans; c'etait le mecontentement des protestans, de n'avoir pas eu dans l'election des officiers municipaux la part qu'ils pouvaient y pretendre. *Compte rendu,* quoted by Baragnon, vol. 3, p. 445.
We may here fairly inquire, how it happened that the intrigues began *before* the municipal elections; and consequently, before the protestants could entertain discontent at exclusion. The elections took place in February, 1790; but Froment proceded to Turin in January; and he declares in one of his publications, that the nobility of Languedoc had held a deliberation at Toulouse, in November, 1789, for the purpose of planning measures to restore the old regime. Lauze dePeret, 2 livraison, p. 198.

In the autumn of 1789, some violent pamphlets were issued against the protestants. *Pierre Romain aux CathoUquesdeNimes* bears no date, but *Charles Sincere a Pierre Romain,* which responds to the appeal, and is apparently from the same pen, is dated 22 Nov., 1789. These libels contain a declaration of mortal hatred against the protestants: a P. S. to the latter declares, that the free exercise of the reformed religion would cause the ruin of the monarchy; and suggests a subscription for publishing a new edition of Caveyrac's *Apologie,* which is called 44 cet ouvrage immortel."

Respecting Froment, we learn from M. Baragnon, that his quarrel with the friends of the revolution, was altogether personal in its origin; that he was never the *real* chief of the catholic party; and that the accounts of his services have been greatly exaggeratedly his wounded vanity. His correspondence with the count d'Artois, and his zeal in the catholic cause, are however admitted, pp. 446-8.

In the terrible episode of the Bagarre, the question is, who was the aggressor? and M. Baragnon unhesitatingly charges the protestant party.'

L'assembl& nationale, indisposeecontrc les catholiques par la petition du 20 avril, savait que l'interet des religionnaires les liait etroitement a la cause de la revolution, et les protegeait ouvertement: l'assemblee electorate etait entierement a leur devotion. ... Touteslescontrees protestantcsetaient en armes, et prevenuesde longue main; c'est sous ces auspicesque l'assemblee electorate devait se reunirle 4 juin, p. 477-8.

This paragraph decides the author's point of view; the version adopted in this volume, will in consequence, wound his historical susceptibilities. We differ widely in our conclusions; and public opinion, is the tribunal which must decide between us.

The writings of M. Lauze de Peret have been violently assailed, by what is termed the *royalist party* in France; yet the author is not aware that any detailed refutation of his statements has been attempted. He is moreover so very minute in dates, names, and places, that if his assertions are unfounded, it would be a very easy task to controvert him. Several highly respectable inhabitants of Nismes, catholic as well as protestant, have borne testimony to his veracity, by correspondence and in conversation; and the best possible reply to M. Baragnon's account of the Bagarre, is a passage from M. Lauze de Peret, published in 1818. Both these writers were advocates of Nismes, and equally near the best sources of information.

En 1788, en 1789, et au commencement de 1790 jusqu'au moment oil Ton discuta la constitution civile dn clerge, l'opinion fut unanime dans presque toutes les classes; la revolution, c'esta-dire une reforme qui n'etait pas encore revolutionnaire, fut recue avec un euthousiasme aussi general qu'en aucun autre lieu de la France. Mais dans cette meme annee 1790, ties hommes qui ne voulaient aucune reforme,fonderent sur l'opjiosition (Icscullcsrcspcrancc d'une opposition politique, d'une division qui troublat les esprits, qui fit preTerer passionnement les interets particuliorsu l'interet public dont la raison s'occupe seule, et qui enfin, malgre les voeux naturcls du plus grand nombre des Francais, fit travailler les Francais euxmemesa l'entier retablissementde cequel'autorite du siecle venait d'abolir. C'est ainsi que Ton parvint a se separer les unsdcs autres les catholiques et les religionnaires. I" livraison, p. 96.

The official report presented to the National Assembly by M. Alquier comprises the depositions of numerous witnesses, who establish the charge of fanatical conduct and threats on the part of the catholics, in the month of *April*; but those statements M. Baragnon does not condescend to notice.

The Bagarre occurred in *June.* The destruction of the capucin convent has been the subject of controversy. The death of M. Massip was the pretext of violence, and according to the statement of one party, he was killed by a shot, fired or supposed to be fired from the convent—their opponents declare it was a malicious colouring, invented to justify the assault. One fact is beyond doubt: M. Mas&ip was killed in front of the convent, and M. Baragnon offers the following *truly ingenious solution* of a charge, rendered more intricate by the depositions of the monks themselves, and especially by that of their gardener, who stated that the shots *appeared to himio* be fired from the convent.

Sil nous est pcrmis de dormer noire opinion,.d'expliquer la morl de M. Massip, et de faire concorder le recit de M. de Marguerittes avec la deposition des religieux, nous dirons que des malveillans, posted autour du Luxembourg ou dans Tangle de la rue Notre-Dame, tirerent sur le rassemblement place a l'esplanade plusieurs coups de feu qui n'atteignirent personne, et n'avaient d'autre but que d'exciter un mouvement; que ces coups de feu mirent l'epouvante dans la troupe, et que, dans le desordro qui en fill la suite, *la maladrem* (fun *legionnaire* donna la inort a M. Massip, p. 501.

A fourth volume, bringing the history of Nismes down to 1830, has been for sometime announced, and the author regrets that the delay in its appearance has prevented his availing himself of M. Baragnon's superior advantages and skilful reasonings, for correcting any erroneous notions which he may have formed, notwithstanding the most scrupulous attention in consulting individuals, residents of Nismes in 1815.

Postscript.—It is due to the memory of the illustrious Colbert, to mention that he died in 1683; and consequently is free from the reproach of sanctioning the Edict of Revocation, and its corollary decrees. They were apparently countersigned by his eldest son, better known as Marquis de Seignelay; who was Secretaire d'Etat de la Maison du Roi, and Minister of the Marine. The practice of using the family name, instead of the titular honour, was common among the old families. The duke de Bouillon signed *Henri de la Tour*—the duke de Soubise, *Benjamin de Rohan*—and the statesman Villeroy, *de Neufville.*